KING ALFRED:
A Man on the Move

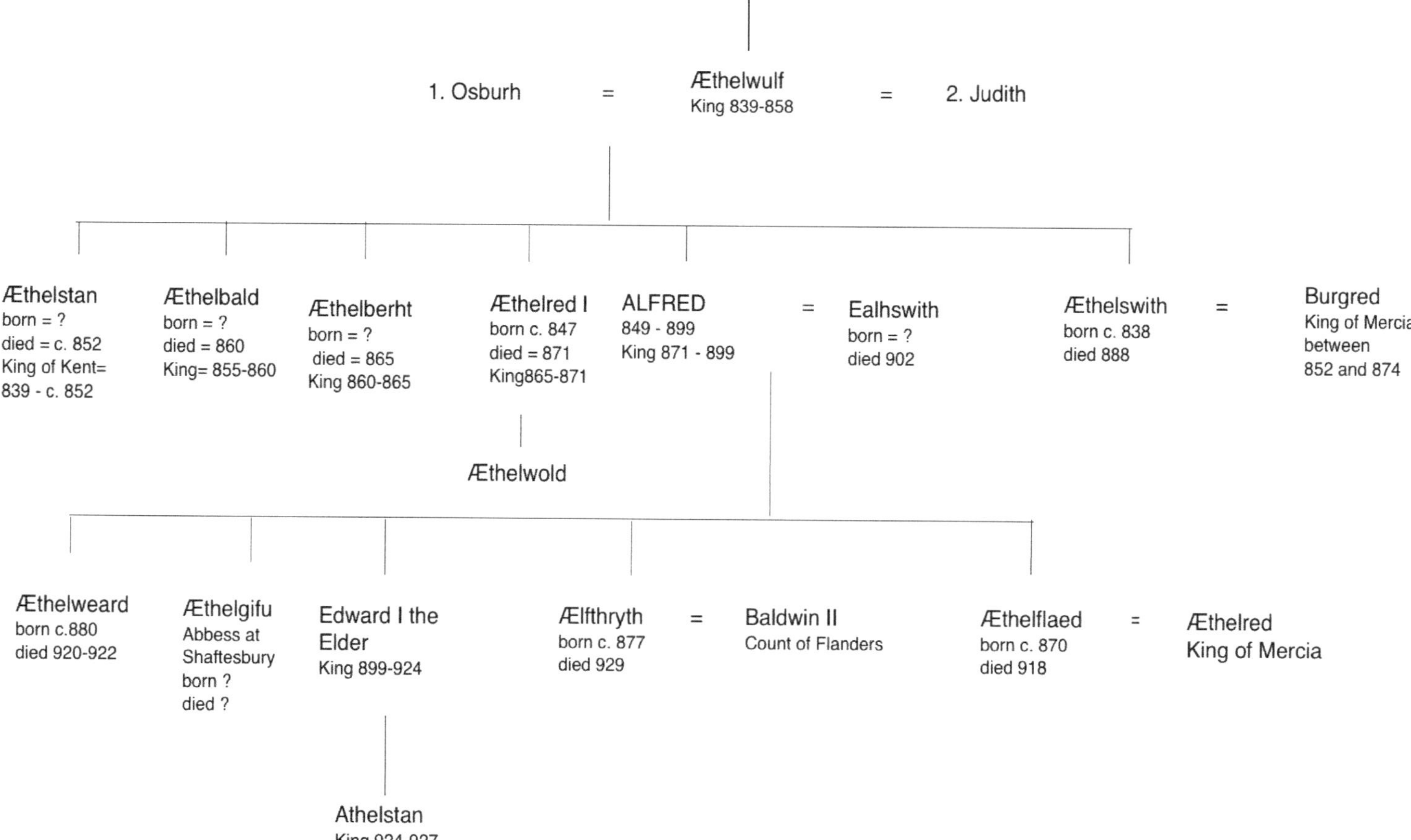
Egbert
King 802-839
1. Osburh = Æthelwulf King 839-858 = 2. Judith
Æthelstan
born = ?
died = c. 852
King of Kent=
839 - c. 852
Æthelbald
born = ?
died = 860
King= 855-860
Æthelberht
born = ?
died = 865
King 860-865
Æthelred I
born c. 847
died = 871
King865-871
Æthelwold
ALFRED
849 - 899
King 871 - 899
=
Ealhswith
born = ?
died 902
Æthelswith
born c. 838
died 888
=
Burgred
King of Mercia
between
852 and 874
Æthelweard
born c.880
died 920-922
Æthelgifu
Abbess at
Shaftesbury
born ?
died ?
Edward I the
Elder
King 899-924
Athelstan
King 924-927
Ælfthryth
born c. 877
died 929
=
Baldwin II
Count of Flanders
Æthelflaed
born c. 870
died 918
=
Æthelred
King of Mercia

KING ALFRED:
A Man on the Move

Dr Paul Kelly

Black Slash Publications

First published 2019

Black Slash Publications
Weymouth, Dorset.
www.black-slash.co.uk

All photographs were taken by the author. Those maps that contain Ordnance Survey data are used under the OS OpenData arrangements. The photograph on the cover was provided by Danielle Wootton.

ISBN 978-1-9161820-0-4

Acknowledgements

I would like to thank Danielle Wootton and Janette Wootton for their constructive criticism and for their many suggestions, which have shaped the creation of this book. I would like to thank the many volunteers who staff our churches, cathedrals and museums. They have been a fount of knowledge. I particularly thank volunteers at Wimborne Minster, Rochester Cathedral, Sherborne Abbey, Edington Priory Church, Ware museum, Godalming museum, Alfred's Tower in Somerset, and St Mary's church, Guildford, where I was also helped by a local historian. I would like to thank a lady at Englefield House, who allowed me access to the ground on a day that it was closed to the public. My thanks also extend to the many other people I talked to on walks, in public houses, or elsewhere. I am also grateful to Danielle Wootton who took the photograph that appears on the front cover of this book. I feel that it is important to acknowledge other writers, many of whom are no longer with us, who have dedicated time to writing about King Alfred. Without this body of work the starting point for writing my own book would have been significantly more barren.

Contents

Introduction

Simply perching on the low open windswept hill at Athelney, or visiting the lovely little church at Aller, or standing in the pouring rain at the location of his burial at Hyde Abbey, was more than enough to inspire me to go on a reflective journey exploring King Alfred's connections with the beauty and diversity of the English rural and urban landscapes. This book is based on my personal journey into the life and travels of King Alfred, taking me across several English counties to discover and explore the places associated with this great man.

As I made my way round the places described in this book I found that I was often alone as there were rarely any visitors at most of the locations, even those that are important to the history of England, such as the location of King Alfred's burial, or the place where his reconquest of Wessex began, or the site where he sealed the defeat of the Viking leader. By contrast, Winchester cathedral and his famous statue in that city, important locations in their own right, were well visited. It became my mission to do justice to these lesser known places and to present them to a wider audience. I am aware that some readers will be interested in legend as much as fact, so I have included some places if they are associated with a particularly strong story, whilst pointing out the lack of supporting evidence if that is the case. It is also important to note at the outset that much concerning Alfred is uncertain. Hard facts are few in number.

I have always felt that it is possible to mentally compress time so that long-past events seem more recent, and that "on location" personal contemplation is the key. I think this is important because it helps us to understand the past. Were those people who lived such a long time ago really that much different from us? What started as a following of Alfred's footsteps soon became my own journey transporting me away from twenty-first century life into the Wessex of old, basking in the life and travels of King Alfred, a king with a purpose. Hopefully, after visiting at least some of the sites in this book, you too will perceive that you are walking in Alfred's country and will be able to appreciate the events of his period even in their contemporary setting. To my mind what could be better than travelling through Alfred's world on a sunny afternoon, drifting into little known historic sites reached through scent-filled lanes, or to browse ancient churchyards with the sound of birds nesting in the hedgerows, and a bench to rest on and ponder the journey? Or to enjoy beautiful sunsets over the fields and valleys of King Alfred's Wessex with a sandwich in hand and a sense of history all around. All this sounds idyllic, and I can tell you that it has indeed been an enjoyable experience.

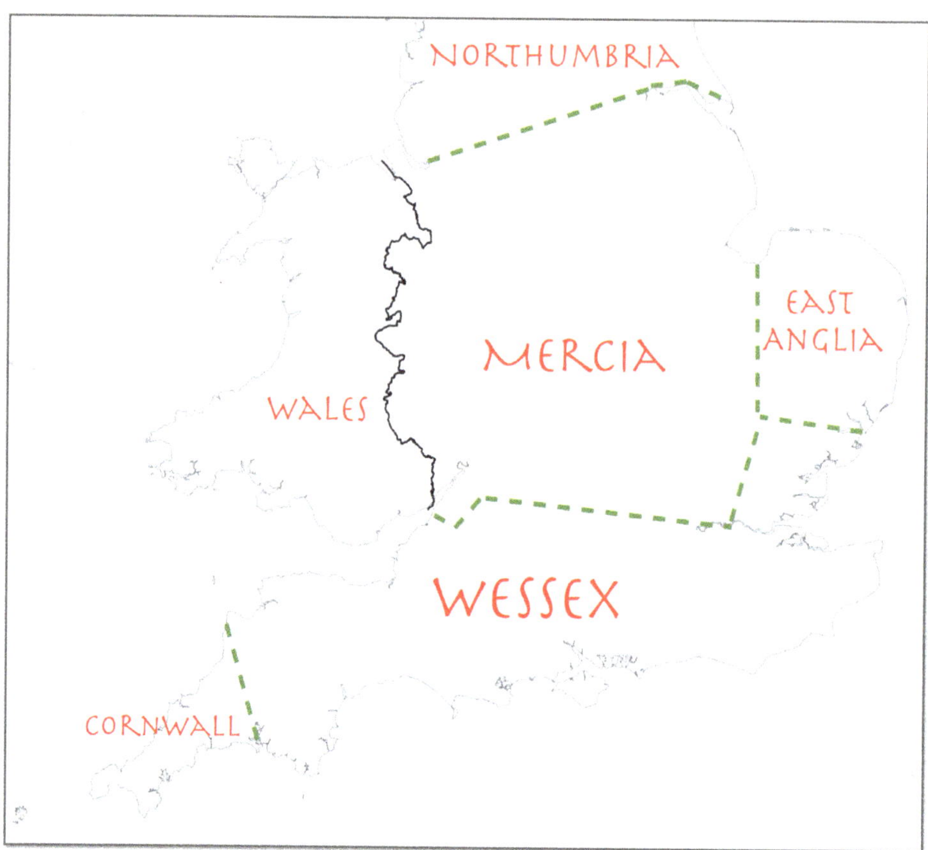

Fig.1 Schematic diagram of territorial divisions at the start of King Alfred's reign. Contains OS data © Crown copyright and database right (2018).

I was in no doubt that people were interested in the Anglo-Saxons generally, and King Alfred in particular. It seemed to me that there must be a reason why some important locations had few visitors, and it occurred to me that a reason was that there was no easy way for people to know where to go. This book aims to solve that problem. Some locations are obvious, others less so, and sometimes there are competing locations for the same event, which made my journey even more compelling because I found that musing over solutions to historical puzzles drew me deeper and deeper into the subject. It was like being an amateur detective in a historical setting.

This book also shows how fighting on through adversity can have stupendous outcomes. By 878 Mercia, Northumbria and East Anglia were under Viking rule, and it was now the turn of Wessex to come under intense pressure. Many must have thought that the odds of King Alfred being able to successfully fight back were too poor to make a struggle worthwhile. This was clearly not what Alfred believed, and he was right.

When Wessex was attacked in 878, Alfred could have done what King Burghred of Mercia had done when his nation was attacked in 874, which was to flee to Rome, but he chose not to do this. Instead, he rode out the storm and then fought back and won, and under his grandson, Athelstan, England would become a single united country.

With his elder brothers ahead of him in the line for the throne, the young Alfred must have considered it unlikely that he would become king. Perhaps of equal importance is that Æthelwulf, Alfred's father, may have thought it unlikely that Alfred would ever become king, and therefore would have planned his development accordingly, perhaps orienting him towards a future of religious dedication. However, it turned out that these elder brothers did die before Alfred, without their offspring being able to succeed them, and in 871 Alfred did indeed become king. I believe that it was at least partly because of this "career change" that Alfred became a great king. An education based around something other than kingship may have resulted in a king arguably more literate and philosophical than might have otherwise been the case. We know that he had these traits because they are apparent from his own writings that are available to us today, but he was great for other reasons as well. There is evidence that Alfred implemented important developments in the the defence of key towns, military reorganisation, and sea-faring capability.

King Alfred was a King of Wessex, and it may be helpful to describe Wessex in King Alfred's time. It included the counties that we now call Devon, Dorset, Somerset, Wiltshire, Berkshire (and some of adjacent Oxfordshire), Hampshire, the Isle of Wight, East and West Sussex, Kent and Surrey. Also included was Essex until it was ceded to Guthrum the Viking in a treaty drawn up around the year 886. It is worth pointing out that there were additional areas where King Alfred had the upper hand in possible power-sharing arrangements. By the end of his reign, this included London, which had earlier been under Mercian control. It also seems from Asser's writings (see p. 4) that at some time before 893 South Wales came under King Alfred's control. Asser tells us that this happened at the time of King Hyffaid of Dyfed, and we learn from the *Annales Cambriæ* that he died around 892. Nor must we forget Mercia itself. After about 879, western and southern Mercia (eastern Mercia remained under Viking control) was ruled by Æthelred, who was the son-in-law of King Alfred, and it seems that it was Alfred who had the upper hand. It may seem bizarre to think that his influence therefore extended as far as what we now know as Liverpool and Manchester, although there is no evidence that Alfred personally visited Mercia's distant northern points. The extent of Wessex control in Cornwall is still unclear. The *Annales Cambriæ* tell us that King Dungarth of Cornwall drowned in 875, but after that there is no mention of who was ruling in Cornwall until 926 where a version of the Anglo-Saxon Chronicles mentions a King Huwal of West Wales, which would have then meant Cornwall. It therefore seems to me that from a monarchical point of view Cornwall remained independent during Alfred's time. However, from an ecclesiastical point of view, we know that the diocese of Sherborne (in Dorset and therefore in Wessex) extended across the whole of Cornwall.

I occasionally refer to routes that Alfred or the Vikings may have taken. However, a caution needs to be raised about the routes available in Alfred's time because we may be unaware of the extent of minor routes at that time. Christopher Taylor[1] drew attention to the intensity of human occupation going back to the Iron Age, and that these settlements would have been connected by tracks. It isn't possible to know how many of these tracks have become our current roads, bridleways and footpaths but it seems plausible that a fair proportion of them must have survived. There is also the problem of uncertainty over how long a particular route may have remained in use. Where a Roman route is still in use today then it seems fair to assume that it would have been in use in Alfred's time. However, where a Roman road has disappeared, we may not know whether it went out of use before Alfred's time. Nonetheless, Roman roads that have gone out of current use are sometimes referred to in Saxon land transfer documents and some late-Saxon sites were on or near Roman roads, [2p.118] suggesting that some continued to be used in the Saxon period. Where sources refer to miles, I take this to be an approximate distance because we cannot be sure what was meant by a mile in Anglo-Saxon times. Old English miles were different to Roman miles, and both of these were different to modern miles (modern mile = 5280ft, Roman mile = 5000ft, Old English mile = about 6800ft). As far as personal names go, I have tried to remain faithful to the original Old English names except where I feel that a replacement spelling has become so accepted that the original would look arcane. I therefore retain the old spellings for the likes of Æthelwulf (Alfred's father) and Æthelred (an elder brother), but I use Alfred (instead of Ælfred or Elfred) for the great man himself.

Although this book contains some maps, it is presumed that the reader will be able to independently view Ordnance Survey maps, something that should usually be straight-forward with internet access. I have provided grid references for places that I feel might be particularly difficult to locate. The chapters are broadly in chronological order and I hope that many readers will read through them sequentially, although I expect that others will wish to skip straight to areas of particular interest. This latter approach should in most cases work out fine, albeit entailing a risk of missing out on some prior and relevant narrative. A lot happens in this book and I have provided a timeline at the end for reference.

Please remember that circumstances might have changed by the time that you read this book and it might be worth checking before you leave to visit a location. Furthermore, it is probably impossible to write a book like this without including some errors and, although I have tried not to commit such errors, you would probably be well advised not to place one hundred per cent reliance on an author who is merely an amateur historian. On a final note, please make sure that you have permission to go wherever you go and most importantly enjoy your journey into the old Wessex of King Alfred.

A note on sources

It is my hope that by now introducing the main historical sources to the reader it will be less necessary to disrupt the rest of the book with repeated explanations about source documents. Although the more important documents are mentioned below, I also used many additional sources, which I shall point out as I go along or in the references at the end of the book.

The most important source is the set of documents known as the Anglo-Saxon Chronicles, with the oldest versions written solely in Old English. The Anglo-Saxon Chronicles are a set of several documents that differ in detail. The version referred to in this book is mainly manuscript A, otherwise known as the Winchester, or Parker, manuscript. Although there are nine known Anglo-Saxon Chronicles (labelled by the letters A to I) we do not know how many there once were. However, none of the versions available to us today are original documents; they have all been derived or copied from earlier documents. Nonetheless, it is thought that there was once a single original document. The parts of this original Anglo-Saxon Chronicle that deal with Alfred are thought to have been written more or less at the same time that Alfred was king. Version A is the oldest and probably the closest to the original text and there is evidence that it was commenced in the last years of the ninth century[3 p. xxi] while Alfred, who died in 899, was alive. Modern English translations are available and I encourage those with an interest to obtain a copy. Where I have obtained dates from the Anglo-Saxon Chronicles, these have been adjusted to accommodate the fact that in the past the New Year did not always commence on January 1st.[3] This may be important as readers may find, particularly in older texts, that a different date (usually one year later) may be provided.

I also refer to a chronicle written by a person called Æthelweard, thought to have been written in the 970s-980s This is considered to be a translation from Old English into Latin of a lost Anglo-Saxon Chronicle that differed from the others in some aspects. Interestingly, Æthelweard was a descendant of Alfred's elder brother Æthelred and he was writing his chronicle for Mathilde, who was an abbess of Essen Abbey in today's Germany, and who also happened to be a direct descendent of King Alfred via his son King Edward the Elder. Æthelweard's chronicle is written in particularly difficult Latin, and the translation by John Allen Giles,[4] published in 1906, has been of great assistance.

I also refer to Geffrei Gaimar's *Estoire des Engleis* (History of the English), written in the Early French language, in Lincolnshire in the 1130s. It seems clear that Gaimar was using a version of the Anglo-Saxon Chronicles, and it is possible that this version may have been lost because Gaimar provides information that is not in the known versions, such as Alfred's fleeing to Whistley after the battle at Reading and the inclusion of Dorset forces in Alfred's army as it came together prior to the Battle of Ethandun.

I also repeatedly refer to the work of Asser, which has become known to us as *The Life of King Alfred*. Asser was a Welsh monk who spent much time with King Alfred and his writings are sometimes viewed as a biography of the King. Asser reveals that he was writing around 893, because he tells us that he was writing in Alfred's forty-fifth year. He was therefore writing at about the same time that the original Anglo-Saxon Chronicle started to be written. However, there has been controversy over whether this work was written by Asser or by a later person pretending to be Asser. The arguments for the latter were strongly put forward by Alfred Smyth, who suggested that a monk called Brythferth, who was attached to Ramsey Abbey (Cambridgeshire), wrote or collated the document around the year 1000. I personally find that if one strips away from *The Life of King Alfred* that which is obtainable from other documents (including the Anglo-Saxon Chronicles) one is left wondering why somebody who was supposed to have accompanied Alfred could have so little to add that was new or different. Although the only known ancient copy of *The Life of King Alfred* was unfortunately burnt in a fire in 1731 the owner, an Archbishop of Canterbury called Matthew Parker, had published a printed (as opposed to hand-written) version in 1574. However, and apparently with a team of people working for him, Matthew Parker added to and "improved" the original text. Although modern eyes have spotted obvious additions, some additions or changes to the original text that was lost in the fire may remain undetectable. We shall visit the problem of additions and "improvements" again in Chapter 5 where I turn to the story of King Alfred's burning of the cakes. However, even if *The Life of King Alfred* had not been written by Asser, it does not necessarily mean that the contents are erroneous, and Matthew Parker's additions may be just decoration on a foundation of truth. For example, while other sources provide no indication of Alfred's place of birth, *The Life of King Alfred* tells us that Alfred was born at Wantage. Even if the work was written around the year 1000 by someone other than Asser, the location of Wantage could have been correct and based on evidence available at that time. It is clear to me through my research that the predominant view is that the work of Asser was indeed written by Asser, although I continue to entertain the possibility that it may have been written by someone else, whilst accepting that the contents may be nonetheless largely factually correct. The document is not, however, infallible as there are known errors that we can point to. For example, the author locates York on the north bank of the Humber, which it clearly is not. Fortunately, however, a large part of the historical events described in *The Life of King Alfred* are corroborated by the Anglo-Saxon Chronicles.

Another source that crops up repeatedly is King Alfred's Will, and the point that I wish to make here in order to avoid later repetition is that I find it impossible to tell whether an estate that he left at a particular place comprised the whole of that named place or just a part of it (the Old English records these places as *ham* or *land*, which takes us no further). For example, when he left the estate at Guildford, was that the part of Guildford that he owned, or the whole of Guildford because he owned all of it? Guildford (and other places) would have been considerably smaller than it is now, so the latter option must be plausible. Therefore, when we are looking for these estates, we might be in fact looking for the Anglo-Saxon settlement as it was at that time.

Readers will note that I sometimes refer to what old documents say in their original language. I have always had an interest in languages and I have picked up some Old English and Latin along the way. I would not, of course, suggest that my abilities are in any way comparable to those of experts in this field, and I apologise for any mistakes that I have made, both in this regard, and anywhere else in this book. Finally, it is worth stating that the Anglo-Saxon Chronicles, and the writings of both Asser and Æthelweard are likely to be biased towards portraying Alfred in a good light. It is, however, impossible to tell which parts of these documents, if any, are exaggerated or false, and all we can do is work with the material that is available to us.

1

The young Alfred

King Alfred's life was relatively short in relation to modern expectations, but in this period he covered great distances politically, emotionally and geographically. In this chapter we look at his earlier life. I have taken this to be from his birth in 849 up to 870 when a series of battles, which are the subject of the next chapter, commenced. Hopefully the reader will appreciate that skipping from one location to another in a series of sometimes unconnected events is due to the fact that there is no continuous record of Alfred's life for us to draw upon. All that is available to us is a series of snapshots, and I write about these where I can relate them to particular locations. Let us start with where Alfred is said to have been born.

Wantage, Oxfordshire

Asser tells us that King Alfred was born at Wantage in 849, with his father being King Æthelwulf, and his mother being Osburgh. We are reliant on Asser for both the date and the location, although there is some evidence that he could have been born in 847 or 848.[5 p.228] This book assumes Asser to be correct, but the reader may wish to bear the alternatives in mind. Wantage was a small Roman settlement on the Letcombe Brook, later becoming the home of the Poet Laureate John Betjeman, and has now grown into a pretty but busy little town. It is now in Oxfordshire, but it used to be in Berkshire.

That Alfred was born in Wantage has been challenged on the basis that in 849 this settlement would not have been in Wessex but in Mercia, and therefore potentially in enemy territory. Indeed, there is evidence that Berkshire had been under Mercian control as recently as 844 because in that year the Bishop of Leicester granted land at Pangbourne (in Berkshire) to Beorhtwulf, the King of Mercia, who passed the land on to a man called Æthelwulf (a different Æthelwulf to Alfred's father), who will re-enter our story when we turn to the Battle of Englefield that took place in 870 (Chapter 2). However, in his book[6 pp.244-245] on Anglo-Saxon England Sir Frank Stenton indicated that at some time before 850 King Æthelwulf, Alfred's father, settled the disputes between Wessex and Mercia in this area and from then onwards Berkshire was part of Wessex. It

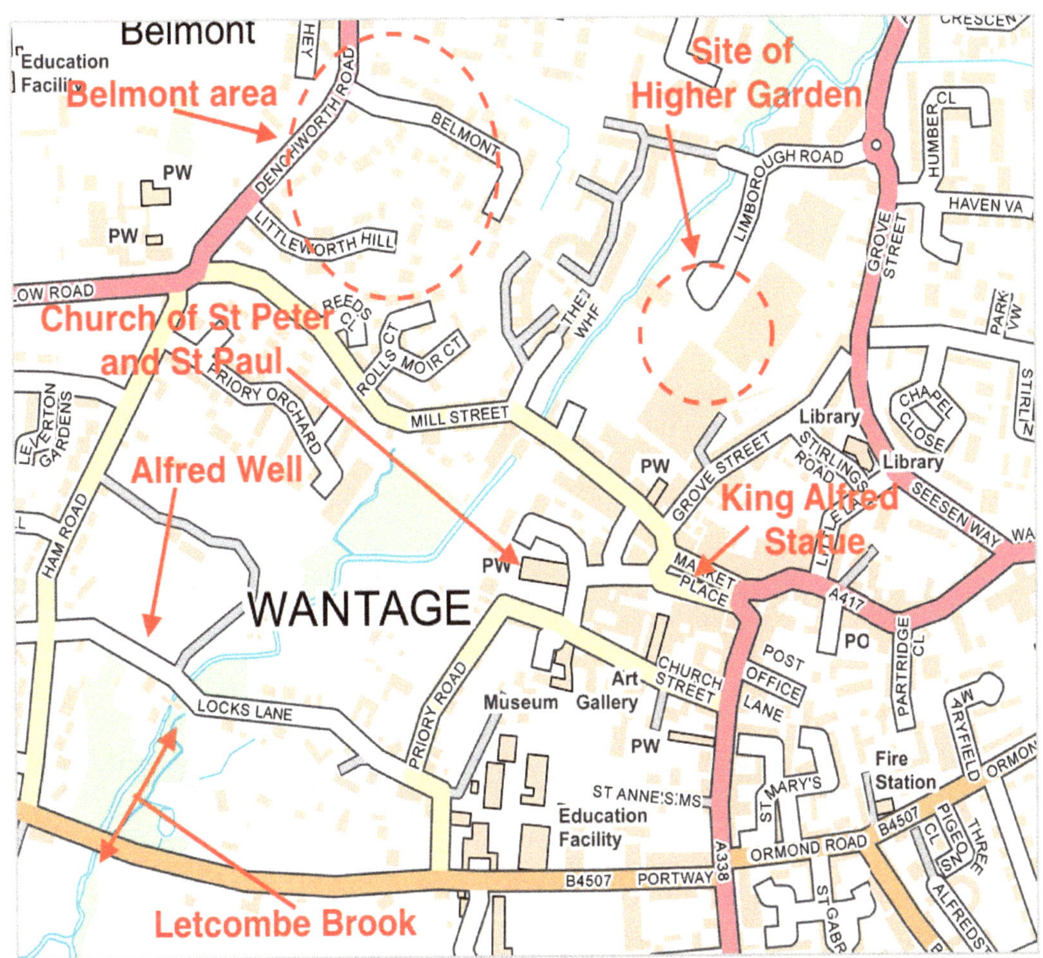

Fig. 2 Map of Wantage with places mentioned in the text. Contains OS data © Crown copyright and database right (2018).

therefore does not seem possible to dismiss Wantage as the location of Alfred's birth on the basis that it would have been in Mercia and not in Wessex.

Even though we can accept now that Wantage was in Wessex, it has also been argued that the proximity of Wantage to a hostile border with Mercia is a reason to doubt that Alfred would have been born there. However, this border may not have been particularly tense. Indeed, Sir Frank Stenton refers to[6] a coin with King Beorhtwulf of Mercia on one side and King Æthelwulf of Wessex, Alfred's father, on the other. This coin must date to when these kings' reigns coincided, which was between 839 and 852, and seems to indicate some sort of partnership rather than enmity. Remembering that Alfred was born in 849, it therefore does not seem possible to rule out Wantage as the location of Alfred's birth on the basis that it was close to a dangerous border with Mercia.

There is a famous statue of King Alfred in the market place where he stands high above the market traders on an eight feet high piece of Sicilian marble resting on granite rock, with an axe in his right hand and a scroll in his left. Woe-betide anybody who misbehaves in their commercial transactions! This statue was created by a Count Gleichen (Prince Victor of Hohenlohe-Langenburg) who was a friend of the Royal Family. It had been commissioned by Robert Loyd-Lindsey and unveiled in 1872 by Their Royal Highnesses the Prince and Princess of Wales, who had travelled by train to Wantage. Alfred in his statute form has settled in well with the town residents, while the square is a nice place to enjoy a beverage and a naughty piece of cake under the scrutiny of his gaze!

The royal unveiling is not the sole illustrious recognition that Alfred has had in Wantage. In his novel Jude the Obscure, Thomas Hardy recognises Alfred's connection to the town when he gives the town the fictitious name of *Alfredston*. It seems to me that Wantage has a thriving town centre, and I think Alfred would be proud of that. Indeed, Wantage won the Best town centre in Britain competition in 2014, with regeneration being an important factor.

In his will King Alfred left an estate at Wantage to his wife Ealhswith, and it seems plausible that this was the same estate at which he was born. As indicated in the Introduction, I find it impossible to tell whether an estate that he left in his will at a particular place comprised the whole of that named place as it existed at that time, because he owned all of it, or just a part of it. Nonetheless, evidence suggests that the focus of settlement had changed from the west of to the east of the Letcombe Brook by Alfred's time[7] which I feel gives us an important clue. Lis Garnish discussed possible locations for Alfred's royal estate at Wantage.[8] Although she found that the location could not be determined, she indicated that the earlier Roman site (west of the Letcombe Brooke) at Belmont was unlikely. She preferred the areas to the north and east of the church of St Peter and St Paul, with another possibility being to the south of this church and to the east of Priory Road. These locations are indeed consistent with the shift in the focus of settlement to the east of the Letcombe Brook. It is pleasant to wander around these areas, which are close together. The 1912 Ordnance Survey map shows a location west of Grove Street to be "Higher Garden. Site of palace", although this area has been developed into a retail park. It does not seem possible to rule this location out.

There is a spring known as "Alfred's Well", but there is no evidence that this was anything to do with King Alfred. Nonetheless, in 1849, the 1,000th anniversary of the birth of King Alfred was celebrated at this location.[9] The location is at Locks Lane (on the section on the west side of the Letcombe Brook - it is not possible to drive from one end of this road to the other), and you may see a corresponding "w" on OS maps (Grid Ref SU39338784). When you arrive at the site you will see an information board that makes no reference to King Alfred but states that the site is named after a certain Alfred Hazel, a 17th century cloth manufacturer.

Rome, Italy

Asser records that Alfred went to Rome twice. However, only the first visit is recorded in the Anglo-Saxon Chronicles, and this was in 853 when Alfred would have been only four or five years old! Asser records that on this first trip Alfred had been accompanied by many nobles and commoners, but it seems that his father did not travel with him as he did on the second trip. It is on this first trip to Rome that Asser records that the pope anointed Alfred as king (although he clearly was not yet king) and metaphorically adopted him as his son. It seems that much of this must have been ceremonial hyperbole, but we cannot know what influence this might have had on Alfred and those around him in later years. The second trip took place just a couple of years later in 855 and Asser records that on this occasion Alfred had been accompanied by his father, Æthelwulf. Asser records that Æthelwulf remained in Rome for a year and it seems likely that Alfred remained with him. There is evidence that there was unrest in Wessex while they were away because King Æthelwulf's son and Alfred's elder brother Æthelbald seems to have taken advantage of his father's absence and seized greater power for himself. It is recorded in the Annals of St Bertin[10] that Æthelwulf, on the return journey from Rome, betrothed (July 856) and married (1st October 856) Judith, daughter of Charles the Bald at a place called Verberie, to the north-east of Paris, and it seems likely that the young Alfred would have been present. It could have been this marriage that triggered unrest at home as further offspring might have changed the succession to Æthelbald's disadvantage. In order for Æthelwulf to be in a position to remarry it seem likely that Alfred's mother Osburg must have died. The Annals of St Bertin indicate that Æthelwulf, Judith and presumably Alfred, returned to Wessex after the marriage and, according to Asser, Æthelwulf was forced by his son Æthelbald to take the less important eastern territories (Kent, Sussex and Surrey) and to let Æthelbald rule the Wessex heartland. It is interesting to note that the 855 entry in the Annals of St Bertin records that Æthelwulf, and therefore presumably Alfred as well, had been received by Charles the Bald on the second outward journey to Rome. It is therefore possible that this is when Æthelwulf first met his second wife, Judith.

The best known route to Rome was the Via Francigena, but we cannot prove that Alfred or Æthelwulf went this way, or even overland. Verberie is about 50 miles off the route of the Via Francigena, but it is likely that there would have been a connecting route to this seemingly important place. Moving on to Italy, Pavia is on the Via Francigena before Rome and it seems that this was a notable location around Alfred's time. King Alfred's sister Æthelswith died in Pavia in 888 after having fled from the Vikings with her husband King Burghred of Mercia in 874, and Eadburgh, daughter of Offa, and wife of King Beorhtric of Wessex, also died in Pavia. A route via Pavia might therefore have been taken, although I have also seen it suggested that the route taken went through Brescia. It seems unlikely that it would have gone through both.

We can't be certain where precisely Alfred went in Rome, but it is highly likely that he spent time at what is today known as the Vatican, and also at what was then the *Schola Saxonum*, which had been built under the instruction of King Ine of Wessex (who reigned between 688 and 726, over a hundred years before Alfred was born). The role of the *Schola Saxonum* was to support Saxon pilgrims and it was located in an area to the east of the Vatican that is known as the Borgo. Today it is the location of the Ospedale di Santo Spirito. When Alfred and his father visited everything must have been dilapidated, new, or under reconstruction because we know that the Borgo had been devastated by fire in 847. I have been to Rome a few times, but this was before I caught the Anglo-Saxon fever. On those occasions I had no idea about the relationship between this part of the city and the Anglo-Saxons, and I would certainly now view it in a different light.

Ireland

In his 14th century writings known as the *Polychronicon*,[11] Ranulf Higden tells us that Alfred went to Ireland to visit a Saint Modewenna because of an incurable infirmity. The same source indicates that later on, after her church in Ireland had been destroyed, King Æthelwulf (Alfred's father) transferred the sisterhood to two abbeys in England with one at *Arderum apud Pelleswortham* (thought to be modern Polesworth in Warwickshire) and the other at *Streneshale* (although very similar to an old name for Whitby, evidence points to it being, like Polesworth, in the vicinity of the Forest of Arden[12]), where Saint Modwenna herself dwelled. Higden also tells us that Saint Editha, King Æthelwulf's sister, was also at Polesworth. Indeed, it seems that Polesworth Abbey had been founded by King Egbert (Æthelwulf's father and Alfred's grandfather) in 827, which would have been made possible by Wessex under King Egbert gaining control over Mercia in the period 825-830. Higden provides us with no dates, but he writes about Alfred's visit after he has described King Æthelwulf's return from Rome, which would have been in 856. Because Æthelwulf died in 858, and he must have been alive in order to assist with the transfer of the sisterhood from Ireland, Alfred must have gone to Ireland in the narrow period between 856 and 858, when he was still a child, and assuming that the story is at all true. Unfortunately, I have been unable to establish where in Ireland he was supposed to have gone. What Higden tells us is also interesting because it raises the possibility that Alfred was suffering from the first of three illnesses. We know that he later had a disorder (possibly haemorrhoids) that he had prayed for to relieve him of his carnal desires and a later ailment that commenced at his wedding celebrations.

Steyning, West Sussex

My journey also took me to the lovely town of Steyning, with its splendid Georgian townhouses and Tudor-styled timber buildings, all because of a record that Alfred's father had been buried there and my belief that it was likely that Alfred would have been present at that event, at the age of about nine. There is also a fascinating legend, pre-dating Alfred, that a St Cuthman built a church here after the wheelbarrow in which he was wheeling his paralysed grandmother had broken down. Indeed, you can meet St Cuthman in sculpture form just across the road from the church. It is interesting to note that in Saxon times Steyning, now inland, was on a large tidal estuary, with a harbour called Portus Cuthmanni, named after the saint. Alfred's father, Æthelwulf, died in 858, specifically on the 13th of January according to the writings of Florence of Worcester, and the Annals of St Neots tell us that he was interred at *Stening* (Steyning), although I couldn't find this place being mentioned in any other source. It seems likely that Alfred would have been at Steyning at some point if his father's funeral had taken place there. However, if Æthelwulf's body had ever been at Steyning, it was later moved to Winchester as the Anglo-Saxon Chronicles tell us that he was interred there. The church of St Andrew and St Cuthman in Steyning has a tombstone in the porch that is said to be from Æthelwulf's grave, although it is now thought to be 10th or 11th century,[13] and therefore too recent to be Æthelwulf's. However, I find that there are plausible reasons why Æthelwulf may have been initially interred at a place like Steyning in the eastern territories of Wessex. We have seen how Asser tells us that on King Æthelwulf's return from Rome his son Æthelbald forced him to be ruler in the east of Wessex, while Æthelbald gained control of the Wessex heartland in the west. It seems from the Anglo-Saxon Chronicles that this split persisted after King Æthelwulf's death as Æthelbald continued to hold the west while the next youngest son, Æthelberht replaced Æthelwulf in the east. It wasn't until Æthelbald died in 860 that the east and the west were reunited under King Æthelberht who, as we have seen, had already been ruling in the east. Perhaps when Æthelwulf died there were still ongoing hostilities with his son, or perhaps he had come to consider the eastern territories of Wessex as his kingdom in the two short years that he ruled over them since his return from France. These considerations may provide reasons why King Æthelwulf may have been interred in the east and perhaps therefore at Steyning, with his remains being transferred to Winchester after east and west came together under Æthelberht in 860. We know that Steyning was a place of some significance as King Alfred left an estate there to his nephew Æthelwold in his will. Although there are no visible remains, it is thought that the Anglo-Saxon minster at Steyning was at the approximate location of the current Norman church of St Andrew and St Cuthman.[13]

After returning from Rome it seems that Æthelwulf had two enemies. The first was the Vikings, and the second was his own son, Æthelbald. It seems difficult to believe that his displacement to the east would have resulted in a peaceful and stable situation. I suggest that he would have minimised his distance from the rest of Wessex that had been usurped from him and it therefore seems logical that he would base himself in West Sussex instead of further east, such as in distant Kent. There are two ancient hill-forts close to Steyning and Bramber (see later) that could have been brought back into use by Æthelwulf for strategic purposes. One is Cissbury Ring and the other is Chanctonbury Ring. It is only by climbing up these that one can get a true impression of how the views would have been important in the context of military intelligence. Taking both together, they provide a 360 degree view for many miles and are also within easy sight of each other. From Chanctonbury I could see Portsmouth, nearly 40 miles to the west. From these locations one could survey across towards the west of Wessex and also monitor Viking approaches on a wide east-west sweep.

There are ruins of a Norman castle at the top of a prominent natural hill at Bramber, just east of Steyning. However, it seems reasonable to wonder whether this hill, which seems as though it would have been crying out for military utilisation, could earlier have been used by Æthelwulf as a base and might explain his burial at nearby Steyning. Furthermore, the name Bramber seems to be derived from Old English.[14] We also know that Bramber was the administrative centre for the Rape of Bramber in the 11th century and It seems plausible that the place had prior significance rather than suddenly having significance thrust upon it after 1066. Maybe Bramber had also been the administrative centre for this area in Saxon times. The prominent natural hill at Bramber would have stood adjacent to the tidal estuary that was present in Saxon times (Bramber, like Steyning, is now inland). Indeed, when looking east from the castle's remains across the flat low-lying land one can easily appreciate where the expanse of water once was. I stayed at Bramber in the lovely Castle Inn Hotel, where I had ample opportunity to sample the excellent range of beers from the Harvey brewery whilst compiling my notes for this leg of the journey.

Beeding (now Upper Beeding), very close to Bramber on the other side of the River Adur, is also a contender for Æthelwulf's base because we know that Alfred left an estate there in his will. This went to his nephew Æthelhelm, which is interesting as the estate at Steyning, very close to Beeding, went to his other nephew Æthelwold (Æthelhelm's brother). That two royal estates were very close together might indicate that greater significance should be attached to this area, and to my mind this increases the likelihood that Aethelwulf indeed had a base in Steyning, Bramber or Beeding. In summary, there are reasons to believe the claim in the Annals of St Neots that Æthelwulf had been interred at Steyning. I have seen a reference to Alfred having fought a battle at Wolstonbury Hill, which is about eight miles east of Steyning. However, I did not find much evidence to support this.

Sherborne, Dorset

Sherborne is a lovely Dorset town with a big brooding ancient abbey. Although I live in Dorset and visit Sherborne frequently, it was with great pleasure that I was able to re-explore this beautiful town through the new perspective of its connections to King Alfred. Sherborne's most important feature is indeed its abbey, and it is here that two elder brothers of King Alfred, Æthelbald (died 860) and Æthelberht (died 865) had been buried, and I consider it likely that Alfred would have been present at their funerals, or would have at least visited their resting places. He would have been about eleven years old at the time of the first death, and about sixteen at the time of the second. It is interesting to note in passing that between the dates of these two deaths Alfred's name appears on a charter (a document transferring rights or land) dating to 862, when Alfred would have been only about thirteen, issued at a place called *Willherestrio*, the location of which remains unknown. To return to the matter of burials, it is possible that a third brother of Alfred was buried at Sherborne as well. The Anglo-Saxon Chronicles, with the exception of the B version, have this brother, Æthelred, buried at Wimborne (Dorset), but the B version tells us that he was buried at Sherborne. I consider that this contradiction can be resolved by considering that Æthelred may initially have been interred at Wimborne and then later moved to Sherborne, probably because of the relative importance of the latter location. That the other two brothers had been interred at Sherborne supports the idea that this place was more important than Wimborne.

There is a plaque in the abbey indicating the approximate location of the burials of Æthelbald and Æthelberht, and there is nearby a small area where the floor has been replaced by glass and some bones can be seen beneath. However, in discussion with a member of staff of the abbey I was told that it is not really known whose remains these are. I was also told that there had been a plan to compare the DNA from these bones with the Anglo-Saxon bones housed in Winchester cathedral, but at the time of writing I am not aware of this having taken place.

It is significant that Asser, King Alfred's companion and biographer, and from whose writings we derive so much information, became bishop of Sherborne at some time in the 890s, while King Alfred was still alive, and it appears that he continued in this role until his death in 909, ten years after Alfred had died. In order to understand the importance of Sherborne in Alfred's time it is important to appreciate that it had a huge diocese, created by King Ine of Wessex in 705, that extended all the way down to Land's End in Cornwall. The Abbey still has Saxon elements despite much of the earlier church being demolished by Roger of Caen to be replaced by a larger Norman one. As you walk around Sherborne it is easy to be unaware of just how important this place would have been. In my opinion it must have been one of the most important places in Wessex, perhaps even the most important in a period before Winchester would be able to claim that title.

Saint Neot, Cornwall

The writings of Asser indicate that Alfred went on a hunting trip in Cornwall some time before he married in 868. We are told that on this trip Alfred made a detour to visit the resting place of a Saint Gueriir, about whom we know very little. Asser tells us that Alfred prayed there to be relieved of painful haemorrhoids, and for this ailment to be replaced by something less severe. We are told that Alfred was indeed cured from his first malady, although it appears that his prayers may not have been fully answered because Asser also tells us that the second condition, which waited until his wedding feast before it struck and then lasted until he was about forty four, was actually worse than the one it replaced. We are told that Alfred had contracted his first disorder after having prayed for it in order to subdue his carnal desires. We do not know whether he had specifically prayed for haemorrhoids or whether haemorrhoids had been effective in calming him down. It therefore seems that he visited St Neot between the age that he would have become susceptible to carnal urges and when he got married in 868 at the age of about nineteen. Perhaps here is the best place to bring in the contentious matter regarding whether Alfred had an illegitimate son, with his wish to restrain his carnal desires possibly being a response to this. The focus of this line of enquiry has been a man called Osferth, who appears as an important person in some charters and is left a large amount of property in Alfred's will. The evidence, however, is not conclusive and it seems to me that we can't go any further than saying that Alfred may have had an illegitimate son called Osferth.

So, where was this place in Cornwall that we are told Alfred visited? Fortunately, Asser tells us that the resting place of St Gueriir was also the resting place of St Neot, and we know where this latter was. The church of St Neot, in the village of the same name, was the initial resting place of St Neot. Corroboration is provided by a document called the Life of Saint Neot (*Vita S. Neoti*), which indicates that the location was about 10 miles from Saint Petroc's monastery, which was at Bodmin. The distance from Bodmin to St Neot is approximately correct, and I am aware of no other candidate for the resting place of St Neot that would fit with this distance. When Saint Neot was later transferred, at some time before 1020, to St Neots Priory in Cambridgeshire, presumably Saint Gueriir remained where he was, as perhaps he does to this day. Recalling that Alfred had been praying for a cure (and a less severe replacement illness), it may not escape the notice of some that "Gueriir" is very similar to the french word *guerir*, meaning "to cure." Perhaps more significantly, there is a Cornish word *gweres*, which means to help or assist. However, the similarities between these translations and the name of the saint may be just coincidence, although I have seen speculation that St Gueriir had been a healer at a castle or court at Liskeard.[15] Asser tells us that Alfred had a tendency to make detours to a church, but it is unclear whether Asser meant that Alfred had a tendency to make a detour to this particular church or to churches in general. He may therefore have visited the location of St Neot on more than one occasion, perhaps on different hunting trips to Cornwall.

I visited the church at St Neot during a torrential downpour and the wind was so powerful it was rocking my car from side to side. I eventually made it to the church and when I re-emerged the wind had dropped, the rain had stopped, and the birds were singing. Perhaps St Gueriir appreciated my visit. The present church is much more recent than the time of King Alfred, but it is possible that there could have been an earlier building on the same site. There has been speculation that a cross in the churchyard may have been given by Alfred, but there doesn't seem to be any evidence to confirm this. There seems to be confusion between the similarly sounding St Neot and a St Anietus, with the original dedication of the church possibly having been to a Saint Anietus. I have seen it mentioned that Anietus was a Celtic saint and Neot was a Saxon one, although I have not been able to tell whether they are in fact different names for the same person.

It has been suggested that Alfred would not have gone hunting in Cornwall because it would have then been hostile territory,[16] although I am unaware of any evidence that confirms that this would have been the case. On close analysis it can be seen that when Asser tells us that the resting place of Saint Gueriir was the same place as that of St Neot, what he is precisely saying is that it had also *become* the resting place of Saint Neot. This is important because it means that St Neot may have still been alive when Alfred visited the location that would later become St Neot. It also means that suggestions that I have come across claiming that they knew each other, and may have even been companions, cannot be ruled out. However, I found no evidence to support another suggestion that St Neot had been a brother of Alfred. There is a tradition that St Neot appeared to Alfred in a supportive dream on the night before the assembly of troops at Egbert's Stone, and again in a vision prior to the battle at Ethandun in 878 (Chapter 7). These traditions may not be compatible with arguments that Alfred and St Neot knew each other in life, because it seems to me that visitations in dreams are more associated with people who have died than those who are still alive.

A defended base must have been available for his visit to Cornwall, and it is interesting to speculate where this might have been. According to his will, Alfred had an estate in Cornwall at Stratton (near Bude), although this is some 30 miles distant from St Neot and we don't know whether this was available to him when he was younger. It is also possible that he was hosted by a Cornish ruler, and this could have been King Dungarth. Although there appears to be nothing to indicate when Dungarth's reign commenced, the *Annales Cambriae* record that he drowned in 876, which makes it possible that he was around at the time Alfred came to Cornwall before 868. I have seen it suggested that Dungarth had a court at Liskeard, which is not far from St Neot and indeed also not far from the mysterious King Doniert's Stone, which has been associated with Dungarth because Dungarth and Doniert are thought to have been the same person. The remains have been dated to the approximate time of Dungarth, and the Latin inscription includes the name Doniert.[17] The site is very easy to visit as it is at the roadside a short distance north-west of St Cleer. Unfortunately, I visited during a torrential downpour. I waited for it to stop but it never does when you need it to, so I left the shelter of the car to examine the stones and got drenched in the process.

Fig. 3 The Church of St Neot in Cornwall

Alfred's Wedding

Asser tells us that Alfred got married in 868, and he tells us this before he tells us that Alfred was involved in the confrontation with the Vikings at Nottingham in the same year. This suggests, but does not make it certain, that the marriage took place before the events at Nottingham, which will be described later in this chapter. Alfred would have been about nineteen when he got married and there were still a few years to go before he would become king in 871. The celebrations, wherever they took place, would have been spoiled because Asser tells us that Alfred's second period of illness commenced at the wedding feast. However, I found it somewhat surprising that Asser, who wrote about the life of Alfred, does not tell us the wife's name. Fortunately, we can work out that she was called Ealhswith because this is the name of the wife (*coniunx*) of King Alfred provided on a list of benefactors to the New Minster at Winchester, drawn up in the reign of King Canute.[18]

It has been suggested that Alfred may have married Ealhswith at the Oxfordshire (previously Berkshire) village of Sutton Courtenay.[19] It seems that at least part of the reason for this is that a charter was issued by Alfred's elder brother, King Æthelred, from Sutton Courtenay in 868, the same year as Alfred's marriage. Tantalisingly, the list of witnesses to this charter includes an "Ælfred", who is described as a "minister." However, I feel that this may not be the same Alfred as the future king because he isn't usually described as a minister. Of course, showing that an Alfred on a charter was a different Alfred to the future king does not mean that Alfred did not get married at the same place that the charter was issued from. Indeed, one could argue that if King Æthelred was there, then Alfred could have been there too, because these two people often appear together. A further complication arose when I looked at the Old English and found that the location was named as *Suðtun*. It seemed to require a leap of faith from me to select Sutton Courtenay from all the other available places called Sutton. However, another charter, issued much later in 983, came to the rescue because it mentioned *Suðtun* in the same breath as a place called *Drætun*, and I knew that there was a place called Drayton immediately to the west of Sutton Courtenay. I therefore believe that it is highly likely that the *Suðtun* of the 868 charter is indeed Sutton Courtenay.

Furthermore, archaeological investigations around Sutton Courtenay, including in the parish of Drayton, have turned up significant Anglo-Saxon discoveries. Time Team found an Anglo-Saxon Great Hall),[20] perhaps big enough to be royal, south of Drayton East Way and west of Milton Road, with its long axis running east-west. The site is on private land but it is possible to look across the area and try to imagine the presence of the great hall. Although it appears that the hall and associated complex pre-dated King Alfred because they were dated to the seventh century,[21] it is possible that the site persisted in some way into Alfred's time. If we are considering Sutton Courtenay as the location of Alfred's wedding, something that can be argued for, but we cannot prove, then this great hall must be a candidate for where it took place. It is also possible that a wedding at Sutton Courtenay might have taken place at a location more towards the centre of the current village. It has been suggested that Sutton became a royal estate in 801, with the location subsequently becoming the site of Sutton's Abbey, which is now a conference centre and retreat. The oldest parts of the abbey, which is private property, are 14th century. Although there may have been an earlier building, I am unaware of any investigations that have demonstrated this, and therefore I was unable to convince myself that this was the site of a royal estate.

The River Thames formed the border between Mercia and Wessex, and Sutton Courtenay would have been on the Wessex side. However, this causes a problem because Asser tells us that the wedding took place in Mercia. At first sight it seems that either Asser is wrong, or the wedding did not take place at Sutton Courtenay. However, it turns out that as recently as 844, Mercia had been occupying at least part of Berkshire, on the other side of the Thames, so it is perhaps possible that Sutton Courtenay had still been in Mercia at the time of Alfred's wedding in 868. There is also a charter issued in

868 by Alfred's sister Æthelswith, Queen of Mercia, granting land at Lockinge in Berkshire (now in Oxfordshire) to a minister called Cuthwulf. With Lockinge being only about 8 miles from Sutton Courtenay, this provides supporting evidence that this part of Berkshire had been under Mercian control when Alfred got married. Furthermore, this charter is countersigned by both Æthelred, the King of Wessex *and* Burghred, King of Mercia (and husband of Æthelswith), which seems to indicate that some sort of joint control was being exercised.

Visitors to Sutton Courtenay may not want to miss the churchyard of All Saints', which contains the graves of Herbert Asquith and George Orwell (Eric Arthur Blair), who is buried in front of his friend David Astor who had secured the plot for both of them. Asquith lived and died in the village (look out for the blue plaque near the sharp bend as you head north out of the village on Church Street). You don't have to walk far from Sutton Courtenay before you arrive at a beautiful stretch of the River Thames, which you can follow upstream to the important town of Abingdon and the site of its ancient abbey.

Gainsborough has also been put forward as the location for Alfred's wedding. There is no doubt that Gainsborough was in Mercia and it has been argued that it got its name because Ealhswith, Alfred's wife, was the daughter of a chief of a tribe called the Gaini. Asser does indeed tell us that Ealhswith was descended from the Gaini, but the place-name of Gainsborough has been referred to as being derived from a person called Gegn. The people called the Gaini and the location called Gainsborough may therefore be entirely unconnected. Even if Gainsborough had got its name from the Gaini, there would be no reason to assume that the wedding took place there anyway. I have also seen it written that the Gaini were located in Worcestershire, which is about 100 miles from Gainsborough! It may be that we cannot do any better than saying that the Gaini, and therefore Alfred's father-in-law, were from some unspecifiable place in Mercia.[5] There is another reason to add to the above why I don't think the wedding would have taken place at Gainsborough. Let me explain. We know that Alfred engaged with the Vikings at Nottingham in 868 and Gainsborough is some 40 miles north-east of Nottingham. The Anglo-Saxon Chronicles tell us that after the confrontation at Nottingham, Mercia made peace with the Vikings and that they returned to York in 869. Although it is difficult for us to have a clear understanding of how peaceful things were in this area at this time, the overall picture does not seem to be one of stability and I suggest that this makes it less likely that Alfred would have gone beyond Nottingham, either before or after the engagement with the Vikings, in order to get married.

The location of Alfred's wedding is therefore open to speculation and remains a great puzzle still in need of further clues, great minds, imagination and a solution.

Nottingham

The Anglo-Saxon Chronicles tell us that in 868 Alfred went to Nottingham with his brother King Æthelred. They were there because King Burhred of Mercia had requested assistance in dealing with a Viking attack. The Chronicles tell us that they met the Vikings at the stronghold (*geweorc*) and peace was made between the Mercians and the Vikings, who then moved back to York. It is difficult to portray this as a victory for the combined Wessex and Mercian force, and it is likely that the Vikings had demanded some sort of tribute as a price for leaving. The stronghold may have been at the obvious location of Castle Rock, where the current castle stands, but there are alternatives. Asser records that the Vikings had over-wintered at Nottingham prior to this engagement and it may have been easier for the Vikings to sustain themselves at a location lower down than that of Castle Rock. Excavations have indicated a line of Anglo-Saxon defences around the area that is now known as the Lace Market[22] and it is possible that the Vikings used these defences as a stronghold after taking them over. It is interesting to note that Æthelweard's chronicle does not mention Alfred and Æthelred going to Nottingham at all. However, because their presence is indicated in the Anglo-Saxon Chronicles and Asser, I believe that it is more likely that they did in fact go to Nottingham.

2

Survival and Kingship. The events of 870 to 871

Alfred disappears from the records in 869, but reappears again in the period of 870 to 871 when an important series of engagements with the Vikings took place. At the start of this period a Viking army arrived at Reading and at the end, for reasons that are not clear, this Viking army left Wessex and went to London where the Mercians made peace with them. This chapter focuses on the battles that took place at different locations across central southern England in this period. For most of this period Alfred fought alongside his brother, King Æthelred, but Alfred himself became king when Æthelred died after the Battle of *Meretun*.

The Anglo-Saxon Chronicles tell us that nine battles were fought in the period covered by this chapter. However, the Anglo-Saxon Chronicles provide locations for only six of these (Englefield, Reading, Ashdown, Basing, *Meretun* and Wilton) and no additional locations are mentioned in other sources. Therefore, three battles are missing from the written record. The Vikings had a base at Reading from December 870 to some point in 871 when, after the battle of Wilton, Wessex made peace with them (perhaps by paying them off) and they went to London. Alfred had become king by the time of the battle of Wilton, so the peace, whatever this constituted, was established under his rule.

It is interesting to note that despite the assistance given by Wessex to the Mercians at Nottingham in 868, there is little record of assistance from Mercia to Wessex for the engagements described in this chapter. The exception is the contribution by Ealdorman Æthelwulf (and presumably his troops) at Englefield and Reading (see below). It has been suggested that the absence of Mercians may have been because Wessex withdrawn its troops prematurely from Nottingham,[23] although there is nothing in the Anglo-Saxon Chronicles to support this. Nonetheless, we are told that the Vikings had over-wintered at Nottingham, so Wessex may have been unable to retain its forces when men needed to return home to deal with the harvest and other matters in a period that was before King Alfred re-organised and improved the flexibility of the military after 878. However, the Vikings may have had permission to overwinter before moving on, which would not have been unique as this would happen again after their defeat at Exeter in 876. It seems more likely to me that the Mercians did not appear in the battles in this chapter because they had become subjugated to the Vikings as part of the price for peace at Nottingham in 868. It is indeed possible that King Burghred of Mercia was a puppet king from 868 until he was finally deposed by the Vikings in 874.

It is thought that Alfred's daughter, Æthelflæd, was born around 870, and I think that she and Alfred's wife, Ealhswith, would have been kept well away from any turmoil. This daughter would go on to become the renowned Queen of the Mercians.

The Battle of Englefield, 870

There is a pretty little village in Berkshire called Englefield, which in 870 had the misfortune to become the site of a battle. Alfred was not present, but I include it here because it was an important precursor to the Battle of Reading, which took place just a few days later in 871. The engagement was between Ealdorman Æthelwulf (not to be confused with Alfred's deceased father of the same name) and the Vikings who had set up camp at nearby Reading just three days previously. Æthelwulf, a Saxon leader in Berkshire, was fighting on behalf of Wessex and he won. He had earlier been granted land at nearby Pangbourne in 844, and it is plausible that he was still based there in 870, and this might explain why it was him who turned up to fight the Vikings at Englefield. His appearance at Englefield would have been facilitated by the Roman road connecting Silchester with Dorchester-on-Thames that passed close to both Pangbourne and Englefield. That this road remained in use in Saxon times is supported by the belief that the stretch of the A340 as it passes Englefield is thought to be on the Roman route. Unfortunately, Ealdorman Æthelwulf lost his life at the Battle of Reading just a few days later. Interestingly, Ealdorman Æthelwulf may have been a Mercian, because Ethelweard's chronicle tells us that after his death at Reading his body was taken to Derby.

Englefield is down a lane that leads nowhere else and at the end there is the lovely St Mark's church and Englefield House. But where precisely did the battle take place? I was consulting my Ordnance Survey map when a lady stopped her big car and stared at me. It turned out that she was from the big house and they were on guard for reporters and so on because an important wedding was set to take place at the church. However, when I explained that I was looking for the site of the battle, this lady was most helpful indeed. She allowed me on to private land to have a view of where the battle site was thought to be. The gardens are open to the public on certain days and you may then be able to go to where I went or close to it. Essentially, the location pointed out to me was the fields to the north-west of the house, known locally I gather as Angle Field or Angles Field (from whence Englefield). I later found out that the wedding was that of Pippa Middleton, who I had indeed heard of.

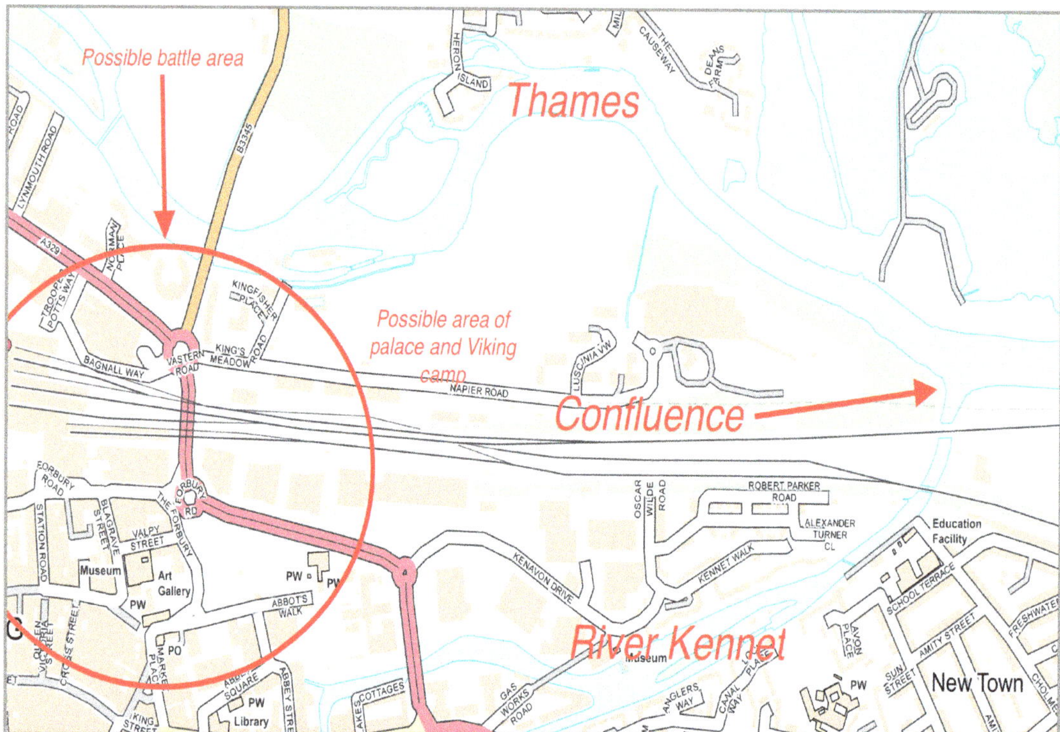

Fig.4 The peninsula at Reading as it is today. Contains OS data © Crown copyright and database right (2018).

The Battle of Reading, 871

Reading is a large town on the Thames in Berkshire. With all the commercial development, the busy roads and the nearby M4 it is all too easy to over-look this place's great historical significance. And it doesn't take much to scratch the surface to discover layer upon layer of questions requiring answers.

We know that in 871 Alfred and his older brother King Æthelred fought, and unfortunately lost, a battle against the Vikings at Reading where they had set up a base. But where in Reading did this battle take place? As a starting point let us examine where the Viking base could have been. An important feature of Reading is that part of the town lies on a peninsula bounded to the north by the Thames and to the south by the Kennet, and to the east by the confluence of these two rivers. We know that the Vikings set up camp somewhere to the west of the confluence, and this would have been partly because being on a peninsula made the location more defendable, but also because, as

Asser tells us, there was a royal estate there. It seems to me that the Vikings would have taken over this royal estate and I therefore believe that the Viking camp and the royal estate would have been at the same place. But this is a fairly large peninsula, so where more precisely was this royal estate? Asser comes to the rescue and clearly tells us that the royal estate was located on the south bank of the Thames.

He also tells us that the Vikings built a rampart south of this royal estate. Clearly, if we can find a rampart, then this may help us identify the location of the Viking camp and the royal estate. Unfortunately, there seems to be no surviving rampart, but there are records of a trench that might have once been accompanied by a rampart. I noticed this feature on a map in a book by John Man, published in 1816,[24] which showed something called the "Plummery Ditch." It seems that this ran north from the River Kennet approximately where Oscar Wilde Road is, and then headed north-west under the railway line. A feature named "Plummery Ditch" is also displayed on the 1879 Ordnance Survey map, to the south of the railway line, although most of the ditch shown on John Man's map seems to have been lost by then. There is now a retail park over the section that is visible on the 1879 map. It is of course possible that the Plummery Ditch was a later feature, perhaps related to the abbey that was founded in 1121. However, if the Plummery Ditch did represent the Viking rampart then the royal site would have extended from the railway line, through King's Meadow to the north, and across to the south bank of the Thames.

Asser tells us that the Wessex forces arrived at the gate of the Viking camp, but the 12th century writer Geffrei Gaimar tells us that the Wessex forces engaged the Vikings in open country, presumably meaning to the west of the Viking camp because to the east was the confluence of the Thames and the Kennet. The two scenarios are, of course, not mutually exclusive. It is possible that the Wessex forces initially went to the Viking stronghold and then the battle took place in, or moved on to, open country.

It therefore seems to me that the most likely location for the battle is in an area extending from the eastern end of King's Meadow. If you are ever waiting at the train station or stuck in traffic on Vastern Road you might find it interesting to consider whether you are on a battle site. I don't know how old the busy Vastern Road is, or how it got its name, but it strikes me that it could derive from Old English, meaning either fortress, or western (the road indeed leads west, and also leads to more or less what seems to me to be the correct area for the royal estate / Viking camp).

Fig. 5 Looking across at the very tip of the peninsula, with the Thames on the right and the River Kennett flowing in from the left.

Much of the relevant area can be easily explored on foot. I parked at the King's Meadow NCP car park on Napier Road, crossed the King's Meadow, which is a large recreational ground, and then proceeded to walk east along the Thames until the confluence with the Kennet, then west along the Kennet until back in the centre of Reading. It was necessary to cross a footbridge near the confluence as it seemed that the only path back into Reading was along the south bank of the Kennet. Near the confluence there is a very pleasant wooded area where deer have managed to hang on (I know because I saw one!).

In his writings of 1838, John Doran indicated that a Dr Stukeley had asserted that remains of the Viking entrenchments could be traced near a place called Catsgrove Hill.[25] The 1879 Ordnance Survey map shows what appear to be earthworks at Katesgrove (taking Katesgrove to be Catsgrove), and in particular a "Bob's Mount." However, this area, now developed, does not appear to be near enough to the confluence of the Thames and the Kennet to be the correct location.

So, Alfred and his elder brother King Æthelred would have fled from the site of the battle, but where did they go next?

Whistley and Twyford

Whistley and Twyford are very close to each other and are both on the River Loddon in Berkshire. Twyford is by far the larger and easier to find of the two places, but if you follow the Loddon south from Twyford on a large-scale map you will soon locate what is marked as Whistley Green.

It is recorded in Geffrei Gaimar's 12th century chronicle that after the battle at Reading, King Æthelred and Alfred, presumably with their troops, fled east to Whistley (*Wiscelet*) and crossed a ford unknown to the Vikings. Gaimar writes that the Vikings went to nearby Twyford (*Thuiforde*), which is named after its two former fords, and Alfred and his brother thereby escaped. To have headed for Whistley from Reading they would have needed to have crossed the Kennet at some point, but where this was is not recorded.

There is currently a ford (Grid Ref SU78227481) near the Land's End pub, where Landsend Lane meets Park Lane, west of the River Loddon and of Whistley. Travelling east from here you will cross a ford through the "Old River" and then a bridge over the River Loddon and then you will arrive at Whistley Green. In the past there could have been two fords, or the watercourse may have been such that the Old River, which is in fact a branch of the Loddon, and the main stream of the Loddon may not have been separated at that time. It is easy to cross the ford if the water is low, but there are signs warning people not to attempt a crossing otherwise. Whilst it cannot be proved that this is the same ford used by Alfred and Æthelred to escape the Vikings, it must at least be very close as Whistley is a small place. It should be noted that the watercourses around Whistley would have been different in Alfred's time. For example, the nearby Loddon Nature Reserve comprises flooded gravel pits.

There is no record of where Alfred and King Æthelred went next. However, we know that they were at the Battle of Ashdown just four days later. The location of this battle has not been determined, but the distance from Whistley to my preferred location at Lowbury Hill (see later) is about 20 miles. Clearly, there was time for the Wessex troops to regroup and make the journey, perhaps by a northerly route in order to avoid the Viking base at Reading.

There are various sources that claim that King Æthelred and Alfred escaped via the fords at Twyford, a place that is very close to and better known than Whistley. I can find nothing to indicate that they took this route and I do not know how this idea took hold, but perhaps it is possible that Whistley and Twyford have in the past been bracketed as the same location, or perhaps Geffrei Gaimar's indication that it was the Vikings that went to Twyford just got distorted across time. Nonetheless it is interesting to take a brief look at the route the Vikings took. It can be seen on maps that when approaching Twyford from the west one has to cross two water courses, the Old River and the River

Loddon (being the same two rivers mentioned at Whistley). The Vikings would have needed to cross these via two fords and it seems that the route would have been approximately that taken by the Old Bath Road. They presumably returned to Reading on realising that Alfred and Æthelred had given them the slip.

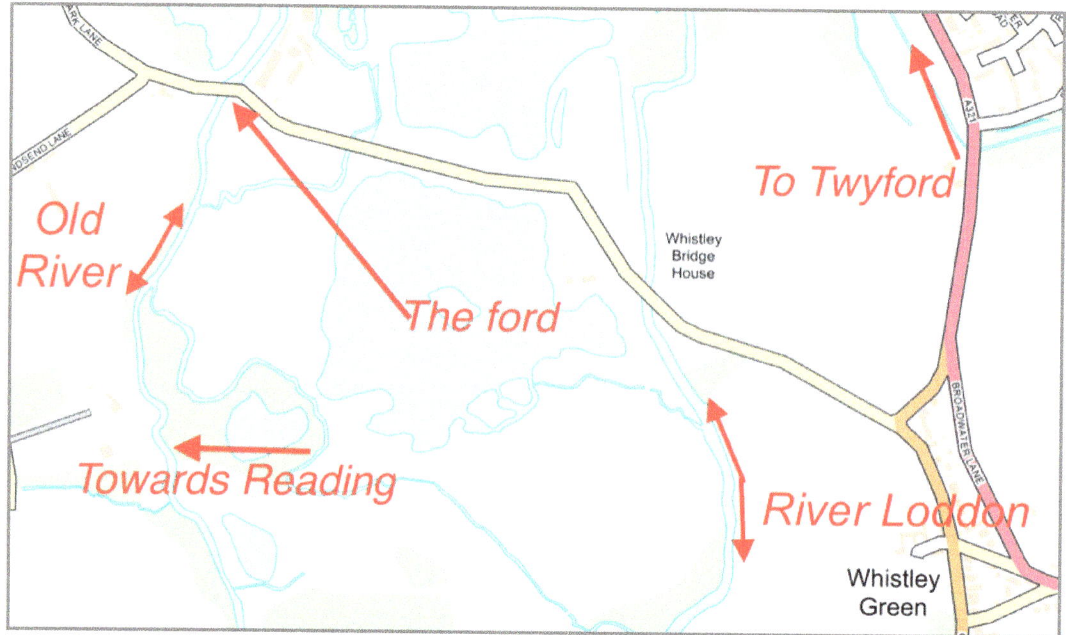

Fig. 6 The area around Whistley, Berkshire, as it is today. Contains OS data © Crown copyright and database right (2018).

The Battle of Ashdown, 871

This battle took place just four days after the Battle of Reading and was an important victory for King Æthelred and Alfred, sandwiched between the two losses at Reading and Basing. However, the location of this battle has not been determined and, unlike Reading, Basing or Wilton, it has not been possible to identify Ashdown with any modern settlement.

Potential locations can be divided into two areas. The first is a group of more western sites that lie near White Horse Hill in Oxfordshire, and the second group is about twenty miles to the east of the first group, on the Downs near Moulsford and Streatley, and being mainly in Oxfordshire but close to the modern boundary with Berkshire to the south.

The Anglo-Saxon Chronicles refer to the location as *æscesdun*, claimed by Asser to mean a hill of ash trees. Of course, there would have been many hills with ash trees on them. However, Asser also refers to the battle taking place near to a solitary thorn tree. It therefore seems that Asser's solitary thorn tree was located on a hill populated by ash trees. Although we can probably picture something like this in our minds, it is of little help in finding the location in today's landscape. However, Asser perhaps gives us another clue about the location when he tells us that after the Battle of Ashdown the surviving Vikings returned to their fortress. As the Battle of Ashdown was four days after the Battle at Reading, and we know that the Vikings had a camp at Reading, it seems likely that they had come from and retreated back to that location. The next recorded battle was two weeks later at Basing, approximately sixteen miles from Reading. All this seems to make sites closer to Reading better contenders for the site of the Battle of Ashdown than the more distant sites. The second geographic area may therefore be more likely to contain the correct location for the battle. This second area is also approximately half way between Reading and the site of the great abbey at Abingdon, which the Vikings perhaps had intended to raid.

Wherever the battle took place, it is important to remember that the Anglo-Saxon Chronicles indicate that it was two simultaneous battles at the same location with both the Wessex forces and the Vikings having split into two groups. King Æthelred took on the army of the Viking kings and Alfred took on the army of the Viking earls. Let us start by looking at the first group of sites.

1. Sites around White Horse Hill, Oxfordshire

White Horse Hill and Uffington Fort

It has been suggested that White Horse Hill is where Alfred prepared his troops prior to the Battle of Ashdown. It has also been put forward as the site of the Battle of Ashdown itself, partly because of the presence of the white horse, with a parallel being drawn with the presence of another white horse near a claimed location for Alfred's other famous victory at Ethandun (Chapter 7).

I had not visited this area for twenty-five years. There are now red kites and ravens present, which I cannot recall seeing on my earlier visits. I had heard that the best view of the White Horse was from Dragon Hill and I could see this distinctive mound whist walking across to the White Horse from the main car park, but I could not initially work out how to get to it. I eventually got there by going over the top of the horse itself and dropping down past its tail. Dragon Hill is a fascinating feature irrespective of how little it improves the view of the White Horse. The only good view must be from the air, which perhaps tells us something about our ancestors.

Uffington Fort[26] is a very short distance west of the White Horse, and is right up against the ancient long-distance Ridgeway route. The ramparts of this iron age fort were much better preserved than I had been expecting, and it has been suggested that the Vikings made their camp here prior to the Battle of Ashdown. You may not wish to miss the opportunity to visit nearby Wayland's Smithy, a famous long barrow, which lies to the west of White Horse Hill along the Ridgeway.

Blowing Stone Hill

This is only a couple of miles along the Ridgeway to the east of White Horse Hill and legend has it that, prior to the Battle of Ashdown, Alfred rode up this hill and summoned his men by calling through a perforated sarsen stone that is now known as the Blowing Stone. It is likely that this is no more than a myth.[27]

You can also head south by road up Blowingstone Hill from Kingston Lisle and there is space to park where the Ridgeway is crossed. Are you now at the site where Alfred summoned his troops by blowing through a stone? Heading up Blowingstone Hill from Kingston Lisle, you can pull in near the first cottage on the left and see the reputed Blowing Stone itself, which was outside on permanent display when I visited. Leaflets were available,[27] which had the following instruction: "The secret is simply to close the hole completely with the mouth and then blow." This presented three problems. Firstly, which of the several available holes should I blow in to? Secondly, hygiene. And thirdly, all of the holes were filled with dead leaves. I gave it a miss. Old maps show that there was once a pub here called the Blowingstone Inn (not to be confused with the nearby Blowing Stone pub).

Alfred's Castle

This enclosure, possibly dating back to the late Bronze Age,[28] was once considered a possible base for the Wessex troops prior to the Battle of Ashdown. It is located near Ashdown House, which is just south of Ashbury. However, there is no evidence to the site being called Alfred's Castle before 1828 - the enclosure was previously called Ashbury, with that name becoming transferred to the nearby village.[29] In my opinion, there is insufficient evidence to connect this site with King Alfred. Ashdown House is a 17th century building and I have wondered whether it derived its name from local legends about the Battle of Ashdown. The site can be accessed by parking in the National Trust car park, which is open when the grounds of Ashdown House are open, and walking west through the woods until you come out on the other side where a couple of gates lead to the enclosure.

I now turn to the second group of sites which are, in my opinion, more plausible locations for the Battle of Ashdown.

2. Sites near Moulsford and Streatley, and the Oxfordshire/Berkshire border

Moulsford and Streatley are settlements that are close to each other on the west bank of the River Thames. The area of land extending west of these settlements contains potential locations for the Battle of Ashdown.

The Anglo-Saxon Chronicles tell us that in 1006, after the time of King Alfred, the Vikings proceeded from Cholsey, now in Oxfordshire, along something called *Æscesdune*, on their way to a place called *Cwicchelmes hlæwe*, which later became called Cuckhamsley Knob. It will be recalled that the name of the location for the battle of Ashdown was *Æscesdun*. Cuckhamsley Knob has now become Scutchamer Knob, which could be seen on my Ordnance Survey map near East Hendred, and about ten miles west of Cholsey. It may therefore be concluded that there was an area of some size west of Cholsey that was known as *Æscesdun* or *Æscesdune*. A line drawn between Cholsey and Cuckhamsley Knob lies just north of potential battle sites described below such as Lowbury and Kingstanding Hills. One wonders whether all of the downs that straddle the current Oxfordshire-Berkshire border were once known as *Æscesdun*.

There are "Byways open to all traffic" in this area. If you decide to drive down these please make sure that you are aware of the regulations, know the conditions, and have a suitable vehicle. Some become deeply rutted, extremely muddy, and it is possible to get stuck.

Kingstanding Hill and Moulsford Bottom

It has been speculated that Kingstanding Hill, a short distance to the west of Moulsford, is the site of the Battle of Ashdown. I could see on my Ordnance Survey map a track near the hill that heads south-west and eventually becomes The Fair Mile. I parked at the beginning of this track and walked up. The views were limited by hedgerows, but there were a couple of good vantage points looking to both north and south. Whilst accepting that this location is on higher ground, making it suitable for Vikings wishing to attack downhill (Asser tells us that the Vikings had taken the higher ground) or for serving as a look-out, I could not see any particular reason for favouring this location as the site of the battle, largely because there are many other places in this area on higher ground.

Moulsford Bottom has also been associated with the Battle of Ashdown, and if the Vikings had attacked down from Kingstanding Hill, then Moulsford Bottom may have been where the battle took place. Generally speaking, Moulsford Bottom lies between

Kingstanding Hill to the west and the Thames to the east. I parked in Moulsford and worked my way through to Moulsford Bottom by following the footpaths marked on my Ordnance Survey map. I came out onto an east-west track, and where this track changed from being north of the field boundary to south of the field boundary, there were unhindered views across Moulsford Bottom, with Kingstanding Hill a short distance to the west.

While at Moulsford you may wish to appreciate a particularly lovely stretch of the nearby Thames Path. This is the section south of the village, accessed by going down Ferry Lane. I remember sitting down there on a warm late spring afternoon and watching three hobbys feeding over the water whilst red kites circled overhead. The Beetle and Wedge Boathouse restaurant, at the bottom of Ferry Lane is at the location where a ferry once crossed the Thames. The name Moulsford, however, strongly suggests that there may have once been a ford here, and it is even possible that King Æthelred and Alfred crossed here with their troops on their way to the Battle of Ashdown.

Around Lowbury Hill

It may not at first be easy to pick out Lowbury Hill on the Ordnance Survey Map (Grid Ref SU54078225). One way is to locate the village of Compton (in Berkshire) and let your eye wander north-east until the boundary with Oxfordshire is only just crossed. There you will find Lowbury Hill. If you can get there in person you will find that the views are magnificent. If one needed to defend a position, or have a lookout, or attack downhill one would, in my opinion, want to use this location. Add to this that the Ridgeway ancient route runs close by to the south, then you have the possibility that the battle took place on the slopes of Lowbury Hill, between the hill itself and the Ridgeway to the south.

Perhaps the Vikings had disembarked from the Thames near Streatley and proceeded west along the Ridgeway ancient route until they came to the lower slopes of Lowbury Hill, which they then occupied, preparing for battle. It is also possible that the Vikings had come over land from Reading, or perhaps they came by both land and water. The Vikings would have got there first and taken Lowbury Hill, as Asser tells us that the Vikings held the higher position. Alfred and King Æthelred may have crossed the Thames at Moulsford, where the name suggests a ford was present, and headed east along the Ridgeway only to find the Vikings atop Lowbury Hill, with battle ensuing.

The best way to get to Lowbury Hill was not immediately obvious from my Ordnance Survey map. On my first attempt I drove west along the unsurfaced Ridgeway (you must check that your vehicle is suitable for this) out of Streatley until I met the track going north that heads up the east side of Lowbury Hill, which I decided to walk up as it was deeply rutted. Eventually I came to an open gate, but sadly the next gate was locked. I was close enough to be able to pick out a tumulus that lies on that side of Lowbury Hill, but little else. I didn't feel that I had wasted my time because the stretch of the Ridgeway that I had travelled down could well have been important in relation to the Battle of Ashdown. Specifically, either the Vikings, or Alfred and King Æthelred, or possibly all of these may have marched to battle along that route. Additionally, if the battle had taken place at Lowbury Hill, fighting could have occurred at any aspect of that hill. It is worth exploring the tracks in this area and looking at the landscape, to see what you think. This, indeed, is how I arrived at my own preference for Lowbury Hill as the site of the battle.

My second attempt to get to Lowbury Hill was via a track leading south from a road in Aston Tirold called Spring Lane. I drove down the track until it became rutted and then proceeded on foot to ascend Langdon Hill, emerging eventually on to Aston Upthorpe Downs. I then used the rights of way marked on my Ordnance Survey map to explore the area.

It is interesting to note that Lowbury Hill sits at the modern boundary between Oxfordshire and Berkshire. In exploring this area you will find that you are frequently switching between counties. There is a feature called Dean's Bottom marked on the Ordnance Survey map immediately east of Lowbury Hill, and I have seen speculation

Fig. 7 Lowbury Hill

that the Vikings were driven down into here. A Roman temple and an Anglo-Saxon burial site have been discovered at Lowbury Hill.

Other sites west of Moulsford and Streatley

Despite my preference for Lowbury Hill as the location of the Battle of Ashdown there are a few more places worth mentioning.

According to the Domesday records of 1086 there was a place called *Nachededorne* at an uncertain location [30] not far from Lowbury Hill. This is of interest because Asser recorded that the battle took place near a solitary thorn tree, and *Nachededorne* could mean "Naked Thorn." Although it seems to me that in some sense naked could also mean solitary, it seems more probable that this name would derive from a more recent tree and not one that would have been present in Anglo-Saxon times, although this cannot be ruled out. It seems that *Nachededorne* was around what is currently Compton, west of Aldworth in Berkshire, a very short distance south-west of Lowbury Hill. There is, however, to this day a Thorn Hill (Grid Ref SU53547815), south east of Compton, although it does not seem possible to know whether it derived its name from *Nachededorne*, or whether it derived its name from Asser's solitary thorn tree, or whether it came from something else entirely. I have seen a suggestion that the Wessex troops could have been at Perborough Castle (an iron age hillfort south of Compton) and may have crossed this Thorn Hill to the east to engage with the Vikings. Because we don't know the site of the battle it is difficult to rule this out. East and West Ilsley, both just north-east of Compton, have also been suggested based on the Domesday place name of Hildeslei which, it has been argued, can be traced back to a term meaning a place of battle. However, it might instead mean a clearing owned by somebody called Hild.[14]

There is folklore relating to the nearby Oxfordshire Astons, which suggests that King Æthelred's contingent may have set out for battle from a completely different location to that of Alfred's.[31] This local story has it that Alfred proceeded from Kingstanding Hill, while King Æthelred proceeded from Blewburton Hill and that the battle then took place around Lowbury Hill. Whilst there seems to be little evidence to support this scenario (which cannot be disproved either), it may be that the two contingents did set out from different locations as this would help explain why there seems to have been some lack of coordination, as revealed by Asser's description that Alfred turned up for battle while Æthelred was still at prayer in his tent. Blewburton Hill is located between Aston Tirrold and Blewbury and can be accessed via footpaths from either. Indeed, my base for exploring this area was in the countryside just outside Blewbury and I have many fond memories of talking to people in The Blueberry pub about King Alfred and the surrounding area. People were really very interested indeed and I knew that I had to find out more.

Finally, it is worth visiting the high ground above Streatley at Lardon Chase and Lough Down. This beautiful area allows an appreciation of some of the local geography, including the course of the River Thames, which would have been a significant obstacle for the Vikings and the Anglo-Saxons alike. There is a car park on the right as you drive west up the B4009 out of Streatley. For those who wish to explore the River Thames in more detail I cannot recommend the Thames Path enough. For those who cannot find the enthusiasm, I strongly recommend Jerome K. Jerome's Three Men in a Boat, which will provide it.

The Battle of Basing, Hampshire 871

So, I turned to the next challenge, which was to try to find the location of the Battle of Basing, where Alfred and King Æthelred lost a battle just fourteen days after they had experienced victory at Ashdown. The Old English of the Anglo-Saxon Chronicles refers to the location as *Basengum*, and in Asser's Latin it is called *Basengas*. This place is known to us today as Old Basing and it is in Hampshire, close to Basingstoke. In Alfred's time Old Basing, or just plain "Basing", would have been the main settlement, with Basingstoke just an outpost. In modern times Basingstoke has become by far the larger of the two settlements.

In my opinion, it cannot be discounted that the battle took place at a central location in Old Basing. This is because I read that an area both sides of the railway line near St Mary's church was possibly the location of a Saxon royal site[32] and that royal status at Basing may go back to at least the seventh century.[33] This might have made Basing a tempting target for the Vikings. However, Basing is not mentioned in Alfred's will, but this could be because it was not owned personally by him. There is a Battledown Farm just to the west of Basingstoke, but I have seen nothing that can connect this to the 871 battle.

My attention was then drawn to a location adjacent to Old Basing called Lychpit, now a housing development of the same name, and which was reputedly a burial site of the dead after the battle at Basing. However, I have not seen anything to suggest whether these were supposed to be Anglo-Saxon or Viking corpses or both. Further confusion is caused by the location's additional reputation as a Civil War burial site. I have also seen it suggested that this was the site of the battle itself,[34] although I have not found any additional evidence to support this. There is still a small amount of woodland left at Lychpit between the roundabout on Great Bindings Road and the west end of the lane called Little Basing. The 1882 Ordnance Survey map shows a Lickpit Farm at this location (Grid Ref SU 6553 7544) and I am struck by the similarity between the "Lick" part of the name and the Old English term *lic* meaning corpse (from which we also get the term "lych gate"). However, even if the farm had been named after burials, it might not mark the exact spot of either the burials or the battle, although it would seem logical that these would be near each other. We can discount the origin of the name being from the Civil War as there is a charter dating to 945 in which King Edmund grants to a certain Æthelnoth a monastery at Basing and land at *Licepyt*. The fact that this was in the royal gift is also perhaps relevant. It seems that Æthelnoth then passed the grant on (and therefore Lickpit) to Hyde Abbey. Basing is not far from Winchester, where Hyde Abbey was located, so it may be unsurprising that the grant went to that foundation. However, it is also the case that King Alfred was buried at Hyde Abbey and one wonders whether the Abbey coming into the ownership of land at the same place where Alfred perhaps lost men in battle is more than coincidence.

It has also been that the site of the battle is located at the north-east corner of Hackwood Park,[35] near to and south of the M3 motorway. This site is adjacent to what seems to have been the ancient trackway called the Harroway (otherwise known as the Harrow Way or Hard Way). Although I have doubts about this being the location of the battle, I think that this ancient trackway, which crops up again (in Wiltshire) later on in Alfred's story, is important and it is worth trying to pin down its route. There is a busy modern Harrow Way in Basingstoke and, assuming that this follows the old Harrow Way, then the north-east of Hackford Park can at least be said to be close to the ancient track. Furthermore, it has been suggested that the road to the north of Hackford Park was a summer route of the Harrow Way that eventually superceded the main route to become the Harrow Way itself.[36] This route is now a road called Dickens Lane, and it is fun to travel down here, perhaps to the evocatively named Polecat Corner, knowing that you are probably on one of Britain's oldest routes.

I explored the general area of this possible battle site by using the public footpaths that go through the Hackwood Estate, starting at Dickens Lane near to where it meets Hackwood Road (Grid Ref SU64455062). At first the entrance to the footpath looks like a closed gate between two white gatehouses, but there is an entrance to the footpath between the two pillars on the right. Once through the gate I walked south and then turned east with the Hard Way (Dickens Lane) to the north and more or less parallel. This is the only public footpath option that takes you through anything that can be described as the north-east corner of Hackwood Park, but it is a pleasant walk and there is a chance that the battle took place here.

However, the case for Hackwood Park seems to be based on an argument that the Vikings were making their way to Winchester and they were therefore trying to reach the Silchester-Winchester Roman road which ran just a few miles to the west of Basing. However, we cannot know from which direction the Vikings approached Basing or even if they had been heading for Winchester. Two weeks had passed since the Battle of Ashdown and where the Vikings went after that we do not know, and if they had been on their way to Winchester, why is there no record of them proceeding there after their victory at Basing? Or is it possible that one of the three battles that are missing from the record took place in this period? Perhaps the Vikings did go to Winchester and engaged in an unrecorded battle there.

To conclude, the evidence is such that the battle could have occurred anywhere around Basing. It is tempting to think that the settlement of Old Basing itself was the location of the battle. The battle was described as taking place at Basing, and Old Basing had been Basing. Furthermore, the archaeological evidence suggests that there was something there worth raiding. However, the evidence for Lychpit seems to me to be greater. It had this name (spelt *Licepyt*) in 945 when it was in King Edmund's possession to give away, and the person he gave it to then gave it to the abbey where Alfred was buried. I think the most likely scenario is that Alfred and King Æthelred intercepted the Vikings as they were on their way to raid Basing and that the battle took place at or near Lychpit. The north-east of Hackford Park seems over-reliant on its proximity to an ancient trackway with little else to support it.

The Battle of *Meretun*, 871

The Battle of *Meretun* took place two months after the battle at Basing but, unfortunately, we cannot confidently identify *Meretun* with a known settlement. Nonetheless, there appear to be two main candidates for the location of this battle, one being Martin in Hampshire and the other being Marden in Wiltshire. Other places that have been suggested include the London Borough of Merton, Marten in Wiltshire, Merton in Oxfordshire, and Merriton, located just beyond the southern perimeter of Bournemouth Airport. The place that seems to make the most sense to me is Martin in Hampshire, which is a village just south of the A354 between Salisbury and Blandford Forum.

It is recorded that King Æthelred (Alfred's elder brother) died after the Battle of *Meretun* and, although we are not given the location of his death, we are told that he was buried at Wimborne. It is therefore possible that he died from wounds sustained in battle but it is also possible that he lived a little longer and died of something else. If he had died of his wounds then it may be relevant to point out that Wimborne is not very far from Martin (about 14 miles) and quite a long way from Marden (about 40 miles). Indeed, the Roman road known as Ackling Dyke runs past Martin on its way to Badbury Rings, which is only four miles from Wimborne. The geographic feature called Martin Down lies a short distance to the west of Martin and there one can explore the famous Bokerley Ditch, which pre-dates the time of Alfred, but perhaps could have been used strategically in battle. Bokerley Ditch also cuts across a Roman road so it could have been used for either side to attack the other coming up that route. To the north this Roman road is still a bridleway and to the south it is now under the A354, so it seems likely that it would have been in use in Anglo-Saxon times. Interestingly, the county boundary between Dorset and Hampshire in this area still follows Bokerley Ditch. One can speculate as to why the Vikings might have been at Martin, and it occurs to me that a contingent from the base at Reading may have been trying to get west, perhaps to Exeter. The Vikings would indeed attack Exeter in 876 and 893, and it therefore seems plausible that they would have liked to have done so in 871. A charter issued by King Edmund between 944 and 946 shows Martin in Hampshire being referred to as *Mertone,* not much different from the *Meretun* of the Anglo-Saxon Chronicles. I found it interesting to note that the literature available at Wimborne Minster also favoured the location of Martin in Hampshire as the site of the battle, and a volunteer I spoke with was convinced that this was correct.

Martin Down is well worth a visit, and there are two main ways of accessing it. One is the car park on the A354, but much more pleasant is the car park at the end of Sillens Lane (Grid Ref SU05751913), which heads west out of the village of Martin itself. Martin Down is tremendously rich in ancient features and I have spent many happy hours exploring these. Also, don't miss the archaeologically highly important area south and west of the nearby village of Pentridge. The features here go back to well before the time of King Alfred but wandering around them gives you a wonderful sense of place.

As we have seen, the small village of Marden in Wiltshire (grid ref SU08555775) has also been suggested as the location of *Meretun.* It may be impossible to disprove that the battle took place here, but the "den" component of the name of this village seems to derive from *dene* meaning valley rather than *tun* meaning settlement.[37] Perhaps more fatal is that Marden seems to have been derived from the even more different name of *Mercdene,* meaning boundary valley, because it is referred to as such in a charter issued in 941. I therefore think Marden is a less likely location than Martin for the battle of *Meretun.*

Marten in Wiltshire (Grid Ref SU28396010, south of Great Bedwyn) has been put forward strongly in the past[38] and I find this location provides the strongest competition to Martin in Hampshire for the site of the battle, with the derivation of the place name also being consistent with *Meretun.* The main point, however, is that there was an ancient route, sometimes referred to as the Inkpen Ridgeway[39] that seems to have connected Basing, the site of the previous battle, to locations close to Marten. This would therefore have provided a potential route of retreat for Alfred and King Æthelred after they had lost the battle at Basing. However, a weakness in this argument is that it would not have taken the victorious Vikings two months to follow them to Marten, only about thirty miles away. Furthermore, Alfred and King Æthelred could have fled from Basing in a different direction. Marten in Wiltshire is also on a Roman road (connecting Winchester and Cirencester) that was likely to have been in use in Anglo-Saxon times as much of it has persisted in use to this day.

Interestingly, there is an earlier Anglo-Saxon Chronicle entry for 757, well before Alfred was born, describing a confrontation at a place called *Merantun.* We are told that King

Cynewulf had been at this place with a woman and a small troop in a stronghold, so at least we know that in 757 there was a place called *Merantun* that was somewhere that a king would go. However, we cannot be certain that this is the same place as the 871 *Meretun* and, even if it was, the location of the 757 *Merantun* is not known either!

The Role of Wimborne, Dorset

Wimborne is a significant historic town in Dorset and is the location of the important Wimborne Minster, which has a history going back to the 8th century. Wimborne is not a site of a recorded battle in this period but I include this location here because most versions of the Anglo-Saxon Chronicles tell us that after the battle at *Meretun* and after, or perhaps over, Easter 871, King Æthelred, Alfred's older brother, was buried here. However, the B version of the Anglo-Saxon Chronicles tells us that he was buried at Sherborne, which seems plausible as the two previous kings and brothers of Alfred, Æthelbald and Æthelbehrt, had been buried there. I consider it possible that Æthelred was initially interred at Wimborne, and then later moved to Sherborne, probably because of the relative importance of the latter location. This may have been because Sherborne was prone to, or had even succumbed to, Viking attack, something suggested by a Dr Reinhold Pauli in a book published in 1889).[40] It is further recorded in Æthelweard's chronicle that Alfred had been present at his brother's funeral rites, which is what we would expect. Nonetheless, a volunteer at Wimborne Minster told me that investigations had been carried out in the 1950s and that a coffin of apparently suitable age and length (Æthelred is thought by some to have been tall) had been found at the approximate location of the pulpit, and that this location corresponded with the altar of the earlier Anglo-Saxon church. I was also told that a university was planning to do further investigations but at the time of writing I am unaware of any further information.

We know that Alfred himself became king after the death of King Æthelred, although the location where this formally took place has not been recorded. I suggest, however, that there is a very good chance that Alfred became king at Wimborne, particularly if he had already been designated as next in line, which Asser tells us was the case. Alfred's immediate elevation on the death of his brother also makes sense in the context of the kingship having run sequentially through Æthelwulf's sons up to that point. It should be borne in mind, however, that just because we are told that Æthelred had been buried at Wimborne does not mean that he died there, with this meaning that Alfred could have become king somewhere else. Nonetheless, Wimborne seems plausible because we know that it had significance because the estate (*ham*) there was seized in 899 by Æthelwold after Alfred's death (if it was significant in 899 it seems likely that had been so in 871). The battles that took place in 871 indicate that Wessex was clearly in a state of emergency at the time King Æthelred died, and perhaps the formal ceremonial arrangements of Alfred's accession were delayed until the relatively peaceful period between 872 and 874 when the Vikings that had been at Reading were causing trouble in Mercia and Northumbria instead. If there was ever a formal ceremony, we have no evidence of it. It has been suggested that Alfred became king in Winchester, but I have seen no evidence of this either. Furthermore, it appears that Kingston-upon-Thames had not yet become (as it would) the favoured site for the consecration of the Anglo-Saxon kings.

It is worth considering for a moment that Alfred became the new king in the midst of conflict with the Vikings, and it seems likely that there would have been some planning as to who would replace him if he also met an untimely death. He was the end of the line of the series of sons of King Æthelwulf, so there was no younger brother to take his place, his son King Edward the Elder had not yet been born, and the sons of the recently deceased King Æthelred were still children. We do not know who would have been next, and fortunately Alfred survived this period.

Alfred was at the Battle of Wilton one month after he became king. At the time Wilton was connected to Wimborne by the Wilton Way, via Cranborne.[39] This makes it credible that Alfred travelled the 25 miles north to Wilton from Wimborne. It is also possible that the Vikings, having received intelligence that Alfred was at Wimborne, were moving towards that place, only to run into Alfred at Wilton.

The Battle of Wilton, Wiltshire 871

Wilton is a lovely small town that once was the "capital" of Wiltshire. Although its importance declined with the building of Salisbury Cathedral (and Old Sarum Cathedral before that), it doesn't take much exploration to start to tap into its Anglo-Saxon past.

King Alfred had only been king for one month when he fought and lost this battle. However, the Anglo-Saxon Chronicles tell us that Alfred had been fighting with a small troop against the entire raiding army, so it is perhaps unsurprising that he failed to win. Interestingly, Æthelweard's chronicle (without mentioning Wilton by name) indicates that Alfred wasn't even there because he was still attending to his brother's funeral, and that the troop was small because of Alfred's absence. However, the Anglo-Saxon Chronicles tell us that the battle took place one month after Alfred had become king, so it seems likely that his brother's funeral would have been completed by then. However, perhaps we ought to bear in mind that Æthelweard's chronicle was written for his relative Mathilde, who was a direct descendent of King Alfred (with Æthelweard himself being a direct descendent of Alfred's elder brother King Æthelred) and there might have been an interest in removing Alfred from a battle that had been lost, or in avoiding having to explain why Alfred had been unable to command a large army.

Wilton, west of Salisbury, has been described as having been a royal sea.[41] Indeed, Wilton has been stated to be "the royal seat" of Wessex, before Winchester took over that role.[42] However, there is no mention of Wilton in Alfred's will, and neither the Anglo-Saxon Chronicles nor Asser mention this to be a royal site at the time of King Alfred. It also seems to me that Sherborne was particularly important at this time, because at least two of his elder brothers who had also been kings had been buried there. Nonetheless, Wilton would have been a strategic location because it is close to where the Rivers Wylye and Nadder meet, whilst also being close to various trackways. The fact that the Vikings won must have been hugely significant. They were already holding Reading, and possibly Basing as well, and later in 871 the Anglo-Saxon Chronicles record that they had left Reading and were in London with the Mercians after having made peace with them. This Viking army then moved to Northumbria and then to Torksey in Lincolnshire and eventually drove out Burhred, the King of Mercia. If King Alfred could have defeated the Vikings at Wilton, the path of history would surely have been very different.

It has been suggested that the location of a royal site at Wilton could have been in the general area of what is now Kingsbury Square,[43] with the place name being a clue, and it has been considered likely that Wilton House is on the site of a Benedictine nunnery founded by King Alfred.[43] Indeed, the 1880 Ordnance Survey map states that Wilton House is on the site of Wilton Abbey.

Asser describes the battle as having taken place at a hill (*monte* in Asser's Latin) called Wilton on the south bank of the Wylye (referred to as *Guilou* by Asser). This is both helpful and unhelpful. If the place was settled, which it appears to have been, why is it referred to as a just a hill? Nonetheless, "south" of the Wylye helps us in that this indicates primarily the area around Wilton House and the former abbey, or perhaps even the site of the current town centre. I remain somewhat uncomfortable that Wilton does not fit the description of being a *monte*, because it seems to me to be fairly flat. Although there are various hills in the vicinity that cannot be ruled out, I find it more likely that the battle took place at Wilton itself, because this is what Asser and the Anglo-Saxon Chronicles state. Furthermore, unlike Asser, the Anglo-Saxon Chronicles make no mention of a hill.

It is unclear from the evidence whether the Vikings had already taken Wilton by the time that the battle took place. If this was the case Alfred may have had to approach from the north-west because of the confluence of the rivers Nadder and Wylye. This approach from the north-west would also have been an option for the Viking take-over of the site if they had got there first, but because we know that they used waterways, they could have come up the Avon and then the Nadder. They could, of course, have used a combination of land and water-based forces. However, Gaimar[44] indicates that the Vikings found Alfred at Wilton (*a Wiltone l'unt trove.*) i.e. that Alfred was there first. If this was the case then Alfred was perhaps lucky to escape as there was the potential for his small troop to be hemmed in between the Wylye and the Nadder by the raiding Viking army.

The grounds of Wilton House, occupying land between the Wylye and the Nadder, are therefore a potential site of the battle. The grounds are opened up to the public for an admission fee, and contain many splendid trees and are well worth a visit in their own right. I found it sobering to think that the beautiful gardens might once have been a bloody battlefield. Once in the grounds I could walk along the north bank of the Nadder until it met an offshoot of the Wylye. There was further land that was out of bounds on the other side of this waterway that appeared to lead to the current confluence of the two rivers but, especially considering that the route of the waterways may have been somewhat different in Alfred's time, I thought that I had done enough to establish as best I could that I was standing at or near the site of the battle. Furthermore, the confluence only gives us the extreme limit in one direction for where the battle was fought. Nonetheless, the battle may have taken place further west, or even outside of the bounds of Wilton House, perhaps at the supposed former royal site at Kingsbury Square. Kingsbury Square, although unfortunately bisected by the very busy A30, is very easy to visit.

I could find no information regarding Alfred's activities between the end of the series of battles in 871 and the recorded recommencement of hostilities in 875, which I shall turn to in the following chapter. It is thought, however, that Alfred's son Edward, who would go on to become King Edward the Elder, was born around 874.

3

Viking Betrayal and Submission: Wareham to Exeter 875 – 876

In this chapter I follow Alfred through the beautiful south-western counties of Devon and Dorset as he confronted the Vikings in the two years of 875 and 876. The Anglo-Saxon Chronicles record that Alfred took part in a sea battle in 875, perhaps before the Vikings came to Wareham. However, although Alfred was victorious, we are not told where this sea battle took place. I shall therefore go straight to describing what I found out about Wareham.

Wareham, Dorset

Today's Wareham is a delightful Dorset market town that seems to have history creeping out of every corner. It is situated at a strategic junction between the Rivers Piddle and Frome, and Poole Harbour can be reached via the latter, making a pleasant boat ride through the reeds accompanied by bird song and the sounds of the sea.

The Vikings turned up and occupied Wareham in 875, but the following year Alfred made peace with them when the Vikings swore on the *halgan beage* (holy ring) that they would leave Wessex. However, they waited for the cover of darkness and went instead to Exeter, in Devon, but also part of Wessex. The Anglo-Saxon Chronicles tell us that the Vikings had given hostages to Alfred as part of the deal, and that these men had been the worthiest of the Viking army. We don't know whether the holy ring belonged to Alfred or the Vikings, or who it was "holy" to, if not to both parties. If it was a Viking ring, then Alfred clearly must have had the upper hand to make them swear on it, which would fit with Alfred having been given important hostages, who could be killed if the Vikings reneged on the deal. On balance, however, it seems to me that it was Alfred's ring. This is because the Anglo-Saxon Chronicles refer to it as "holy" and it seems unlikely to me that this source would refer to something unchristian in this way. The Vikings must have seen Exeter as a great prize if it meant sacrificing their worthiest men. One can imagine how some Vikings might have viewed the subsequent loss of 120 ships near Swanage in a storm as they fled to Exeter as divine retribution for breaking an oath sworn on a holy ring and for condemning the hostages to death.

But where exactly was the Viking camp at Wareham and how did they get there? Both Asser and Æthelweard indicate that the Vikings had arrived at Wareham from Cambridge, and it seems that they must have had a combination of land and sea forces

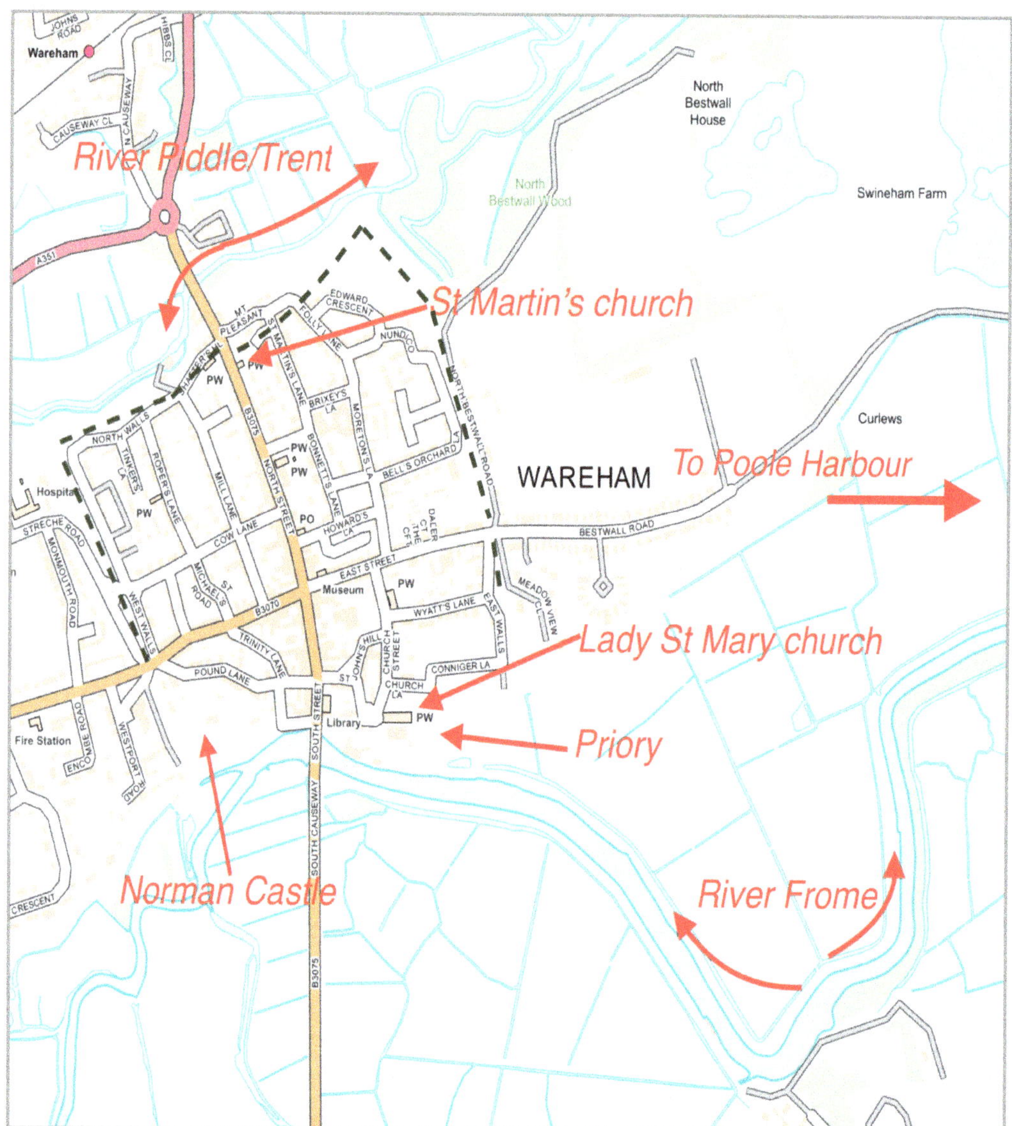

Fig. 8 Features relating to Wareham that are described in the text. The approximate outline of the remaining walls is shown by the dashed green line. Contains OS data © Crown copyright and database right (2018)

because that is what left Wareham when they fled to Exeter. We also know that the sea-borne force must have been considerable because the Vikings lost as many as 120 ships in a storm near Swanage when fleeing, so the total number of ships must have been even higher than that. To get to Wareham, the Viking ships must have entered Poole harbour, and perhaps they only took some of their ships up the Frome to Wareham. Presumably, with that many ships they would have been able to defend their rear by perhaps occupying Brownsea and other islands in Poole Harbour and by defending the harbour entrance. This was clearly a very serious situation for Wareham and this part of Wessex. Try to imagine over 120 Viking ships in Poole harbour coinciding with the arrival of a land-based Viking army. Ultimately, although the Vikings broke their oath, Alfred's intervention had saved Wareham and the surrounding area from further destruction and subjugation, and we should also recognise that when the Vikings got to Exeter they had not escaped Alfred because they had to deal again with him there, and this time they would leave Wessex.

The route that Alfred and the Viking land-based forces had taken to get to Wareham is open to speculation. There may have been a Roman road from Wareham to Woodbury Hill (Grid Ref SY85689469), near Bere Regis,[45] which may have been in use in Alfred's time because there is still today a straight road that heads in that direction. However, for the Vikings, this seems to head in the wrong direction (being north-west instead of north-east) because we are told that they had come from Cambridge.

Asser describes Wareham as having been a *castellum* (fortification) and also the location of a monastery. The current Priory Hotel is on the site of a priory that may have been derived from this monastery, which may have been a target in the 875 attack. It has been suggested that the Vikings took advantage of the part of Wareham not defended by a wall, which is where the River Frome runs to the south of the town, and which was also where the priory was located. However, Wareham may have had no walls in 875, with the walls being built later as part of Alfred's programme of defending a range of towns and settlements in a period after his victory over the Vikings in 878.[46] It is possible that the section against the River Frome was protected by a wooden structure. We can still see these walls today, although we know that they have been modified over subsequent centuries.[46] The fortification mentioned by Asser therefore probably covered a different area to what is circumscribed by the walls that we see today. Indeed, we know that the Normans built a castle by the River Frome at the western extent of the walled area (Grid Ref SY92168715). I have, however, been unable to find any evidence that there may have been an earlier fortification at this location in Anglo-Saxon times. I believe that this location should nonetheless be seriously considered as the site of the Anglo-Saxon fortification, as if a site was suitable for the Normans, it probably had also been suitable for the Anglo-Saxons too. In this case the Normans would have taken over the pre-existing Anglo-Saxon fortification and made it theirs. Although the site of the former Norman castle is on private land, Wareham's walls can be easily walked.

Asser's reference to a *Castellum* could also relate to an ancient or Roman construction, for which there is no remaining evidence, although even this could have been at the site of the Norman castle. However, it is worth bearing in mind the possibility that Asser may have been referring to the status of Wareham at the time he was writing in the 890s, after King Alfred's post-878 defence programme, as opposed to the situation in 875. This seems less likely to me as Asser would have been aware of the potential confusion that this might have caused. It would be a bit like me saying that 20 years ago I went for a walk in London where the Shard is. It would mislead people into thinking that the Shard was there 20 years ago, which it wasn't.

However, things become even more complicated when we look at Æthelweard's chronicle. He describes the Vikings going to near (*iuxta*) Wareham and occupying a location alongside (*coniecit statum communem cum*) a Western Army. We cannot tell whether this Western Army was a Wessex army or another Viking army. Unlike Asser, Æthelweard makes no mention of a fortification (neither do the Anglo-Saxon Chronicles), but describes Wareham as an *oppidum* (town). Assuming that the Western Army was a Wessex army it seems plausible that the Vikings may have set up camp outside of Wareham and with the Saxons inside the town. The use of words meaning "near" and "alongside" would then appear to make sense. A further difference between the writings of Æthelweard and Asser is that only the latter states that the Viking army entered (*intravit*) the *castellum* of Wareham. However, these two sources may just be providing two snapshots of a sequence. Taking it all together it appears that the Vikings camped outside of the settlement of Wareham and then took it over, including entering the *castellum*, perhaps after besieging it. Æthelweard goes on to tell us that the Vikings also ravaged most of the province of Wareham, which perhaps corresponds to the part of Dorset that we know today as Purbeck.

Asser describes Wareham as being between the rivers *Frauu* (Frome) and *Terente*, which some may find surprising because Wareham is today between the Frome and the Piddle. However, the Piddle is also known as the Trent, which is not to be confused with Dorset's River Tarrant that flows into the Stour near Tarrant Crawford. Wareham's situation is similar to other locations subjected to Viking attack, such as at Reading, in that it was bounded by water on three sides (with the third side at Wareham provided by Poole Harbour), presumably because this made the location easier to defend.

The nearby church of Lady St Mary, although subject to much rebuilding, has an important history going back to at least the 8th century[47] and may well have been associated with the monastery mentioned by Asser, which may indeed have been adjacent at the location of the former priory. The church is beautiful inside and several pieces of Anglo-Saxon masonry are on display. One version of the Anglo-Saxon Chronicles (E) tells us that King Edward the Martyr was initially buried at Wareham after he had been murdered at nearby Corfe in 978. Although it seems that he was later transferred to Shaftesbury, his initial burial would probably have been at or near the site of the church of Lady St Mary. I have seen it written that King Beorhtric of Wessex had been buried at Wareham in 802, but I have not found any evidence to support this. If King Beorhtric had been buried here, then Wareham might have been more important in 875 than we might otherwise have thought, and this could perhaps explain why it was attacked by the Vikings. Another important location in Wareham is St Martin's church, which has a history that may go back to the 7th century, although the current building dates to about 1030. This church is generally locked outside of the main tourist season, but there is usually an indication of where to obtain the key. The area immediately to the east of Wareham, and therefore closer to Poole Harbour, has provided archaeological finds suggesting that there was much industrial activity up to and including the Middle Saxon period.[48] Most references that I have seen regarding Anglo-Saxon periods places King Alfred's reign at the end of the Middle Saxon Period.

The events of 875 would not be the last that Wareham would see of the Vikings, because they attacked Dorset again via the Frome, which runs past Wareham, in 998 and again in 1015.

Exeter

We now journey on to Devon, and specifically Exeter, a vibrant city situated on the River Exe and the home of the majestic Cathedral Church of St Peter, founded in 1050. A pleasant moment can be taken sitting in a cafe in the shadow of the cathedral enjoying the mild Devon climate and a cream tea before taking off to explore the history of this important city.

The Chronicles tell us that in 876 the Vikings that were at Wareham went to Exeter, but that their fleet lost 120 ships in bad weather at Swanage in Dorset. But not all of the Vikings had fled by sea and Alfred pursued on horseback those Vikings that were fleeing over land towards Exeter, although he was unable to overtake them before they got there. On reaching Exeter the Vikings secured themselves in a fortress, but their situation does not appear to have been particularly positive, perhaps because of the large loss of ships, and they settled for peace with Alfred. After over-wintering (permission to do this being presumably part of the peace settlement) the Vikings left Exeter and went to Mercia, and specifically to Gloucester according to Æthelweard's chronicle.

I asked myself whether it was possible to work out from the available information where exactly in Exeter the Vikings went. The Anglo-Saxon Chronicles implies that the Vikings occupied a fortress that had already been there, as opposed to building one when they got there, as they would do in Rochester, in Kent, in 884. Exeter's Rougemont Castle goes back to 1068 and the rebellion against William the Conqueror, so we are looking for an older fortification, which might even have been a previous construction on the same site as Rougemont Castle. The case for this is strengthened by the discovery of Anglo-Saxon masonry at Rougemont Castle. We also know that Exeter had (and largely still has) Roman walls[49] with four entrances and it appears that these were repaired and strengthened in Anglo-Saxon times. It seems unlikely to me that Exeter would have had a fortification beyond the perimeter of its walls because there would have been a security risk of it being taken over by hostile forces (like Vikings). The Old English of the Chronicles says that the Vikings came *into* Exeter, which fits with the idea that the Vikings had managed to get into Exeter through one of the four entrances in the walls and then either occupied a fortification within the walls, or used the walls themselves as a fortification. The circuit of the walls was 2.35 km,[50] so this would have stretched the Viking troops, but with only four entrances[50] perhaps it was possible for them to secure the site. I feel that it is more likely that the depleted Viking force took over a fortification within the walls rather than the walls themselves, and it seems to me that the site of (or part of the site of) Rougemont Castle would have been the most likely location for this fortification. The outer walls of Rougemont Castle can be easily visited. Just get off a train at Exeter Central train station, come out of the entrance, turn left and then take the first left into Northernhay Gardens. Then just follow the wall on your right. By passing through Athelstan's Tower you can then wander into the adjacent Rougemont Gardens as well. It is in Northernhay Gardens that you can see (although you may need an expert eye - you need to be on the sloping path that leads to the passageway through Athelstan's Tower on the outside wall of Rougemont Castle) elements of Anglo-Saxon construction in the remains of the wall. It is thought that King Athelstan (King Alfred's grandson) restored the city walls in around 928. The site of Rougemont Castle is now called Exeter Castle, and is a commercial enterprise. Perhaps the best way to appreciate the site is to walk up Castle Street to the main entrance and the surviving Norman gatehouse.

It is possible that the land-based Viking contingent, with Alfred in pursuit (the deal was that the Vikings would leave Wareham and Wessex swiftly, so Alfred probably remained at or near Wareham to make sure that the Vikings did in fact leave), took the Roman road to Bridport via Dorchester and then the Roman road that now approximates to route of the A35 to Honiton, and then finally the Roman road that is more or less on the current route of the A30 to Exeter. Alternatively, they could have branched off this route onto another Roman road near Charmouth in order to reach Exeter via Colyford and Sidford, approximately following the route of the current A3052. It seems likely that these routes would have been in use in Alfred's time, because much of these routes have persisted from Roman times right through to today.

It seems that either route would have brought them to a gate to the south-west of the walled city at a spot that is towards the southern end of South Street of today's Exeter. There is still some wall there today (and a plaque) to help you find the precise spot. This South Gate must be, therefore, the most likely point of entry for the Vikings, and also for King Alfred in pursuit, in 876. Unfortunately, there is no gate present there now as, after serving as a prison, it was finally demolished in 1819. Nonetheless, it is possible to explore on foot how these routes come together just outside the former location of the South Gate. However, I found this location to be a difficult place to be a pedestrian and

I also found it generally unsightly. If you do make it down here, there are other places of interest such as the old Eye Hospital and the Dissenters' Graveyard.

Having come through the South Gate, and with Rougemont Castle (as it was later called) at the extreme north end of the walled city, Alfred would have needed to cross the centre of the city to get to this location, which seems to me to be the most likely place that the Vikings would have headed for. Although these events took place prior to Alfred's post-878 rebuilding programme, it seems likely that there would have still been a road leading from the South Gate up to the main city intersection where today South Street, North Street, Fore Street and High Street meet. It seems that High Street would have

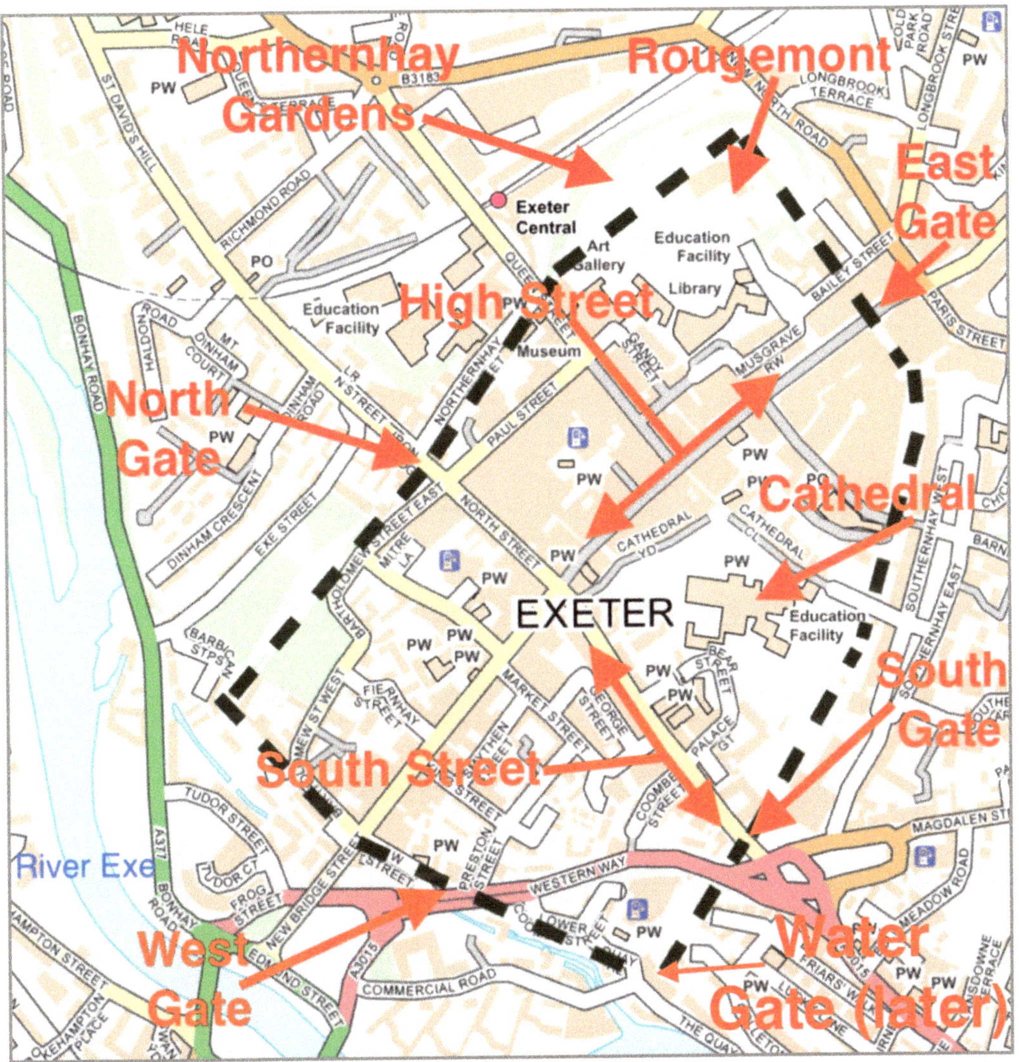

Fig. 9 Places in Exeter referred to in the text. The line of the Roman walls is shown in green dashes. Contains OS data © Crown copyright and database right (2018)

been present in Alfred's time, and this leads in the general direction of Rougemont Castle. I therefore suggest that Alfred and his troops proceeded up what is now South Street and turned right on to what is now High Street, with the land-based Vikings having taken the same route just a short time before. Any surviving sea-borne Vikings would have made their way up from the harbour, via the West Gate or perhaps via a lost Roman gate in the wall nearer to the port (the Water Gate may have been a later development not present in Alfred's time). They may have even disembarked at nearby Topsham and then made their way, like the others, to the South Gate. However, it seems to me that the land-based Vikings may have surrendered even before the later arrival of the sea-borne troops, which may have turned back and regrouped somewhere else. This is because it would have taken Alfred and his troops less time to ride to Exeter than it would have taken the Viking fleet to sail there.

It is not known why the Vikings went to Exeter, but it is possible that they were responding to requests from Briton populations in the South West for the Vikings to join them in fighting against the Anglo-Saxons of Wessex. If this had been the case, the loss of much of the Viking fleet off Swanage might have made an alliance pointless. However, the Vikings could have gone to Exeter just because it was a centre of wealth, with possibly few other options remaining open to them when they fled from Wareham.

Although Alfred had liberated Exeter, it would not be long before Wessex would be subject to a further Viking attack, which would this time be even more serious. These events unfold in the following chapter and start with the Vikings arriving early in 878 at Chippenham, in Wiltshire and part of Wessex. This set off a chain of events that would lead to the eventual downfall of the Vikings at the Battle of Ethandun later that same year.

Before we leave Exeter, I wish to briefly skip forward to a period that is more comprehensively covered in Chapter 8, because we find a reference in the Anglo-Saxon Chronicles to King Alfred heading again to Exeter in 893. While on his way to assist his troops that were besieging a Viking contingent near London, he received word that other Viking forces had landed in North Devon and that Exeter, in South Devon, had also been besieged. The Anglo-Saxon Chronicles indicate that Alfred and his troops therefore diverted towards Exeter, although there is no confirmation that he arrived there and there are no records of any engagement with the Vikings either at Exeter or in North Devon at this time. Perhaps King Alfred's post-878 programme of improving defences at key settlements had worked and on this occasion the Vikings had not managed to breach Exeter's walls.

4

Prelude to Athelney

It will be recalled from the last chapter that the Viking army departed from Exeter, and left Wessex, in 877. However, any peace would have been short-lived because the Vikings returned to Wessex and took Chippenham early in 878, an act that would set off a chain of events that would eventually lead to the important defeat of the Vikings at the Battle of Ethandun later that same year. Athelney is the location of King Alfred's famous base in the Somerset Levels from which he commenced his reconquest, but in this chapter I shall look at locations associated with Alfred before he arrived there, including those that might relate to his whereabouts in a period in which he was "missing." This chapter is therefore mainly based in the narrow time period of January 878 to Easter 878, although later events at Chippenham are included in order to avoid having to take the reader to the same location twice.

Chippenham, Wiltshire

The chain of events relating to the battle of Ethandun starts and finishes in the same place, Chippenham. Although the intervening events are examined in subsequent chapters it seems sensible to bring everything that happened in Chippenham together under one heading.

The Anglo-Saxon Chronicles tell us that the Vikings came to Chippenham after or over (*ofer*) Twelfth Night in January of 878. But where had they come from? The Anglo-Saxon Chronicles record that when the Vikings left Exeter in 877 they went to Mercia, with Æthelweard being more specific in telling us that they went to Gloucester. Asser's account differs in that it states that the Vikings went straight from Exeter to Chippenham. It seems to me more likely that that the Anglo-Saxon Chronicles and Æthelweard are correct and that Asser is wrong. Furthermore, it seems that Alfred would have had the power to see that the Vikings left because they were a defeated and depleted force.

The arrival of the Vikings at Chippenham was an important turning point because the Anglo-Saxon Chronicles tell us that the Vikings over-ran Wessex, and King Alfred went into hiding. It is worth reflecting on what the Chronicles tell us, which is that the Vikings did not just over-run the area around Chippenham, but probably most of Wessex, and all of Wessex if we take the Chronicles literally, which means all the way from the west of Devon to the east of Kent. There were, however, parts of Wessex that clearly remained beyond their control, such as the area in North Devon where the battle of *Cynuit* took

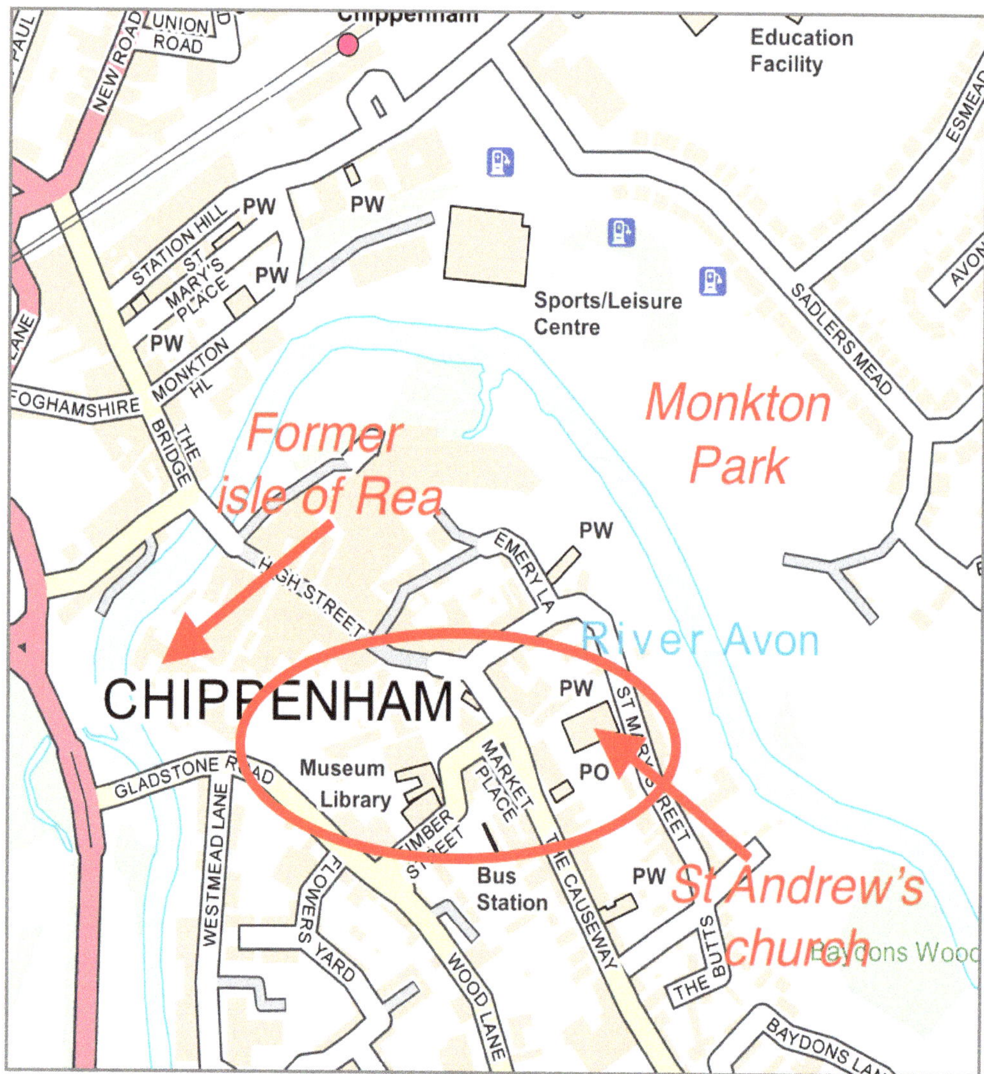

Fig. 10 Map showing locations referred to in the text. The speculative combined location of the Viking base and the Anglo-Saxon royal estate is outlined by the red oval. Contains OS data © Crown copyright and database right (2018).

place (the precise location of *Cynuit* is not established but the fact that the Vikings had to engage in battle tells us that they did not have it under their control) and Athelney, where Alfred found a safe haven for a while. But the implication is that for a short period in 878 Wessex had effectively been lost to the Vikings. As Wessex was the last kingdom in what we now call England still independent of Viking rule, this also means that between Twelfth Night and some time after Easter in 878 the Vikings had control over the whole of England. With King Alfred on the run they must have seen a permanent victory as a plausible outcome.

I think it is worth reflecting on the huge impact of Alfred's decision to stay in Wessex and not to flee to, for example, Rome, which King Burghred had done when Mercia collapsed to the Vikings in 874. It can be strongly argued that the course of history would have been very different had Alfred fled in the wake of the Viking onslaught. But from a position that many must have thought irrecoverable he instead fought and won back his kingdom and eventually, during the reign of his grandson Athelstan, all of England would be relieved from Viking rule.

It has been claimed that King Alfred was at Chippenham on Twelfth Night when the Vikings attacked,[51] although I can find no evidence that he was indeed there. However, his presence would have given the Vikings a reason to attack Chippenham at this particular time, and Asser tells us that Chippenham was indeed a royal estate, which is confirmed by Chippenham's appearance in Alfred's will. Asser also tells us that Chippenham had also been the location of Alfred's sister's marriage to Burghred, King of Mercia, in 853, although Alfred may not have been present as this was the same year that the young Alfred first went to Rome.

Chippenham then disappears from our story while we look at the events leading up to the Battle of Ethandun (see Chapter 7), but then immediately re-emerges because the Anglo-Saxon Chronicles tell us that Alfred pursued the Vikings as far as an unnamed fortification (*geweorc*), which seems most likely to have been a base that they had established at Chippenham, [19] some 15 miles to the north of Ethandun. That Chippenham served as a Viking base across this period is supported by Asser's telling us that they overwintered at Chippenham after their arrival in 878 and the Anglo-Saxon Chronicles' telling us that it was here that they relocated from in 879 to go to Cirencester after their leader's conversion to Christianity. It has also been suggested that the unnamed fortification was Bratton Camp, on the north-west edge of Salisbury Plain, although it seems unlikely that this would have been a main base as provisions for troops and animals would have been difficult to provide on this elevated landscape over an extended period. The Anglo-Saxon Chronicles tell us that after Alfred had pursued the Vikings to the fortification, he besieged it for fourteen days, after which the Vikings surrendered. Asser provides further detail and identifies the location of Alfred's besieging camp as being in front of the gates of the Viking fortification.

Asser tells us that prior to the Battle of Ethandun the Vikings were on the eastern bank of the Avon as it runs through Chippenham. It seems difficult to establish the navigability of the Avon as far as Chippenham in Alfred's time, although the Vikings may not have arrived by water. It seems likely that any fortification at Chippenham that the Vikings retreated to after the Battle of Ethandun would be at the same location. Examination of a map shows that there is a bend in the Avon that would allow the Vikings to defend a peninsula, as they had done when they were at Reading. Today, the old town is located on this peninsula. I parked in the Sadler's Mead car park and walked down to the River Avon, which is the same river that flows through Bath and emerges at Avonmouth near Bristol. I walked along the path that heads west and then south along the outer bank, allowing me to appreciate what may have constituted Asser's east bank of the Avon. It is important to note that the river today is not the same as it appears on old maps, and It would have been even more different in the time of Alfred. But even going back to the Ordnance Survey map of 1886, one can see an Isle of Rea, which no longer exists as such, just south of the town bridge (High Street). My impression is that this island is where much of the deeply unaesthetic Borough Parade shopping centre now stands. This area can therefore probably be excluded from being Asser's east of the Avon because it may have been an island even in Alfred's time. I use the word "probably" because I cannot prove that this island was not man-made after King Alfred's time. Just south of here the river once divided again into a main stream and a Hardenhuish Brook, forming yet another island called The Ham. However, it seems like it is the brook rather than the main stream that has disappeared so that when we now look across the river at this point, we are looking at the east bank of the Avon as opposed to the eastern edge of a former island. So, I proceeded to walk all the way down the western bank looking across at the eastern bank. Today, this area has been developed, except at the point where one reaches some playing fields.

The Viking base could have been anywhere along this east bank, allowing for the disappearance of the Isle of Rea. However, because the Avon bends sharply, there is a second eastern bank a little further east, where Monkton Park is located. However, I feel that this is a less likely location because of the pattern of the Vikings usage of water to defend themselves on three sides, which the latter site could not provide. But there is a third option. Neither Asser nor the Chronicles state whether the Vikings set up a new fortification or took over what was already there instead. I believe it likely that the Vikings took over the royal estate which, especially considering its northerly location compared to the rest of Wessex, presumably had defences. It is perhaps inconceivable that the Vikings would drive the Saxons out of Chippenham and not use a defended Saxon site as their base. Establishing the location of the royal estate may therefore also establish the location of the Viking base. I searched for clues that might tell us where the royal estate may have been. St Andrew's church has been described as probably being at the site of the Saxon church[53] and is near the Market Place, which was the main focus of the Saxon town[54] It is possible that the Saxon church may have been associated with the royal estate. Anybody who walks down nearby St Mary's Street will sense that it is very old and indeed it is considered to be part of the Saxon settlement, with the area to the north of St Andrew's church considered to be a possibility for the location of the royal estate.[54]

Ordnance Survey maps from 1900 to 1967 indicate a "site of King Arthur's Palace" between the Market Place and Gladstone Road. Although it is named after King Arthur, who we cannot prove existed, one wonders how this royal connotation came about. The area indicated is to the rear of the current Museum and Heritage Centre and also appears to be at the northern end of a restricted parking area accessed off Timber Street opposite a good restaurant serving Caribbean food.

Therefore, we have two potential sites for a royal estate, one to the west of The Causeway and one to the east. Both of these would meet Asser's description of being east of the Avon, although the latter would probably be better described as being west of the Avon as it is closer to the other side of the peninsula. It seems to me that the royal site could have ranged across both of these areas and perhaps we should not consider them separately. Therefore, for me, the most likely area for the location of both the royal estate and the Viking fortification extends between Borough Parade shopping centre car park in the north, Timber Street in the south, and St Mary's Street to the east, encompassing the site of St Andrew's church.

We now turn back to Twelfth Night of 878 to examine some clues regarding where Alfred might have gone next. Readers will note that I mention a place in Devon called Appledore, which is not to be confused with Appledore in Kent, which enters our story in Chapter 8.

Where did Alfred go?

We do not know where Alfred was between the Vikings' arrival at Chippenham on Twelfth Night in January 878 and when Alfred developed the fortification at Athelney at Easter in the same year. If Alfred had not been at Chippenham on Twelfth Night, and there seems to be no evidence that he was, his last recorded location is Exeter in 876. Because the historical record indicates that control of Wessex had been lost to the Vikings after their arrival at Chippenham, much of Wessex would have become unsafe for Alfred. The Viking penetration deep into Wessex is supported by entries in both the Anglo-Saxon Chronicles and in the writings of Asser that describe Alfred, after he had arrived at Athelney, attacking Vikings from this remote location on the Somerset Levels. The Anglo-Saxon Chronicles tell us that, after the Viking attack at Chippenham, Alfred had been in woods and defensive positions (*morfæstenum*) in swamps or moors. This does not necessarily mean that he was in the Somerset Levels in the period when he is missing from the record, because other places could fit those descriptions. The entry also indicates that Alfred was at more than one secured place (*morfæstenum* is plural) amongst marshes, and this means that even if Alfred had headed straight to the Somerset Levels, Athelney would not have been the only secured site. It is possible that Alfred was in the Somerset Levels for the whole period between the Viking attack on

Chippenham and his departure from Athelney, with additional *morfæstenum* located in the Somerset Levels being used prior to the development of a definitive base at Athelney. Indeed, Athelney is not the sole area of higher ground in the Somerset levels. Locations such as Burrow Mump or Aller could also have been used, which might even help explain why Aller was significant enough for Alfred to have the Viking leader Guthrum baptised there after the Wessex victory at the Battle of Ethandun (see Chapter 7).

Although there is no evidence to support it, there are legends that refer to Alfred's presence in the north of Devon. It cannot be ruled out that after the arrival of the Vikings at Chippenham he retreated as far as this county, with the later encampment at Athelney in Somerset being the commencement of his reconquest. Indeed, he may already have been in Devon because, as we have already seen, his last recorded location before the Vikings arrived at Chippenham was at Exeter in 876.

The Anglo-Saxon Chronicles tell us that in 878, and in the same winter that the Vikings attacked Chippenham, the Vikings also attacked Devon with 23 ships under the leadership of an unnamed brother of Ivar and Halfdan, although Gaimar tells us that the name of this brother was Ubbe. Asser provides further detail and states the location to be *Cynuit*, and also that the Vikings had sailed from Dyfed in Wales. The location of *Cynuit* remains uncertain to this day. There is no proof that the attacks on Chippenham and on *Cynuit* had been co-ordinated, although this cannot be ruled out. However, it might be that the Vikings attacked *Cynuit* because Alfred had been in that area, and it is this that inspired me to investigate this battle further.

Whilst not explicitly stating who won, the Anglo-Saxon Chronicles imply that the Vikings lost at *Cynuit*, because we are told that their leader had been killed, along with many other Vikings, and that their raven banner had been taken from them. However, Æthelweard's chronicle confusingly states that the Vikings had won, despite their leader having been killed. However, Asser's account certainly gives the impression that the Vikings had lost. I therefore feel that most of the evidence points to the Vikings having lost. Additionally, it is only in the writings of Asser and in Æthelweard's chronicle that a Wessex stronghold is mentioned. Asser indicates that the location had been secure from all directions except from the east and that it was not adjacent (*contigua*) to water, presumably meaning fresh water as siege conditions were being described. Asser also indicates that the Vikings besieged the stronghold but the defending Saxons then won when they stormed out of the front of the stronghold at dawn. The Viking leader, Ubbe, died along with over 800 other Vikings. However, in Æthelweard's chronicle the Viking leader is identified as Halfdan. It is generally considered that Æthelweard's chronicle is less contemporaneous than the Anglo-Saxon Chronicles, which say that the leader was a brother of Halfdan, making it reasonable to conclude that the leader had not been Halfdan. Æthelweard's possible error perhaps allows us to also doubt his claim that the Vikings had won. Geffrei Gaimar is even less contemporaneous than Æthelweard, but his naming of Ubbe as the killed Viking leader fits better with the Anglo-Saxon Chronicles' telling us that the leader was a brother of Ivar and Halfdan.

I wondered whether it was possible to find out where this *Cynuit* was, and whether establishing the location might shed light on where Alfred may have been before the Easter of 878. Bearing in mind that the attacking Vikings had sailed from Wales it seems more likely that the battle took place in North Devon rather than in South Devon. It has been suggested that the battle took place at today's Countisbury on the North Devon coast,[5] [6] although this has been challenged.[55] Countisbury Castle, an iron age promontory fort, appears to fail Asser's description as the eastern aspect was defended by a ditch and rampart,[56] although we cannot be certain of the later status of these defences in King Alfred's time. Nonetheless, the discrepancy with Asser's description seemed good enough reason for me to consider other locations for this battle.

A 2008 newspaper article announced that the location of the Battle of *Cynuit* had been discovered to be Castle Hill (Grid Ref SS52271681),[57] a site of a prehistoric hillfort not far from Beaford in Devon, and near where the River Torridge bends to create a peninsula. The location seems to fit Asser's description of being secure from all directions except the east and not being adjacent to water (although only just as the River Torridge flows nearby). Viewing Castle Hill presented a challenge as it is high up on private land. However, I managed to obtain a view by looking across from a tiny place called Homer (Grid Ref SS51251648), which is in an elevated position on the other side of the Torridge. There is a Kenwith Nursery at the end of the peninsula, and the similarity of Kenwith to *Cynuit* is striking. However, I understand that this is a coincidence and that this location was not always associated with the name Kenwith.

The name Kenwith/Kinwith crops up elsewhere in North Devon. Sir John Spelman, in a book published in 1709 (although he was writing in the first half of the seventeenth century), speculated the location of *Cynuit* to be "not far from the mouth of the *Tau*",[58] with the *Tau* seeming to be the same as the River Taw, which meets (at arguably its "mouth") the River Torridge near Appledore. However, I was unable to work out why it was that John Spelman felt that *Cynuit* had been at this location and I could find no indication of *Cynuit* there, although I did come across an earthwork called Kenwith Castle (Grid Ref: SS43272737) that had become associated with *Cynuit* at a nearby location west of Bideford. Unfortunately, this location appears to have once been called Henniborough or Henni's Castle, and it appears to have only acquired the name Kenwith in the early nineteenth century based on the speculation of a local man called Robert Studley Vidal. Furthermore, this location may not meet Asser's description of *Cynuit* because there is water running adjacent to the site.[59] Kenwith Castle was marked on my Ordnance Survey map but the site is on private land. An impression can nonetheless be gained by viewing from nearby roads. A river called the Kenwith flows from this area to enter the Torridge at Bideford, although I have been unable to establish for how long it has had this name. It would be especially interesting if it could be discovered to have been called the Kenwith prior to the nineteenth century as this might mean that the name of the earthwork had not in fact changed, and could increase the chances of this being the real location of the Battle of *Cynuit*. Please be aware that there is nearby an eighteenth century house (now a care home) that is also called Kenwith Castle.

Fig. 11 The monument at Bloody Corner. The inscription reads "Stop stranger stop, near this spot lies buried King Hubba the Dane, who was slayed by King Alfred the Great in a bloody retreat."

It has been suggested that Cannington in Somerset could have been *Cynuit*, partly because the nearby village on the River Parrett called Combwich had a similar name to *Cynuit* (personally, I don't recognise a similarity). Furthermore, the battle is described by all the main sources as having taken place in Devon, and Cannington and Combwich are, and were then, in Somerset. The proximity of these locations to the River Parrett would have nonetheless given them strategic importance and it is notable that an earlier Viking force had been defeated at the mouth of the River Parrett in 848. The Parrett also provided access to the Somerset Levels, and therefore Alfred's base at Athelney. Although not *Cynuit*, it would therefore not be surprising if Cannington and Combwich had played a role in this period that has not been recorded. I have spent some time in Combwich, which to me has an end-of-the-world appeal and is mysterious in the way that places of past importance tend to be. Indeed, it seems that the Romans had a port at Combwich.

It has also been suggested that *Cynuit* may have been reclaimed by the sea,[59] although there is no supporting evidence. It seems that we can discount Cannington, and the claim for Countisbury does not seem to be better than that of Castle Hill. Ultimately, I found that I could not determine the location of the Battle of *Cynuit* beyond that it was fought in Devon. Although I have lingering suspicions that Kenwith Castle could be the site, it seems that Castle Hill, near Beaford, is perhaps the best option on the table.

The 1889 Ordnance Survey map shows a location just to the east of Northam, near Bideford, indicated to be: "*Bloody Corner. Supposed Site of a Battle Between the Vikings & Saxons (A.D. 878).*" Bloody Corner remains on modern maps, although the supposition that it is a battle site has been removed. I parked near here and used the public footpaths to wander around in contemplation. Although this location seems to have been called Bloody Corner for a long time, I could find no evidence as to when it acquired this name. However, in 1804 an antiquarian claimed that it was so-called because the Vikings had fought against the Anglo-Saxons here whilst on retreat from Kenwith Castle (with the writer presumably assuming Kenwith Castle to be the location of the Battle of *Cynuit*).[59] There is still a monument by the road that declares that Hubba (an alternative spelling for Ubbe) was killed by Alfred at this location and then buried nearby. Tradition has it that Hubba landed at Boathyde,[60] not shown on my Ordnance Survey map, but I found out that this was on the River Torridge just east of Hyde Barton, and accessible by a footpath from Bloody Corner. For those who don't mind a longer walk there is an even better option, which is to catch the bus from Appledore to Bideford and walk back along a section of the South West Coast Path, passing the location of Boathyde on the way. Legend has it that Hubba was buried on the local shoreline under a large and the location became known as Hubbastone. Nobody has been able to conclusively identify such a stone, but in 2010 a new one was erected at Irsha Street in Appledore.[61] It has been said that there was once a place near Appledore called Whibblestone, and that this name had been derived from Hubbastone,[59] although I could not find this place. Geffrei Gaimar states that Ubbe was killed at *bois de Penne* (wood of Penne) and that the Vikings built a mound in Devonshire called Ubbelawe, which has been translated to Ubbe's Barrow.[44] However, place-names have changed so much that we may not be able to follow the thread back. I have read that there is a King Alfred's Cave near Northam (just north of Bideford), where legend has it that Alfred hid from the Vikings,[60] although I was unsuccessful in locating this as well.

Ultimately, we cannot determine Alfred's location in the short period prior to the construction of a fortification at Athelney at Easter of 878. Although *Cynuit* may be a clue as to Alfred's location, it is important to recognise that no source indicates that he was anywhere near this battle, the objective of which might have been simply to suppress a part of Wessex that was holding out against Viking control. In the following chapter I reconnect with the known life of King Alfred at around Easter of 878, when he was building his fortress at Athelney.

5

Athelney and the Somerset Levels

Athelney

King Alfred built a fortification at Athelney at Easter in 878, at a time when Wessex had fallen to the Vikings, and it was from here that Alfred set out on the successful reconquest of his kingdom. Athelney, often known as the Isle of Athelney, is an attractive and small settlement located between Burrowbridge and East Lyng. In Alfred's time much of the area would have been impassable and swampy, and the difficulty in besieging such a location must have been a factor in Alfred's decision to set up a camp here. Even now the area is highly prone to flooding with much of the Somerset Levels being below sea level. The legend of Alfred burning the cakes has become associated with his time at Athelney, although there is no evidence that this incident occurred here or anywhere else. His wife, Ealhswith, and their two young children (Edward and Æthelflæd) may have been with him during this period, but it seems plausible that they might have been sent out of the country for their protection.

When you are at the site it is clear that Athelney has two small summits, sufficient to have made this location an island in the watery Somerset levels of Alfred's time. It is thought that Alfred's 878 fortification was on the western summit (evidence of metalworking here suggests the manufacture of weapons for use in Alfred's reconquest of Wessex), whilst an abbey, founded later by Alfred in 893, occupied the eastern summit[62] where a monument dedicated to King Alfred now stands. The monument was erected in 1801 by Sir John Slade who owned Athelney Farm at that time and who, interestingly, was also the Lord of the Manor at North Petherton, just a few miles to the north-west, which is where the famous Alfred Jewel was found, in a field at the north-west corner of Petherton Park[63] in 1693. However, the landowner there at that time was a Thomas Wroth, but perhaps because he was only eighteen when the jewel was found, it passed into the ownership of his guardian, and uncle, Nathaniel Palmer of Fairfield in the parish of Stogursey (Somerset).[64] When he died the jewel was gifted to the University of Oxford and it can still be seen in the Ashmolean Museum in that city. A replica was

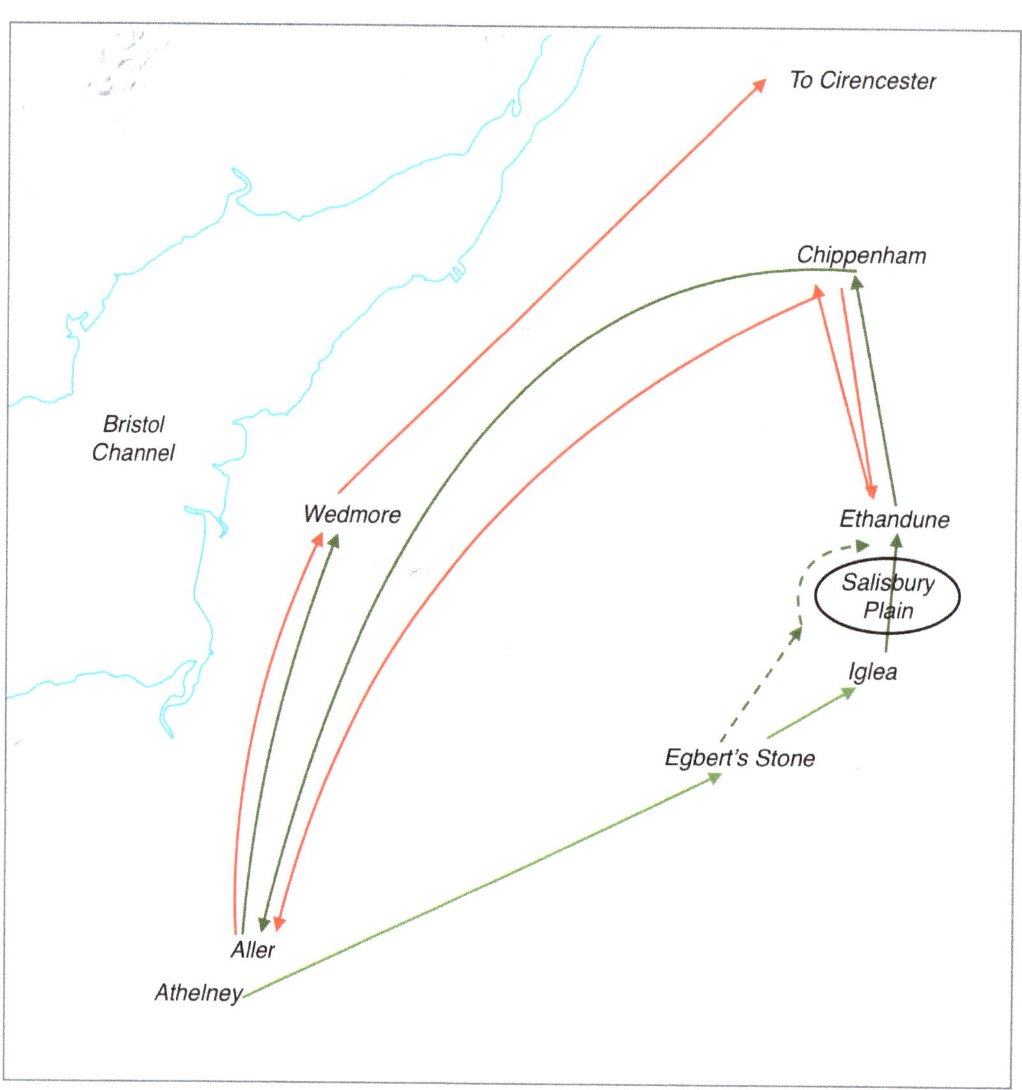

Fig. 12 Schematic diagram showing the movements of King Alfred (Green, with an alternative route shown dashed) and the Viking leader Guthrum (red) in the events discussed in Chapters 5 to 7. Contains OS data © Crown copyright and database right (2018).

made and had been on display at the Church of St Mary in North Petherton. However, it was stolen at least once and, when I visited, I was told that it is no longer on display. The image of this jewel still has significant local importance attached to it - there is a replica on the chain of office of the local mayor and the local bowling club uses a picture of it on their badge. There was a significant Saxon presence at North Petherton,[63] and it seems possible that the find at Petherton Park could be connected to this. At this point I would like to mention an interesting coincidence. There was once a forester at Petherton

Park who was no less than the famous Geoffrey Chaucer, and one of the works of this fourteenth-century writer was a translation from Latin into Middle English of a work by a Roman writer called Boethius, which King Alfred had translated into Old English about 500 years before. The Alfred Jewel therefore connects these two translators of this work, called The Consolation of Philosophy, to the tiny location of Petherton Park. The "jewel" is thought to be a pointer (an *æstel*) used to assist reading, and indeed Alfred tells us in his preface to his translation of Pope Gregory's Pastoral Care that he is going to accompany each copy, to be sent to each bishop, with an *æstel*. At St Nicholas' Church at Moreton in Dorset, famous as the burial place of Lawrence of Arabia, the engraver Lawrence Whistler has created a window that is inspired both by the Alfred Jewel and an Old English poem, which Alfred would perhaps have known, called the Dream of the Rood. Other "jewels" dated to the 9th century have been found, but none includes any text like the Alfred Jewel does, which amazingly states, in translation, "Alfred ordered me to be made." These additional items, all aestels, include the Minster Lovell Jewel, the Bowleaze Jewel (found in the debris of a cliff fall at Weymouth), and the Warminster Jewel.

According to Asser, the abbey at Athelney was one of a pair that was ordered to be built by King Alfred, with the other one being Shaftesbury. I could find no record of when the abbey at Athelney was built but in the section on Shaftesbury I speculate that the abbey there was in use by 882, so it seems appropriate to extend this date to the abbey at Athelney. This date also seems plausible because he could have created these abbeys as a thanks to God after his success in defeating the Vikings at Ethandun in 878. This abbey was later replaced by a medieval monastery, although there is nothing visible above ground today.

But let us now return to the period before his victory at Ethandun and to the time when he was hiding out at Athelney. There is evidence that Athelney may have already been a royal site that was known to Alfred, and this may explain why he went there. When I look at the Anglo-Saxon Chronicles (version A) Athelney is referred to as *eþelingga eige* and *eþelinga eigge*, which seems to me to read as "island of the princes" (*eþeling* or *æþeling* meaning prince, and *eig* meaning island). The impression gained from both the Anglo-Saxon Chronicles and Asser is that this site was already called this when Alfred arrived, rather than it having been given this name retrospectively.

The royal connection may be to a hermit called Æthelwine, recorded as living at Athelney in the 7th century, because he is said to have been the son of Cynegils, king of the West Saxons, and the brother of the subsequent King Cenwealh. It is therefore also possible that Alfred's abbey at Athelney could have been an enlargement of an existing religious site that had persisted at this location since the time of Æthelwine.[65]

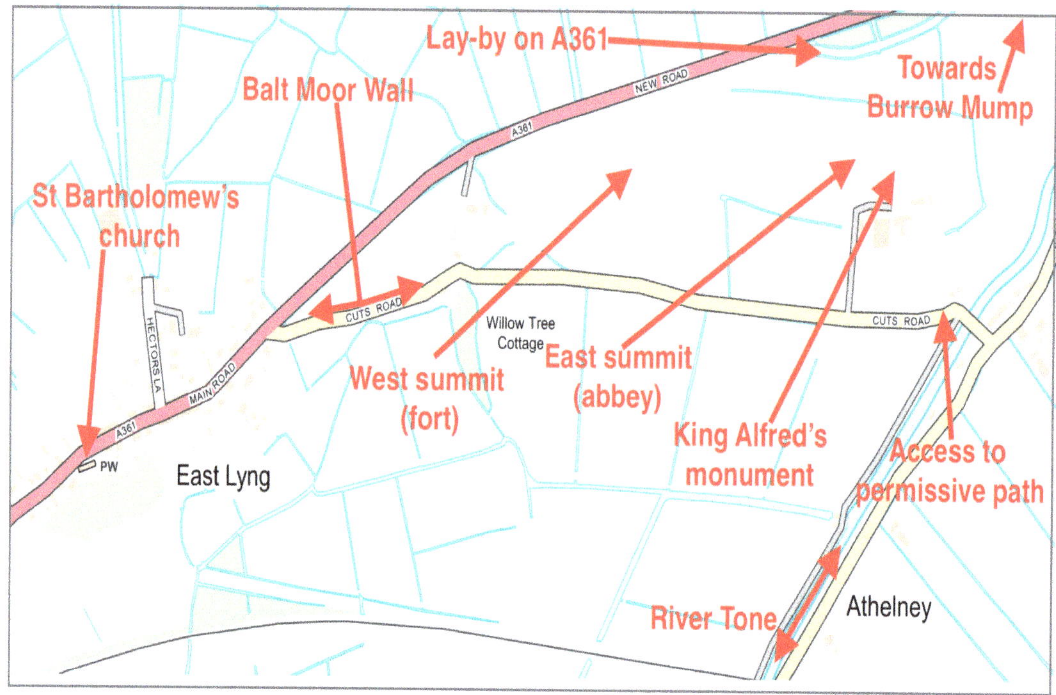

Fig. 13 Features at Athelney and East Lyng. Contains OS data © Crown copyright and database right (2018).

Nowadays, you will rarely find anyone else here at this important location making it easier to picture Alfred's world. I got to the site by taking Cut Road from East Lyng and parking near Athelney Farm. The hills are on private land but there is a signpost indicating a route to the monument. Athelney Hill can also be observed from the lay-by on the nearby A361. Its elevation above the surrounding area is immediately obvious, and one can see the hill of Burrow Mump not far away to the north-east, which suggests that this could have have been used for advance defence and signalling back to Athelney. There are other areas of potentially strategic high ground in the area, such as Windmill Hill to the south-west, Oath Hill to the south-east and, slightly further to the east, the high ridge of Aller Hill. Asser records that Alfred struck out at Vikings from Athelney, which indicates that Vikings had been in the vicinity.

The Anglo-Saxon Chronicles tell us that Alfred left Athelney for Egbert's Stone in the seventh week after Easter in 878. He was therefore at the fortress at Athelney for about seven weeks, although he could have also been at Athelney prior to the construction of the fortress. We shall follow Alfred's route in the next chapter, but first I would like to draw your attention to a couple of other places of interest and then explore the matter of the burning of the cakes more fully.

Burrow Mump

Burrow Mump, which always reminds me of Glastonbury Tor, is an unmissable natural hill close to the settlement of Burrowbridge in the Somerset Levels. It is located close to where the River Tone flows into the River Parrett, with the River Tone having just flowed past Athelney. It is also close to where the River Cary once joined the Parrett, although the Cary now runs into King's Sedgemoor Drain to the north. Although it is difficult to fully understand the network of navigable routes for King Alfred's time, it appears that this location therefore would have been strategic in the defence of Athelney, particularly as Burrow Mump can be seen from Athelney and vice-versa. There is church atop Burrow Mump, which is incomplete because funding ran out in the late 18th century, and there is evidence of an earlier structure going back to the 12th century. The hill was later given to the National Trust as a memorial to those killed in the Second World War. Those who clamber up the steep incline are rewarded with great views. Although the surrounding water has long since been drained one can still look around for other areas of higher ground, which would have been islands in Alfred's time. Unfortunately, at times of bad flooding, we are still today reminded why the inclusion of the word "Isle" in the place-names of some of the areas of higher ground is so apt.

An interesting story was told to me regarding the King Alfred pub in Burrowbridge, which once had a three-legged so-called "Alfred Table." Although I was told that it was eventually dated to be much more recent, it still sold for a handsome sum to a visitor. I enjoyed this tale and the pub is a pleasant place to engage in local stories while having a pint.

East Lyng, Somerset

East Lyng is a small settlement on the A361 and is very close to Athelney. Asser tells us that the fortress on the western summit of Athelney Hill was connected to another fortress by a causeway. This second fortress appears to have been at East Lyng which, like Athelney, is on higher ground.

However, it is important to note that Asser tells us about the causeway and the second fortress in relation to the later founding of the abbey at Athelney. There appears to be no evidence that the fortress at East Lyng or the causeway had been present when Alfred had been hiding out at Athelney in 878. Indeed, the causeway may have been built at this later time in order to facilitate access to and from Athelney's abbey and fort. The fort at East Lyng may have been built as part of Alfred's defence programme, which he commenced after 878. A document called The Burghal Hidage was compiled during the reign of Alfred's son King Edward the Elder and it is a list of settlements that would have been fortified during this defence programme. Lyng, although without any distinction between East and West, is named in the Burghal Hidage. Athelney is not listed, perhaps because it was protected by Lyng at that time.

I wondered whether it was possible to see any remains of the fortification at Lyng. Whilst not being able to specifically find the fortification, I was able to observe some evidence of the burgh's perimeter. My research had indicated that a bank and ditch to the west of East Lyng, and in line with the east wall of St Bartholomew's church, might be the remains of the western perimeter of the burgh defences. I went to the location described above and I could indeed see what looked like earthworks in the field to the south of the church. I could not explore further because the field appeared to be private land but, fortunately, the presenters in the first ever episode of Time Team (1994) gained access and their programme confirmed that I had indeed been looking across at approximately the correct spot, although the alignment appeared to be more with just beyond the west wall of the church, running to the south under a disused petrol station! Once I spotted the bank and ditch, I wondered how I could ever have been confused in the first place as it is quite obvious. The bank and ditch would have extended north on the other side of the A361, but there appears to be no remains left in the landscape. It seems likely that the eastern boundary would be near Cuts Road and the old causeway that remains in use today. It therefore seems that most of the settlement of East Lyng might be sited within the outline of the Alfredian burgh of Lyng.

I also investigated the causeway itself, which can still largely be seen as it heads to Athelney. Coming from East Lyng one drives over the first section, and it then passes onto private land but with the route remaining visible. The structure is now called the Balt Moor Wall. I have not seen any reference that dates this to before the 12th century, so we cannot be sure that this was precisely the same route that the causeway would have taken in Alfred's time.

Burning the Cakes

Although I have already mentioned that there is no evidence that Alfred burnt any cakes it seems appropriate for me to say a few more words about this famous and persistent legend, particularly as when talking to people about King Alfred it is often the first thing that comes up. The story first appears in the anonymous *Vita S Neoti* (Life of St Neot), which seems to have been put together in the late tenth century, and we are clearly told that this baking mishap took place at Athelney. The story found its way from there into a twelfth century compilation of documents that became known as the Annals of St Neots. Then in the sixteenth century it was lifted from there and inserted, probably by the theologian Matthew Parker, into Asser's Life of King Alfred. This must have given the story a real boost and is probably why it is so famous today. We cannot ultimately prove that it was inserted by Matthew Parker (as opposed to somebody even before him) because the document that he would have been working from was destroyed in a fire in 1731 and there are no other known ancient copies. The result, however, was that for a significant period of time the story of the cakes was treated as an integral part of the writings of Asser (and therefore may have seemed more credible), when this in fact was not the case. In brief, the earliest version of the story tells us that Alfred turned up on his own as an unknown person at a pig farmer's cottage at Athelney where he was taken in and stayed for some days whilst he awaited God's mercy, whilst keeping in mind the patience that had been demonstrated by the biblical Job. One day, while the pig-farmer was out taking his animals to a field, the farmer's wife started baking loaves of bread (not cakes), but then became occupied with other domestic duties. The loaves started to burn and the wife pointed out to Alfred that although he was quite happy to eat them, he hadn't been so keen to turn them over when he could see them burning. It appears that Alfred was shaken but not stirred, and he proceeded to then turn the loaves over. The word used for swineherd, *subulcus*, was changed in the Annals of St Neots to *uaccarius*, cowherd, for reasons unknown. The tale was recast many times subsequently and I suspect a whole book could be written tracing these variations.

6

In search of Egbert's Stone

In the seventh week after Easter in 878 Alfred left Athelney and went to a place called Egbert's Stone. He was joined there by additional troops before eventually moving on to a place called *Iglea* and then on to his important victory at the Battle of Ethandun. This chapter examines the alternative locations for Egbert's Stone. For me this is one of the great puzzles relating to the story of King Alfred and I hope to encourage the reader to be similarly intrigued. If Alfred's wife and two children had been with him at Athelney, it seems most likely to me that they would have been sent elsewhere for their safety when Alfred departed for Egbert's Stone. This refuge would probably have been across the English Channel or at least in a location where the crossing could quickly take place if Alfred was defeated.

The Anglo-Saxon Chronicles refer to Egbert's Stone (*Ecgbryhtes stane)* as the place where the armies from Somerset, Wiltshire and the part of Hampshire that is mysteriously described as being on this side of (*behinon*) the sea, came together to fight alongside Alfred. It is notable that Devon and Dorset are not mentioned. However, Dorset may be an omission because the 12th century writer Geffrei Gaimar indicates that this county had indeed been involved. Devon may have had enough on its plate, recalling the recent attack by the Viking Ubbe at *Cynuit* (chapter 4) and the relatively unknown relationship between Wessex and adjacent Cornwall at this time. There has been speculation about the meaning of *behinon* - what does the part of Hampshire on this side of the sea really mean? It has been suggested that the sea refers to either Southampton Water or the Solent, meaning that forces from either eastern Hampshire or the Isle of Wight respectively did not take part (it seems that the Isle of Wight was part of Hampshire at this time). However, I think it is possible that the Anglo-Saxon Chronicles may have been referring to the men rather than the land of Hampshire, particularly as we are also told that after their arrival at Chippenham the Vikings had driven many people overseas.

The Anglo-Saxon Chronicles tell us that the location of Egbert's Stone was *eastan Sealwyda,* which can be translated to "east of Selwood." Selwood was an ancient wood, of which very little is left, that covered a large area extending from the north of Dorset to almost as far as Bath. We can therefore be tempted to rule out anything that would have been in Selwood. However, Asser says that the location was in the eastern part of Selwood, which temps us to rule out everything outside of Selwood! It may not be possible to resolve this conundrum, but at least we can perhaps rule out places that were neither in the eastern part of Selwood or east of Selwood. The eastern part of Selwood would have been approximately 30 miles east of Athelney and the sources indicate that Alfred rode. However, no source tells us how long it took to get from Athelney to Egbert's Stone, so we are unable to exclude anywhere because of distance. King Egbert was Alfred's deceased grandfather and one suspects that the location of this stone was at a place significant to the life or the death of that ruler. I found seven potential sites for the location of Egbert's Stone, and I shall commence with the one that I consider more likely and work down through those that I consider less likely.

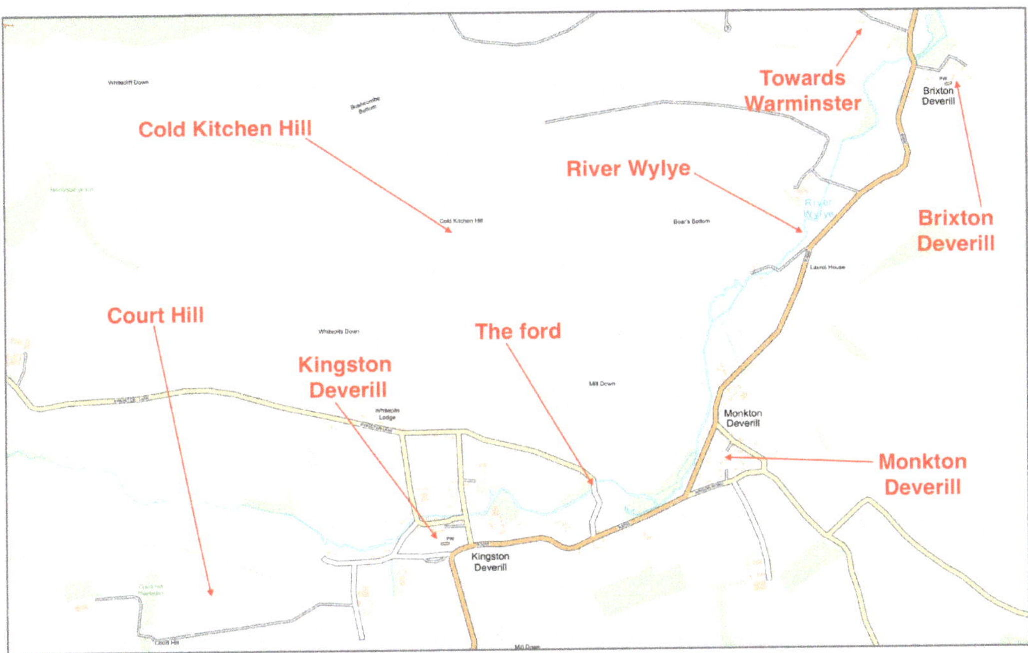

Fig. 14 Features relating to the Upper Deverills that are mentioned in the text. Contains OS data © Crown copyright and database right (2018)

The Upper Deverills (Wiltshire)

The Upper Deverills are a short distance south of Warminster and consist of three small villages on the River Deverill. These villages are Kingston Deverill, Monkton Deverill and Brixton Deverill. When walking in the hills here I rarely saw anyone else and it seems to me that this beautiful rural area is relatively under-visited. I recommend the stiff climb up towards Cold Kitchen Hill (itself an important site in pre-historic and Roman times) for the elevated views over the Upper Deverills that this provides.

There is another hill to the west of the village of Kingston Deverill called Court Hill, or King's Court Hill, and it has been suggested that it got its name from King Egbert having held a court there. There is also a story that a farmer brought three large stones down from this hill and used them as stepping stones to a barn. They were then mounted in a rectory garden, and are now on private land to the east of the church. I could see only two, although this fits with a reference I have seen to the third one disappearing during World War 2.[66] Of course, these stones could have just been lying around on the hill, or maybe they were from a collapsed dolmen that had nothing to do with Egbert.

Fig. 15 The ford at Kingston Deverill

Court Hill was marked on my Ordnance Survey map and there is a bridleway running up it and also a track that goes to a gliding club. The views up here are rewarding and one can imagine troops coming from different directions to meet at this place. You need permission to access private land, and it might be worth contacting the Gliding Club, who also have open days. However, it seems to me unlikely that the troops would have assembled on high ground, away from water and where they would have advertised their presence to the Vikings.

However, the location of Kingston Deverill throws up a further possibility in that the village lies close to where the Roman road coming up from Badbury Rings (Dorset) meets the Roman road that connected Old Sarum in Wiltshire to Charterhouse in the Somerset Mendips. Furthermore, there is evidence that the Roman road from Badbury Rings extended north beyond Kingston Deverill to Bath.[67] It has been claimed that the two Roman roads crossed at the ford at Kingston Deverill, with this location also being at the boundary between Kingston Deverill and Monkton Deverill.[68] I visited the ford, which was marked on my Ordnance Survey map (Grid Ref ST85113728) and found it to be a lovely spot that also seemed well cared for. Please note that there are signs saying that the ford is not suitable for vehicles to cross. If you visit Kingston Deverill, remember to visit the 15th century St Mary's church (although there may have been an earlier structure) where I was delighted to find a banner depicting King Alfred, indicating that his connections with this area had not been forgotten. Furthermore, the important ancient route known as the Hard Way (and also as the Harrow Way) runs east-west a short distance to the south of Kingston Deverill. It seems that this was a well-connected area.

Monkton Deverill is approximately an equal distance east of the ford as Kingston Deverill is west of it. There is a legend that Alfred prayed at a church here before the Battle of Ethandun, and this church later became dedicated to St Alfred the Great.[68] The church is now a private residence, and appears to have been constructed more recently than the time of King Alfred, although there may have been an earlier structure on the site (I am not aware of any evidence of this). Finding this church was not easy, because my Ordnance Survey map appeared to indicate that the church is set on the road, which is not the case. A friendly gardener eventually told me that it was up a footpath that I had driven past several times, and indeed this footpath cutting through the village was shown on my Ordnance Survey map.

There has also been speculation that Egbert's Stone was at nearby Brixton Deverill, and there is undoubtedly a strong resemblance between the names Brixton and *Ecgbryhtes stane*. However, caution is required because the name of this village is thought to be derived from a person called Beorhtric[14] and, indeed, the Domesday Book tells us that in 1086 the lord here went by the name of Brictric (whether this was the same person as Beorhtric I do not know). It seems therefore that there are good reasons to doubt that the name of this village could have been derived from *Ecgbryhtes stane*. There is a legend that the story of Alfred burning the cakes took place in a field south of the rectory at Brixton Deverill,[68] therefore competing with Athelney as the location for this baking mishap, if it happened at all (see Chapter 5).

I found the following entry in the Anglo-Saxon Chronicles to be most interesting: *he for ymb ane niht of þam wicum to Iglea*. This can be translated to "he (Alfred) then went one night from the settlements to *Iglea*." I am no expert in Old English but I was expecting to see "settlement" rather than the plural "settlements", with the latter indicating that Alfred may have had multiple encampments at Egbert's Stone, and I suggest that these camps may have been at the locations of what are now the different Upper Deverill villages. It is worth considering the strategic fit of the Upper Deverill villages collectively with Alfred's potential route to *Iglea*, which is where he went next. Following the valley of the River Wylye north-east would have taken Alfred close to a potential location of *Iglea* in the current Eastleigh Wood, near Sutton Veny (see Chapter 7).

Other potential locations for Egbert's Stone are also near ancient trackways, but for me the Upper Deverills stand out because they fit so well with a sensible route to a location where Alfred plausibly went next. It also appears that the Upper Deverills would have been in the eastern part of Selwood,[69] therefore fitting the description of the location of Egbert's Stone provided by Asser. All in all, I find that the Upper Deverills is the most likely location for Egbert's Stone. The evidence, however, is a very long way from conclusive and further possibilities are described below.

Willoughby Hedge, Wiltshire

Willoughby Hedge may be better known to some as the service station on the A303 in Wiltshire near West Knoyle and indeed there is little else there. Nonetheless, the service station is just a very short distance south west of our point of interest, which came to my attention in a book by John Peddie.[70] The location, just a short distance south of the Upper Deverills, is also just west of where the A350 meets the A303 (Grid Ref ST87433377). I would advise that you do not walk down the very busy A303 to get to the specific point of interest. There was a Willoughby Hedge and an Old Willoughby

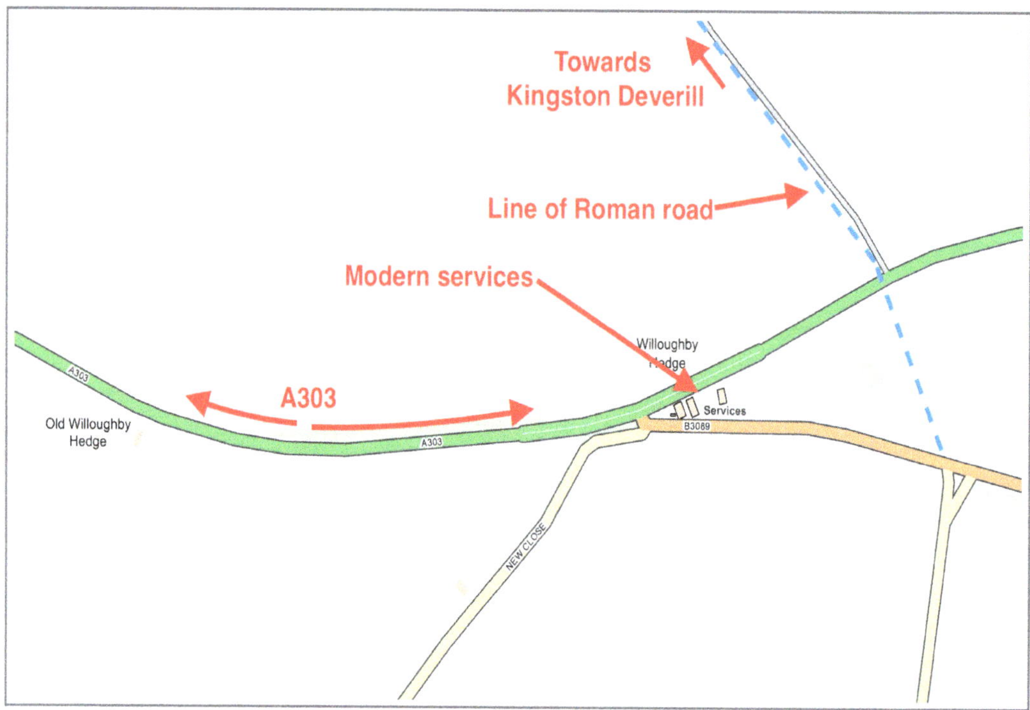

Fig. 16 Features mentioned in the text that relate to Willoughby Hedge. The indicative route of the Roman Road is shown in blue dashes. Contains OS data © Crown copyright and database right (2018)

Hedge marked on my Ordnance Survey map, although these precise locations should be disregarded because what is relevant to us is the realisation that the A303 is on the route of the ancient Hard Way (also known as the Harroway) and that it is crossed by the same north-south Roman road that runs to the ford near Kingston Deverill. This crossing can be more or less pinpointed. Although the Roman road was not marked on my Ordnance Survey map it seems that the crossing was near to where a track leading up to Keysley Farm (which is on Ordnance Survey maps) leaves the A303. The maps also show a right of way that still crosses the A303 at approximately the correct point. That the Hard Way would have still been in use in Alfred's time is supported by the fact that the A303 at this point still lies on this ancient route. The Hard Way will crop up again when we look at further potential locations for Egbert's Stone at King Alfred's Tower in Somerset and Kilmington Common in Wiltshire.

It seems plausible to me that this location would have been relevant to the coming together of troops on their way to Egbert's Stone, rather than it being Egbert's Stone itself. The Upper Deverills are, after all, only a very short distance north of here.

King Alfred's Tower, Somerset

This location, several miles west of the Upper Deverills, is frequently suggested as being at or near the site of Egbert's Stone. The tower is an unusual three-sided folly, built from 1762 onwards, and set in a lovely location surrounded by woodland on Kingsettle Hill in Somerset. It is strikingly large and indeed an aeroplane crashed into it in 1944. When I first visited the tower, it was at dusk in winter and I had a strong sense of solitude despite the over bearing presence of the tower and the proximity of the road. The trees surrounding the tower gave a protective feeling almost like a castle moat and as night descended there was a strange perception of the trees closing in. But is this romantic site also the location of Egbert's stone? The road that goes past the tower is on the line of the ancient Hard Way, with the name surviving at the nearby Hardway Farm. However, it seems difficult to describe this location as being east of or in the eastern part of Selwood which is required to fit the descriptions given by Asser and the Anglo-Saxon Chronicles. Its location adjacent to an important ancient route therefore does not seem enough to determine this to be the location of Egbert's Stone.

A man called Dugald Macfadyen, writing in a book published in 1901, indicated that there had been a local tradition that the signal for the gathering at Egbert's Stone had been provided by a beacon being lit at the site of the tower, although the gathering itself was at Brixton Deverill.[71]

Kilmington Common, Wiltshire

Kilmington Common, put forward as a location for Egbert's Stone by Dr Williams-Freeman in the 1950s,[35] is a village that lies about a mile east of Alfred's Tower and back across the border into Wiltshire. The west-east road and track, named Tower Road and Long Lane respectively, lie on the route of the ancient Hard Way. I walked down the track called Long Lane, partly to appreciate that this was a potential site for Egbert's Stone and partly for the simple enjoyment of walking on the ancient Hard Way. I looked over to where "the common" was marked on my Ordnance Survey map, but there was little to see apart from crops. Although the case for this location is supported by evidence that tracks ran in other directions near here, it seems difficult to define this location as east of or in the eastern part of Selwood. I therefore consider this to be a less likely location for Egbert's Stone.

The Roman Road and Junction near Pertwood, Wiltshire

It was Geoffrey Wright's 1988 book on ancient trackways that drew my attention to a potentially significant ancient intersection[39] to the east of Lower Pertwood in Wiltshire and not far from the A350 (Grid Ref ST89763654). I found the number of routes that come together here to be quite striking. Even today there are tracks leading off in six different directions, but there would have once been seven because the Roman road heading east is no longer visible today, although the section to the west survives on the Ordnance Survey map as a bridleway. This was the Roman road that led from Old Sarum to the Mendips in Somerset, and is the same road that passes by Kingston Deverill. Geoffrey Wright points out that seven parishes (I only managed to count six) met at this location. From this location one of the routes leads north to the village of Sutton Veny. This may be significant because the nearby Eastleigh and Southleigh Woods are potential locations for *Iglea,* which is where Alfred went after he left Egbert's Stone (see Chapter 7).

To get to this location I parked near the start of the byway that runs north-east from the A350 and where there is a sign announcing Kingsdown Farm. From there a lovely track heads south-east. I walked along what increasingly looked like an ancient track, with slight ditching and banks either side until I arrived at the elevated site of the intersection. However, when I visited the two bridleways heading west, including the one on the line of the Roman road, were not discernible due to recent ploughing.

Could this location be Egbert's Stone? Although the possibility cannot be ruled out, I feel there is a risk of inappropriately assuming an association between the number of routes that converge at a particular point and the likelihood that this was King Alfred's meeting place. I therefore still find that the Upper Deverills are a more likely location for Egbert's Stone. Nonetheless, it cannot be ruled out that this location may have served as a meeting point for additional troops that had not arrived at Egbert's Stone but joined him at *Iglea* instead.

Where Dorset, Wiltshire and Somerset meet

Tradition has it that Alfred's grandfather, King Egbert, marked the point where Dorset, Somerset and Wiltshire met with a large stone on the bank of the River Stour. However, it may not be safe to assume that the counties met at the same location in Egbert's or Alfred's time as they do now. The woodland of Selwood would have then extended further south into today's Dorset,[72] and because there is some evidence that the edges of the wood were used as boundaries, it is possible that the border could have been further south than it is today. However, I have not seen anything to indicate where any older boundary might have been.

I drew upon John Peddie's reference to Coombe Street, which is west of Zeals (Somerset) and north of Bourton (Dorset), as a claimed location for Egbert's Stone.[70] Travelling west, this road crosses the Stour where a sign (Grid Ref ST77153137) indicates that you have arrived at Penselwood. The river is narrow at this point, which is unsurprising as its source is at nearby Stourhead. However, I saw no evidence of a significant stone. There seems to be an impression locally that a standing stone on a nearby golf course, just north of Bourton, is Egbert's Stone, although it has also been suggested to me that this is not the case. Nearby Factory Hill crosses the Stour at a point where there was once a mill, although this area was in the process of being developed for housing when I visited. Nonetheless, there is a nearby footpath that comes off Kite's Nest Lane that takes you close to where the three counties currently meet (Grid Ref ST77323102) and I could see a lake on the right as I walked up this path. However, maps show that the exact point at which the three counties meet is on private land, so I was unable to establish the presence of a significant stone. Nonetheless, my quest was not necessarily to find the stone but to find the location where Alfred brought his troops together, and if this indeed took place where the three counties now meet, then I was satisfied that I had found the location.

However, it seems logical that Alfred would have used a meeting point that was strategic in terms of route-ways and other factors rather than a location where three boundaries met. It also seems unlikely that this location would have been east of, or in the eastern part of, Selwood, which is required to fit the descriptions of Egbert's Stone provided by Asser and the Anglo-Saxon Chronicles. For these reasons I consider this site to be a less likely location for Egbert's Stone. It is possible that somebody long ago wished to mark the junction of the three counties with a stone and that this has somehow become tangled up with the record of Alfred's assembling of troops from different counties.

The location of Egbert's Stone has also been attributed to Penselwood,[73] which is in Somerset but close to the junction between the three counties. Penselwood is also the supposed location of the Battle of Peonnum, which had been an important victory for the Saxons in 658. However, this was before the time of King Egbert so I cannot see how this would have resulted in that king's name becoming associated with a stone there, and nor does it seem likely that this location could have been described as east of or in the eastern part of Selwood.

Dalwood, East Devon

Mathew of Westminster, a shadowy fourteenth century character, who is now thought to have never existed, had referred to Egbert's Stone having been on the eastern side of a wood called *Dalwde,* now the location of the pretty East Devon village called Dalwood. The argument goes that copyists of the ancient manuscripts at some point must have accidentally exchanged the correct *Dalwde* for the incorrect Selwood. However, Asser and the different versions of the Anglo-Saxon Chronicles record that Egbert's Stone was located east of (or in the eastern part of) *Sealwyda, Selewuda* or *Seluudu* and I believe it unlikely that these sources would all be wrong. Asser also refers to Selwood as a great wood, *sylva magna,* and I am not aware of any evidence that *Dalwde* could have qualified as such. This location would also take us in an entirely wrong direction for the most likely site for the Battle of Ethandun at Edington in Wiltshire. Although I therefore believe that Dalwood can be dismissed from our enquiries regarding Egbert's Stone, the village nonetheless remains interesting as it used to be part of an exclave of Dorset (an island of Dorset in a sea of Devon) that may go back to 934 when King Athelstan, in a charter issued at Dorchester (Dorset), transferred some land there to Dorset's Milton Abbey. I have spent many a happy hour exploring the hills in this beautiful less-visited part of East Devon.

It is interesting to speculate on the route taken by Alfred to get from Athelney to my preferred sites for Egbert's Stone. Perhaps he made his way to Somerton, Somerset, and then eventually connected with the Hard Way at some point before Redlynch (near Bruton in Somerset). The route of the Hard Way south-west of Redlynch is unclear, but it has been suggested that it came down near Yeovil in Somerset.[39] Travelling north-east, the Hard Way then passes Alfred's Tower, Kilmington Common, and Willoughby Hedge, three potential sites for Egbert's Stone, and then runs a short distance to the south of the Upper Deverills, which is my preferred location. It is also possible that Alfred may have travelled to Egbert's Stone on minor routes, considering that Wessex had fallen under Viking control at this point.

So, we end this chapter with King Alfred camped at Egbert's stone, but in the following pages I will pick up the story of Alfred's continued journey towards his victory at the Battle of Ethandun.

7

Victory

This chapter covers the period from King Alfred's departure from Egbert's Stone up to his successful reconquest of Wessex from the Vikings after his crucial victory at the Battle of Ethandun. There has been significant disagreement about the route Alfred took to get to Ethandun, and even the site of the battle has not been determined with certainty. I decided to study and visit the alternatives and I found that I was able to arrive at a sequence of events that I believe to be the most likely to have occurred.

Iglea

The Anglo-Saxon Chronicles tell us that one day after Alfred's troops came together at Egbert's Stone, they went to a place called *Iglea,* a place that is referred to in Asser's Latin as *Aecglea.* Unfortunately, we do not know with certainty the location of this place.

Aecglea was Alfred's final stop before the Battle of Ethandun, which took place in Wiltshire at Edington or, less likely in my opinion, at the location of the Iron Age hillfort called Bratton Camp (see later). In the last chapter I explained that the most probable location for Egbert's Stone was the Upper Deverills, and it seems to me that after leaving there he would have had two main routes to get to the battle site. One would be to follow the Ridgeway (marked on maps) to skirt around the north-west of Salisbury Plain in order to reach Bratton Down or to continue on to Edington. The other option being to go straight across Salisbury Plain instead of around it (Fig. 12, Chapter 5). It seems likely that the location of the encampment at *Iglea* would depend on which route was taken. Alfred had lost Wessex and was operating in enemy territory and it therefore seems likely that he would have gone across Salisbury Plain rather than around it in order to avoid as many significant settlements as possible. Crossing Salisbury Plain from south to north also implies that Alfred knew that the Vikings had already taken Bratton Camp or Edington, because this route would have made little sense if he had been heading to the Viking base at Chippenham. I shall therefore start my exploration of possible locations for *Iglea* that fit better with a direct approach to Edington (or Bratton Down) across Salisbury Plain. These locations are in an area to the south and east of Warminster and are not far from the village of Sutton Veny.

Iglea is similar phonetically to "Iley" and there was an ancient meeting place called Iley Oak in what is today known as Southleigh Wood, previously called Sowley Wood, to the south-west of Sutton Veny. The precise location of Iley Oak in this area may have been where five roads and paths used to meet[37] at a point where today the access to a Long Ivor Farm comes off the road connecting Longbridge Deverill to Sutton Veny (Grid Ref ST88234176) at the southern edge of Southleigh Wood. I find it striking, and perhaps relevant, that there are the remains of a henge very close to this location. These are rare, with only about eighty examples across the whole of England,[74] and it is thought that they may have been ceremonial sites. The most famous henge of all is, of course, Stonehenge, which is located about 13 miles to the east. Although they date to the Late Neolithic, it is possible that some henges, or the places at which they were located, might have retained a societal significance beyond that period, perhaps even through Anglo-Saxon times. The henge is on private land, but I found that that I could make it out when peering over the hedge from the aforementioned road. Take care if you decide to do this as the traffic here can be very fast. It is worth remembering, however, that the Anglo-Saxon Chronicles and Asser refer to the location as just *Iglea* or *Aecglea,* without making reference to any oak. It does, however, seem striking that there was a meeting place that seems to fit phonetically, was close to a henge, and in a location that fits with a subsequent route across Salisbury Plain to potential sites for the Battle of Ethandun.

Southleigh Wood provides one more tempting possibility, which is to be found immediately north of the location described above. I refer to Robin Hood's Bower, which was marked on my Ordnance Survey map (Grid Ref ST87674232). This is a small ancient enclosure that, like the henge referred to above, would have been present long before the time of King Alfred. The outline of the enclosure is clearly discernible and it has been enigmatically planted with many monkey-puzzle trees. I read a suggestion that this was carried out by the Longleat Estate in the 1960s, but I have not been able to confirm this. There are two very large tree stumps present, so clearly there were large trees here, but I have seen no indication that this was the Iley Oak meeting place. Nonetheless, I have also seen Robin Hood's Bower referred to as a former place of worship for non-conformists, so the place clearly holds local significance, and it cannot be ruled out that this significance could go back further to a time when it might have been the location of *Iglea*.

Adjacent to Southleigh Wood there is an Eastleigh Wood and to further complicate matters there is some evidence that the word *Iglea* could have become Eastleigh through the intermediate stage of *Eleigh*.[37] This provides an unsatisfactory situation where *Iglea* could be either at Eastleigh Wood or the southern end of Southleigh Wood. I did much of my exploration from Five Ash Lane, which runs north-west out of Sutton Veny. I found that I could pull over near to where my Ordnance Survey map showed bridleways crossing this road (Grid Ref ST87844299), which I could then follow north into Eastleigh Wood and south into Southleigh Wood.

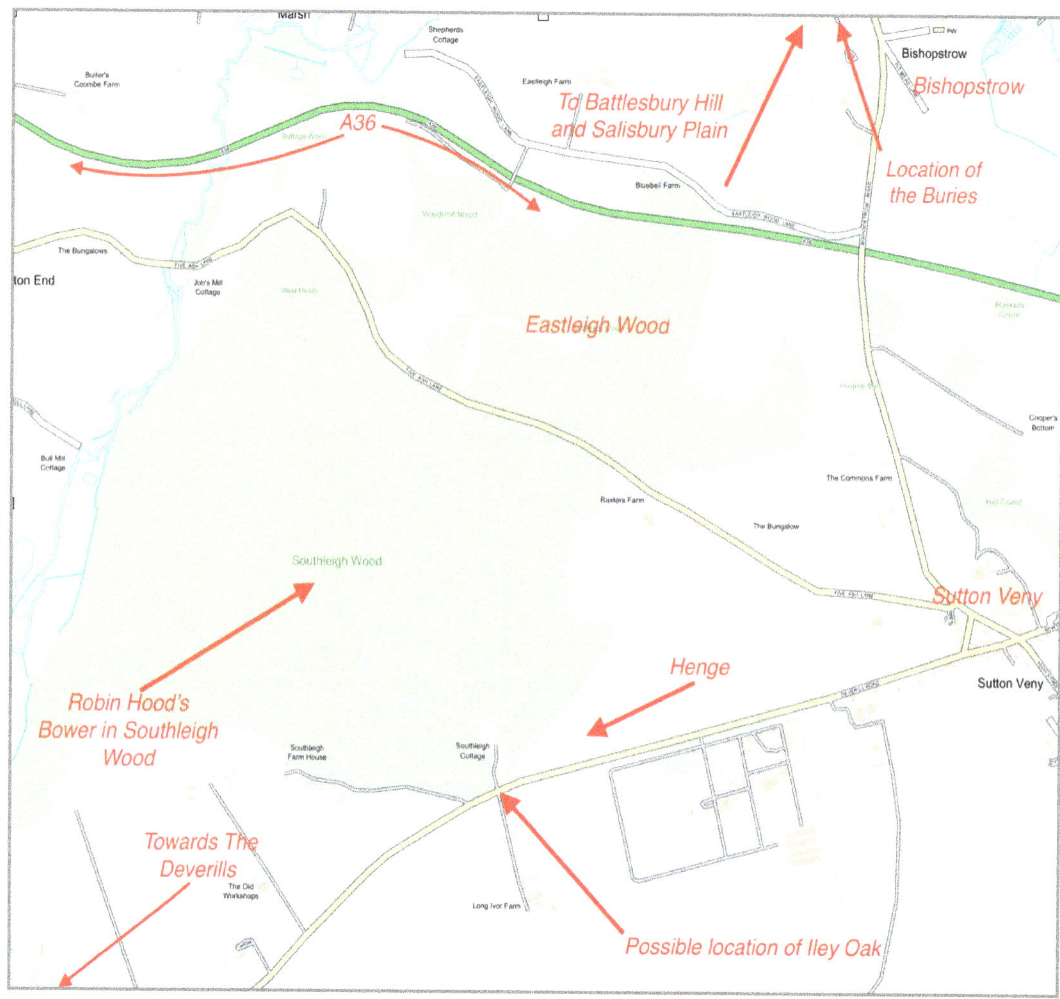

Fig. 17 Map of significant features near Sutton Veny, Wiltshire. Contains OS data © Crown copyright and database right (2018)

However, there was more to discover and explore about potential locations for *Iglea*. We now move a mere one mile north of Eastleigh and Southleigh Woods to look at some locations around the small settlement of Bishopstrow, just south-east of Warminster. We are now back on the Wylye, which is the same river that flows through the Upper Deverills. I read in an old journal dating to 1872[75] that Iley Oak had been located next to a "camp" (presumably meaning Roman camp as Roman discoveries had been made) called "The Buries." On the 1887 Ordnance Survey map, the location of "The Buries" is indicated and this corresponds to a location very close to the south-east of Boreham Mill at Bishopstrow. It seems that today this would be very close to the current Bishopstrow

College or maybe even in its grounds. The argument that Iley Oak was located here seems to be tied up with another argument put forward by a Dr Prior that *Iglea* would probably have been an Island (having argued that the *Ig* part of the word *Iglea* means island) in the River Wylye, with Iley Oak then presumably being named after the nearby island. There is an island in the Wylye as it flows past Bishopstrow at Boreham Mill and the road that leads north out of Bishopstrow goes right across the middle of it (look out for the two bridges). However, it seems that we cannot prove that there was an island there in Alfred's time (it could be the result of later human alteration to the watercourse). All in all, I did not find the arguments for this location to be strong enough to outweigh those that can be applied to the location near the henge at the south edge of Southleigh Wood. I did, however, find the argument that *Ig* indicates an island sufficiently plausible to make this my second favourite.

I also considered the possibility that the intersection of ancient routes near Pertwood (Wiltshire), described in the previous chapter in relation to Egbert's Stone, could have been the site of *Iglea* instead. Although it is impossible to rule this site out, particularly as it was connected by a Roman road to Kingston Deverill, it is heading off in somewhat the wrong direction compared to locations at Eastleigh or Southleigh Wood near Sutton Veny. As discussed in the previous chapter, one needs to be careful not to ascribe a particular meaning to a location on the basis that a number of tracks converge there.

It has also been argued that because Asser tells us that Alfred's troops left Egbert's Stone at first light, this must mean that they had marched a greater distance, perhaps as far as Berkshire and the area once known as the Hundred of Eagle (Eglei),[75] which later became part of the Hundred of Kintbury Eagle. Although I can see that there is a similarity between Eglei and *Iglea* I do not wish to distract the reader too much with this location, which I found difficult to pin down in any case. Perhaps it is somewhere near Hungerford in Berkshire, because it seems too far for a day's march (about 40 miles from the Upper Deverills) and does not seem to fit with the main alternative locations for where the Battle of Ethandun took place on the following day. I also disagree with the assumption that leaving at first light means that they marched a long distance because I can see good reasons for a shorter march when the next day strength would be required for an additional march followed by a battle.

I now turn to the possibility, which I believe to be less likely, that Alfred went around the western edge of Salisbury Plain to get to the site of the Battle of Ethandun (represented by the dashed line in Fig. 12, Chapter 5). He could have ascended to the Ridgeway near Warminster or perhaps he could have taken a lower route passing modern Westbury and Bratton (only the Ridgeway would provide a sensible route to the less likely site of the battle at Bratton Camp). As he would have been in enemy territory, I suggest that if he had indeed gone around Salisbury Plain, he would have taken the higher Ridgeway route to avoid significant settlements. If Alfred had circumnavigated Salisbury Plain by either of these routes it seems that the main contender for the location of *Iglea* is Cley Hill, just west of Warminster.

This prominent location seems too good to have not been used as a look-out by either Alfred or the Vikings. However, it seems to me unlikely that Alfred would have taken his troops up and down this steep hill, away from water, in the midst of what had become enemy territory. However, it could have served as a combined camp and observation post with most of his troops camping at the base of the hill. The site would have potentially offered easy advancement towards Chippenham, until perhaps they realised that the Vikings had moved south to Bratton Camp or Edington. There is clearly a similarity between the modern name of Cley and *Iglea* or *Aecglea*. Therefore, it seems to me that Cley Hill would be a plausible location for *Iglea* if Alfred had circumnavigated Salisbury Plain.

I visited Cley Hill, the site of an Iron Age hill-fort, on a sunny Saturday afternoon. It is indeed spectacular, as are the views from the top, which I found particularly useful in helping to understand the western edge of Salisbury plain, which is clearly visible from here. Legend has it that the Devil had been offended by the town of Devizes and he was planning to bury it under a giant hump of earth. When he asked an old man the way he was told that he had been travelling to Devizes for so long that he had turned grey. On hearing this the Devil gave up his journey and dumped the earth at what is now Cley Hill. There are other legends associated with this geographic feature and it clearly has been a place of superstition. For me, however, it is a place of beauty and solitude, and I recommend a visit.

The sites for *Iglea* described so far are quite close to each other in the vicinity of Warminster. However, a place called Iley Mead, near Melksham, and about 12 miles north of the other sites, has also been put forward as the location for *Iglea*.[71] Whereas the other locations are *en route* to where the battle of Ethandun is thought to have taken place, this one requires that Alfred would have overshot the site of the battle by about eight miles to the north and would therefore have needed to have turned back to attack the Vikings from behind. It has been suggested that this would have been a clever move as it would have also cut off the Viking's ability to retreat back to their base at Chippenham, as Melksham is between Chippenham and Edington. I could not find Iley Mead on any Ordnance Survey map going back to 1886, but I learnt that it had also been called Iley Common. I managed to find this on a map in an 1834 publication,[76] which showed it to be a short distance west of Melksham and on the River Avon. Although I would not want to rule it out, I could not find out anything more about this elusive location, including whether it had a similar name going back further in time.

To conclude, it seems to me more likely that Alfred crossed Salisbury Plain and that *Iglea* was in the area of Eastleigh and Southleigh Woods, with the site near the henge seeming to be the most probable, closely followed by the island at Bishopstrow.

Battlesbury Hill, near Warminster

If Alfred and his troops had been, as I suggest, at Eastleigh/Southleigh Woods, the shortest route to the most probable locations for the Battle of Ethandun would have been to go straight across Salisbury Plain. It has been suggested that they would have got up to the Plain by ascending Battlesbury Hill, which seems plausible because this hill leads to a ridge that extends further on into the Plain. Indeed, today a current military road takes advantage of this ridge and it is possible to travel along it on open days. It seems to me that Alfred and his troops would not have needed to climb up to the top of Battlesbury Hill, but would have probably skirted around the edge in order to get to the ridge. It is possible that they would have gone from *Iglea* to Warminster and then followed the line of the current Imber Road, which ascends to the Plain and becomes the military road. Evidence indicates that there was a settlement, and even a royal manor, at Warminster at this time,[77] but with Alfred's loss of control of Wessex to the Vikings he might have avoided significant settlements. He may therefore have taken a more direct route from *Iglea* to Battlesbury Hill, possibly via Bishopstrow, a place where legend has it that the staff of St Aldhelm had grown into an ash tree.[78] St Aldhelm's church at Bishopstrow is 14th century, but it could have been built over an earlier Saxon church.[78] It is therefore possible that the pious Alfred could have prayed here before the final march to the battle at Ethandun. Readers will recall that a location near Bishopstrow was discussed earlier in this chapter as a potential, but less likely, location for *Iglea* itself.

Battlesbury Hill is on the north-east edge of Warminster and can be reached by public footpaths from the adjacent road. The Iron Age Battlesbury Camp, which occupies the top of Battlesbury Hill, is impressive, being much larger than I had been expecting, with fairly well preserved walls, and with excellent views in all directions. There are clear views to nearby Scratchbury Hill to the south east, which I have also seen mentioned in relation to Alfred's ascent on to Salisbury Plain. However, it seems to me that Battlesbury Hill offered the better route, and I therefore think that this is the one Alfred is likely to have taken.

The Battle of Ethandun

It was crucial that Alfred won this battle, and his achievement of this quickly led to Wessex being recovered back from the Vikings. The Anglo-Saxon Chronicles tell us that the battle was fought at a place called *Eþandun* (*þ* is pronounced "th"), which I shall continue to refer to as Ethandun. It is generally accepted that Ethandun is today's Edington in Wiltshire. Although the identification of Ethandun is most helpful, this does not allow us to determine the precise location of the battle in that area.

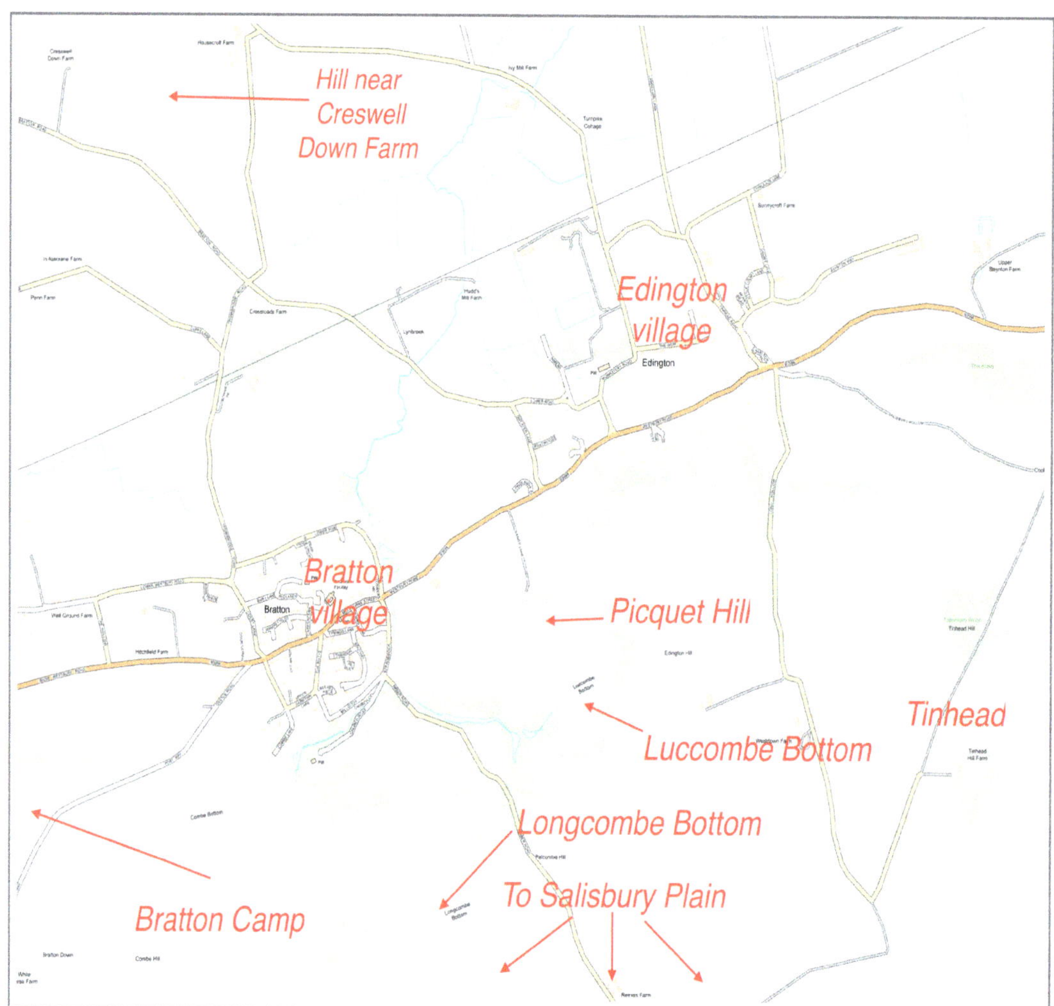

Fig. 18 Map showing places mentioned in the text in relation to the Battle at Ethandun. Contains OS data © Crown copyright and database right (2018).

I started my explorations at the village itself, which I considered to be the most probable site for the battle, quite simply because the Anglo-Saxon Chronicles name the place specifically. However, there is no hard proof that the battle took place at that location so I explored other options as well.

Edington village and parish, Wiltshire

This pretty village lies on the B3098 just a few miles east of the town of Westbury, and we know that Alfred had an estate here because he left it in his will to his wife. In 878 Wessex had fallen to the Vikings and it seems likely that they would have taken over this royal estate that was now available to them and only 15 miles from their base at Chippenham. Finding the royal site may therefore also be to discover the site of the battle, because the royal site may have been all that there was to Edington at that time. Edington is quite small but it has a very large church linked to its monastic past. It is tempting to consider the grounds around the church to be potentially the site of Alfred's estate, although a local resident suggested to me that it might have instead been where the road leading down to the church meets the B3098 at a point where the land is elevated.

Although I believe the most probable site of the battle is the village itself, there are other alternatives in the surrounding area that are worth considering because we can't be sure that when the early documents refer to Edington they don't mean "in the general area of" or what we might today call a parish. The current parish of Edington extends a fair way south onto Salisbury Plain, to an extent that is approximately level with, and just to the west of, the deserted village of Imber. Although it is perhaps unsafe to assume that the same area was under the auspices of Edington in Alfred's time, I could not rule it out. On some days the Ministry of Defence allows public access to Imber and some other parts of Salisbury Plain where access is otherwise restricted. I travelled on one of the special services run by Imberbus, where vintage buses go from Warminster to permitted locations on the Plain, including Imber and New Zealand Camp Farm. Although this was a delightful way of getting around, there is much of Salisbury Plain where there is never public access, including an area not far south of Edington. The best I could do in that area was to explore the roads and paths south of Edington but to the north of the restricted area. Out of these I emphasise the following suggestion because it seemed most interesting and informative in terms of views, and is also within the Edington parish boundary. Just as you approach Edington coming from Bratton there is a lay-by on the right (Grid Ref: ST92215280), with a footpath leading south. Heading from here towards the north edge of Salisbury Plain, this fairly steep path takes you up Picquet Hill and over the top of Luccombe Bottom. As you ascend you will pass ancient tumuli and pillow mounds, and the view opens up in a way that allows one to start to understand this landscape.

It has been suggested that the site of the battle is to the north-west of Edington, near Cresswell (formerly Crosswell) Down Farm, which may have been near the meeting place of the area that was once known as Whorwellsdown Hundred.[79] Whorwellsdown is said to be a lost name for a low hill[80] near this farm and my view is that this must mean the hill (Grid Ref: ST90755421) between Cresswell Down Farm and Housecroft Farm. As with other nearby locations it seems impossible to either prove or disprove that the battle took place here, although it seems to me that a location's role as a meeting place doesn't necessarily indicate the site of a battle.

Bratton Camp and Bratton Down, Wiltshire

Bratton Camp lies on Bratton Down and this area has also been claimed to be the site of the Battle of Ethandun. These features can be found just a short distance south-west of Edington and were marked on my Ordnance Survey map. There is a figure of a white horse marked out on the hillside, which is today sadly made out of concrete. It does, however, seem odd that potential locations of two important battles (the other being Ashdown) had been fought in areas with prominent white horses. However, there is no evidence that a white horse would have been present at Bratton Down at or around Alfred's time. Furthermore, the alternative site for the Battle of Ashdown near the white horse at Uffington in Oxfordshire seems to me to be the wrong one (see Chapter 2) and I do not find that Bratton Camp is the most likely site for the Battle of Ethandun either. It is preferable to avoid the unreliable practice of divining battle sites via horse-led inquiry. Although I prefer Edington as the site of the Battle of Ethandun, it doesn't seem possible to rule out that it took place at Bratton Down or somewhere between there and Edington, so it is worth looking at a few features. At the eastern aspect of Bratton Camp one can look down into the geographic feature called Combe Bottom, which extends past the village of Bratton. One can only wonder at the strategic, or even accidental, implications of the landscape for the combatants if the battle had taken place here. Beyond Combe Bottom are the features called Longcombe Bottom and Luccombe Bottom, which were both marked on my Ordnance Survey map. I found that the best way to view these was to head south down Imber Road from Bratton village where Luccombe Bottom appears on the left and Longcombe Bottom on the right. As with Combe Bottom, one can only wonder about the strategic implications of the landscape. I also came across a legend that Alfred had ordered some Vikings prisoners to be killed at Luccombe Bottom, and indeed a skeleton was found there in 1955. However, these remains were dated to a period some hundreds of years before Alfred.[81] Tinhead, now part of Edington, but which once was a separately named settlement a very short distance to the east, has also been suggested as the location of the battle.[82] However, I have not found anything to support this.

It has also been suggested that Bratton Camp had been the Viking base for the Battle of Ethandun rather than the site of the battle itself (although it could have been both). It is easy to imagine how the Vikings may have come from their apparent main base at Chippenham, to the north, and made the climb up to Bratton Camp to await and then engage with Alfred's forces.

It is recorded that after their defeat the Vikings were pursued as far as their fortification. Unfortunately, the sources do not tell us whether this was their base at Chippenham or some sort of advance camp somewhere else. It is generally thought that Chippenham is meant, although it has been suggested that this could have been the role played by Bratton Camp[55] with the battle taking place elsewhere, perhaps at Edington village. I can see the temptation to consider Bratton camp as the Viking base, but the evidence for a base at Chippenham seems to me to be stronger. Of course, Bratton Camp could have been an additional Viking forward base for the battle, but many other places could have been used as such and it is possible to be mis-led by the combined presence of a hill-fort, a white horse, and wide-ranging views. There is also the matter of maintaining provisions for troops and animals at an elevated position away from water.

Further suggested battle locations

Other locations have been suggested in addition to the areas around Edington and Bratton Camp. Although none of these seem to me to be more credible than the area around Edington in Wiltshire, I shall take a brief look at these sites.

An 1853 translation from Latin to English of a work by Henry of Huntingdon[83] tells us that Alfred fought the battle at Heddington, a village and parish in Wiltshire that is about twelve miles north-east of Edington. However, looking at an untranslated version I found the location written as *Edendune*, and I do not know why the translator opted for Heddington over Edington. Heddington is, nonetheless, recorded as *Edintone* in the Domesday Book (1086), so based solely on the place-name derivation Heddington does challenge Edington, which is recorded in Domesday as the very similar *Edendone*. The only other factor that seems to be in Heddington's favour as the site of the battle is that it is closer to Chippenham (the Viking base) than is Edington. Although it is impossible to rule out Heddington, there are, however, some important considerations that in my view seriously weaken the case for Heddington. In the Domesday Book Edington had a recorded value four times that of Heddington, it had more households, and it covered a much larger area. Domesday also tells us that Edington was under Hampshire's Romsey Abbey in 1086 and there is a charter dating to 968 showing that King Edgar, Alfred's grandson, had given land at *Edyndon* (which seems to have been Edington, given that it was under Romsey Abbey in 1086) to Romsey Abbey. Connections between Romsey and Edington can be traced up to the Dissolution of the Monasteries, so it seems that we can be almost certain that the Domesday *Edendone* is the same place as Edington. We also know that Alfred left *Eðandune* to his wife, confirming that the place that went by that name was in royal hands, which fits with King Edgar being able to give land away at *Edyndon* in 968. It also seems to me very much more likely that the Vikings would have targeted what is now Edington instead of Heddington, where there was no evidence of a royal estate. The evidence therefore seems to be in favour of Edington, and not Heddington, being Ethandun.

It has also been proposed that the battle took place near Edington in Somerset instead of the Edington in Wiltshire.[84] I agree with other writers who find this unlikely. Both Asser and the Anglo-Saxon Chronicles describe Alfred as going to Egbert's Stone after leaving Athelney and, critically, describe this as being east of, or at least in the eastern part of, the great wood of Selwood. This would have taken him to a position about 30 miles east of Athelney. It seems to make little sense that Alfred would make this journey and then travel approximately thirty miles west again to engage the Vikings at Edington in Somerset. Additional evidence against the Somerset Edington comes from the Domesday survey's recording of the place as *Eduuintone*, whereas the Wiltshire location is recorded as *Edendone*, which is closer to Ethandun. If you do make a visit to the Somerset Edington, don't forget to visit the Holy Well at the bottom of (perhaps unsurprisingly) Holy Well Road.

Eddington, near Hungerford has also been suggested, but difficulties arise when we learn that in Domesday it was called Eddevetone and Stevenson states that the Old English form would have been *Eadgifetun*.[55] There has also been speculation that the battle took place at the parish of Slaughterford (Wiltshire) and that the fort that the Vikings retreated to was at Bury Camp, which is marked on the Ordnance Survey map.[85] The argument seems to be that Vikings were slaughtered at Slaughterford. However, there is an Old English word *slohtre* that seems to have meant "muddy",[14] so perhaps Slaughterford was just a settlement by a muddy ford. Yatton, near Slaughterford, has also been suggested as the site of the battle.

Finally, in a publication dating to 1834, I saw it suggested that the Battle of Ethandun had been fought at a place called Woeful Vikings' Bottom, near Minchinhampton in Gloucestershire.[76] The location is marked as a track and a farm on Ordnance Survey maps. However, the belief that this was the site of Ethandun is thought to be based on a misunderstanding of the derivation of Woefuldane, with the "dane" component deriving from den, meaning valley,[86] and not from any miserable circumstances a particular Dane might have suffered.

To conclude, I find that the most likely site for the Battle of Ethandun was at the village of Edington. We now move on to the period where Alfred had regained control of Wessex after having defeated the Vikings in battle. He gained their submission after the fortification that they had fled to (most likely at Chippenham) had been besieged by his forces. However, this was not a typical military submission. Alfred was preparing to baptise the Viking leader and thereby turn him into a Christian.

Aller, Somerset

The Anglo-Saxon Chronicles tell us that the Viking leader called Guthrum, accompanied by thirty of his men, travelled to a place near Athelney called Aller in order to be baptised into Christianity, and that this took place three weeks after the Viking surrender. Asser tells us that Alfred himself raised Guthrum from the baptismal font and that he then became Alfred's adopted son, with a new Christian name of Æthelstan (not to be confused with King Æthelstan, who was Alfred's grandson).

St Andrew's church at Aller, like Athelney, is on raised ground in the Somerset levels, suggesting that the church would also probably have been on an island in Alfred's time. The oldest parts of the current church are 12th century, so the events of 878 must have taken place at a preceding structure. It has been claimed that a font in the church (the more bowl-shaped of the two fonts), recovered from the rectory pond in the nineteenth century, was the one used to baptise Guthrum. The church also has a small but beautiful King Alfred Window, which is a memorial to the two reigns of King Alfred and Queen Victoria. The church (Grid Ref: ST39632880) can be tricky to locate because it is to be found well off the main road. Coming from Langport, take a left turn onto the road called Church Path and then turn left again where there is a wooden sign for the church. This is a peaceful spot and I never cease to be amazed at how this modest location that was so important in the history of England is so under-visited.

It can be speculated as to why Aller, about fifty miles distant from Chippenham, was chosen as the place to baptise Guthrum rather than somewhere nearer. Perhaps Alfred did not trust Guthrum and this was deemed to be a safer location being deeper into Wessex and in a landscape that he knew well, or perhaps Aller was a more significant place then than it appears to us today. It might even be that the church at Aller had become important to Alfred if he went there to pray when he was based at nearby Athelney.

Aller is only a few miles north-west of Langport, which must also have been a significant place in Alfred's time as it is included in the Burghal Hidage (a list of defended locations), drawn up under his son, King Edward the Elder. Although there is nothing that I could find to specifically connect King Alfred with Langport, it seems likely that he would have been there at some point.

Wedmore, Somerset

We are told by both Asser and the Anglo-Saxon Chronicles that after his baptism Guthrum spent twelve days with Alfred, and at least part of this time was spent at Wedmore, which Asser describes as a *villa regia* (royal estate). We are told that after this period the Vikings left Chippenham and went to Cirencester and then re-located again to settle in East Anglia.

It has been suggested that the royal site at Wedmore was north-west of St Mary's church at or near the location of a manor house,[87] and it seems to me that the wall visible from the churchyard could have been the perimeter of the manor's grounds. It occurred to me that the location could have been elsewhere in or around Wedmore, so I decided to explore further. I had been intrigued by marks in the ground visible in an aerial photograph in a field north of Manor Lane, although I could see nothing relevant when I arrived there at ground level. I also explored the hill to the north-west by taking the footpath heading west off Lascot Hill. I eventually decided that I could not improve on the suggestion that the royal estate was at the location of the former manor house.

It was once thought that the Saxon royal residence was at Mudgley,[87] just a short distance south of Wedmore. Although excavations have found no evidence of an Anglo-Saxon residence, the location appears to have been associated with Wells Cathedral so may be of some significance even if it cannot be connected to King Alfred. Near to Mudgley is a place called Aller Moor. It is most helpful that the Anglo-Saxon Chronicles tell us that the Aller of Guthrum's baptism was close to Athelney, because we could otherwise be misled into thinking that he was baptised at a church at Aller Moor. Aller Moor is not close to Athelney, but Aller is. I also noticed that there is a Castle Lane to the south-west of Wedmore, and I wondered whether it could in some way be connected with a former royal estate. However, I was unable to connect the name of this road to any castle or indeed anything else, although there has been some evidence of Roman presence in this area.[88]

It is interesting to speculate as to why Alfred baptised Guthrum and did not kill him. It seems, however, that Alfred managed to turn his enemy into his friend and as a result made at least part of East Anglia an ally of Wessex. Having Guthrum as a strong man in East Anglia might have reduced the Viking threat both there and in adjacent areas. Indeed, although there is a record of further Vikings arriving at Fulham in 879, there is no record that they attacked further, but instead left for Ghent (Belgium) the following year. Alfred and Guthrum, now named Æthelstan and to become King of East Anglia, drew up a treaty. Oddly, however, this may not have been signed until 886, some eight years after the circumstances that gave rise to it. We can work out that there was such a delay because the dividing line described by the treaty left London in Alfred's hands, but he did not take London until 886.[89] The reasons for the delay are unclear. It is possible that an earlier treaty might have been drawn up at Wedmore, but there is no evidence of this or any other intermediate treaties that may have been drawn up. The treaty that has survived defined the boundary between the land under English control and that under the control of the Danes. This boundary is described as going up the Thames as far as the River Lea, then up the River Lea to its source (which is in Luton), then to Bedford, and finally following the River Ouse to the Roman road called Watling Street. We are not told where the border went (if anywhere) beyond this point, which would have been at Stony Stratford, near Milton Keynes. The institution of this border was an important part of the evolution of the Danelaw, although this term was not used until the 11th century.

So, we leave this chapter with Guthrum's Vikings having left Wessex in 878. As we shall see in the next chapter hostile Vikings would return to Wessex-controlled Kent in 884 and 892. Although there could have been unrecorded attacks, the period after 878 seems to have provided the opportunity for Alfred to make some important changes. Most significant among these was the development of defences for a network of settlements, the reorganisation of land-based forces to allow more effective deployment, and an improvement in sea-borne capabilities.

8

Controlling London and defending Kent

I have brought together the events in London and Kent not only because they are adjacent geographically but also because Alfred's recorded presence in London in 886 occurred between two separate episodes of Viking attacks in Kent in 884 and 892. The first episode was the Viking attack on Rochester in 884, with the second being the series of events that followed the Viking landings on both the north and south coasts of Kent in 892. I discuss the role of London in its chronological position between the two episodes of Viking attacks on Kent. This sequence therefore takes us first to Rochester.

The 884 Attack on Rochester, Kent

Rochester is a large town on the River Medway with a majestic cathedral and an imposing castle. It has strong associations with Charles Dickens and is blessed with many delightful old buildings. However, just scratch the surface and it is possible to go back much, much further. The town lies on the important Roman Watling Street, which probably would have been in use in the Anglo-Saxon period because the current High Street still runs close to its route.

Rochester was clearly a target for the Vikings. They had already raided it in 842, before Alfred was born, but it was Alfred who saw the Vikings off after they besieged it in 884. The Anglo-Saxon Chronicles tell us that Alfred did not arrive until 885 and that the Vikings did not leave until the summer, presumably shortly after Alfred's arrival. Because the Anglo-Saxon Chronicles tell us that the town held out until Alfred's arrival, we can conclude that this was a long siege and it is entirely possible that many people would have perished.

The records indicate that when the Vikings arrived, they built a fortress around themselves, and we know that this must have been outside of Rochester's walls because we are told that the inhabitants were standing firm. Asser tells us that the Viking fortification was at the entrance to the town but, unfortunately, there were four entrances and he doesn't tell us which one. I felt that if it were possible to locate the site of the Viking fortification, then this would shed light on where and how Alfred's forces engaged with the Vikings in order to relieve Rochester. It has been suggested that there would have been no Saxon-built stone walls,[90] so the configuration of the walls and entrances in 885 are likely to have been the same as in Roman times and, fortunately, the outline of Rochester's Roman walls is known.

There were four gates in the Roman walls).[90] A North Gate, which is more east than north, an East Gate that is more south than east, and a South Gate that is more west than south, and a "Bridge Gate" that gave access to the Roman bridge over the River Medway. I became less confused by these orientations when I realised that the names seem to indicate the direction in which one could travel after passing through a particular gate rather than the position of the gate itself. But at which gate did the Vikings build their fortification?
I learnt that the East Gate was on High Street [91] approximately outside of where the City Wall Wine Bar now stands, and when I got there I could see that there was a pattern of bricks in the pavement and road at this point, with a metal plaque in the pavement confirming that this was the location of the East Gate.

The North Gate appears to be preserved in the current road name of Northgate. It has been suggested that this may have been a postern gate with marshes beyond,[91] although there has also been speculation that it may have led to a harbour. This gate may have been approximately where Northgate meets Corporation Street,[91] and this would indeed seem to line up with an existing piece of wall that can be seen at the back of The Common car park on the other side of the railway line. However, I could see a line of bricks in the road on Northgate, outside the Corn Exchange and short of the junction with Corporation Street. Although I couldn't find a reason as to why those bricks were there, it is possible that they were placed there to mark the position of the North Gate.

The Romans built a bridge across the Medway at Rochester and there is later evidence of a bridge still being present at 960, meaning that it is plausible that a bridge may have been present when the Vikings attacked in 885. It is thought that today's bridge runs approximately along the same line as the Saxon bridge.[91] The location of a gate near the bridge has not been established,[91] but it seemed to me that one must have existed and that it would most likely be in line with the bridge. Although the modern bridge is much wider than the older bridge, the entrance to the old bridge is marked by two black lions, which allowed me to speculate that the gate would have been where a line drawn from this bridge entrance would have met the town wall. It seemed to me that this would be not far from where The Crown public house stands today.

So that is three gates down, with just one to go, and this is the South Gate, which would have once stood at a point just before where Boley Hill meets St Margaret's Street.[91] Fortunately, there was a plaque on a wall that confirmed that I had found the correct location. Remembering that the Vikings built their fortification outside of a gate, I wondered whether this could have been at where Boley Hill House and Lodge now stand, near the junction of Boley Hill with St Margaret's Avenue.

Although I could not exclude any of the entrances as a possible site for the Viking fortification, I developed a preference for the Bridge Gate, and this was because the Vikings had a tendency to use waterways and by blocking this gate they could also try to fend off any Wessex forces that might try to cross the bridge. I was told by a volunteer at the cathedral that the Bridge Gate indeed appears to be the current favourite! If there had indeed been a harbour beyond the North Gate the Vikings could have disembarked there and set up their fortification outside of that gate. Alternatively, the Vikings could have disembarked at Chatham and then proceeded up Watling Street to arrive at the East Gate. Watling Street is a Roman road stretching from Dover in Kent all the way to Wroxeter in Shropshire and passing through Canterbury, Rochester, London, St Albans and Dunstable. Finally, it seems worth pointing out that the Vikings may not have built their fortification at the particular gate at which they first arrived, but instead at the most relevant one for a siege, and this seems to return us to the Bridge Gate, where they could have cut off the connection to both the river and Watling Street. Undoubtedly, given sufficient numbers, they would have blocked the other gates as well. We don't know how Alfred resolved this situation, but Asser tells us that the Vikings fled when Alfred suddenly turned up with a large army. It seems therefore that no battle took place, and nor was there a negotiated settlement. I suggest that Alfred would have arrived from the south, as crossing a bridge would have been perilous because this would have restricted the flow of men as it approached the enemy.

886AD. Alfred and London

It is recorded in the Anglo-Saxon Chronicles that in 851, when Alfred was perhaps only two years old, London (along with Canterbury) had been stormed by the Vikings, driving out the Mercian King Beorthwulf. The Vikings then crossed into Surrey and Alfred's father and brother, King Æthelwulf and Æthelbald respectively, fought against them at a significant battle at *Aclea,* which is sometimes translated as Oak Field. The location is unknown, but places with names such as "Oakley" and "Ockley" may be relevant.

We now fast-forward to 886 where Æthelweard's Chronicle tells us that Alfred besieged (*obsidetur*) London (*urbs Lundonia*), and with the twelfth century writer called Henry of Huntingdon suggesting that the opportunity arose because of a weakened Viking presence because some had left to join Viking forces on the continent. Both The Anglo-Saxon Chronicles and Asser record Alfred in London (named *Lundenburg* in the Chronicles and *Lundonia* by Asser) at this time, but neither source mentions that Alfred had taken London by force, as implied by Æthelweard. Furthermore, the Anglo-Saxon Chronicles use the Old English word *gesette*, which seems to suggest settlement rather

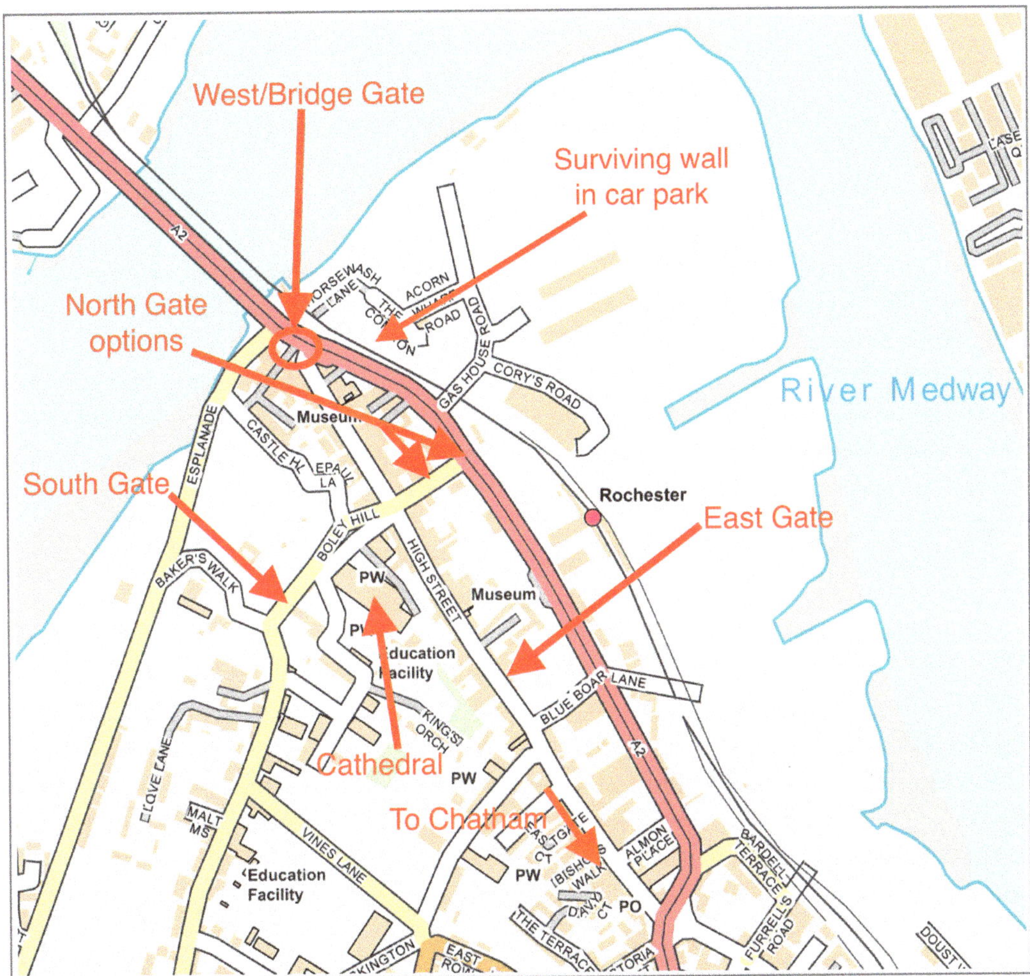

Fig. 19 The locations of former gates in Rochester. Contains OS data © Crown copyright and database right (2018)

than invasion. The Anglo-Saxon Chronicles also indicate that Alfred had been in sole control of London for less than one year because we are told that, later in 886, he entrusted the city to Æthelred, who was ruler of Mercia and also his son-in-law as he had married his daughter Æthelflæd. London had been a Mercian city and perhaps there was resentment after the Wessex take-over, with this being to some extent negated by Alfred handing London over to Æthelred in order to control it on behalf of both of them.[23] It is worth noting that Æthelred was not in control of all of Mercia, as part of it (what we might call the East Midlands, and including Derby, Leicester and Nottingham) was under Viking control.

However, it is possible that Alfred was playing a role in London prior to 886 and there is evidence from coins suggesting that London may have been under Alfred's protection as early as the late 870s. We know from the Anglo-Saxon Chronicles that London had been under Viking occupation in 871 after they had moved there from Reading, but the Chronicles also tell us that these Vikings left for Northumbria in 872, and it was perhaps then that Alfred started to extend his power to London.

But what was this London that Alfred was gaining control over? It has been suggested that after Roman control ended the population left the walled area where the current City of London stands and went to a place called *Lundenwic*, approximately one mile to the west. The *wic* element of *Lundenwic* persists in the modern name Aldwych. It seems that people later moved back to re-use the Roman site (as also appears to have happened at Winchester) and it seems plausible that this happened because of a combination of the risk of Viking attacks and Alfred's redevelopment of the site of Roman London after 868. It does not seem possible to quantify the depopulation of the Roman site after Roman control ceased but, in the other direction, archaeological evidence suggests that people stopped living at *Lundenwic* in the late 9th or early 10th century.[92] When Alfred took control of London it could therefore have comprised what is now the City of London and the area around Aldwych, with the two settlements connected by what we now call Fleet Street.[93]

It has been suggested that the site of King Alfred's redeveloped burgh within London's Roman walls extended along the north bank of the Thames from near Queenhithe in the west to near Billingsgate in the east, and extended inland by about 300 metres.[92] It is interesting to note that this area only occupied a small part of the Roman walled area, but in Alfred's time much space might have been taken up by crops and livestock. Much of the river-side component of this area can be walked and for me the most interesting location is Queenhithe, where I have spent much time gazing out across what would have been a dock in Alfred's time. We can't know what it would have looked like then, but today it is hemmed in by modern office blocks, with a new one being constructed when I last visited. Queenhithe is named after Matilda, the wife of King Henry I, but the location had previously been called Æthelred's Hithe, named after Alfred's son-in-law.

There is an undated entry in the *Liber Monasterii de Hyda* (a book of old documents from Hyde Abbey in Winchester)[94] indicating that Alfred attended a Council in London and he is quoted as saying that ignorant public and religious officials should either resign or engage in the study of wisdom. The speech is very similar to what Asser (in his Chapter 106) has Alfred saying, but without specifying a particular meeting or date. Although

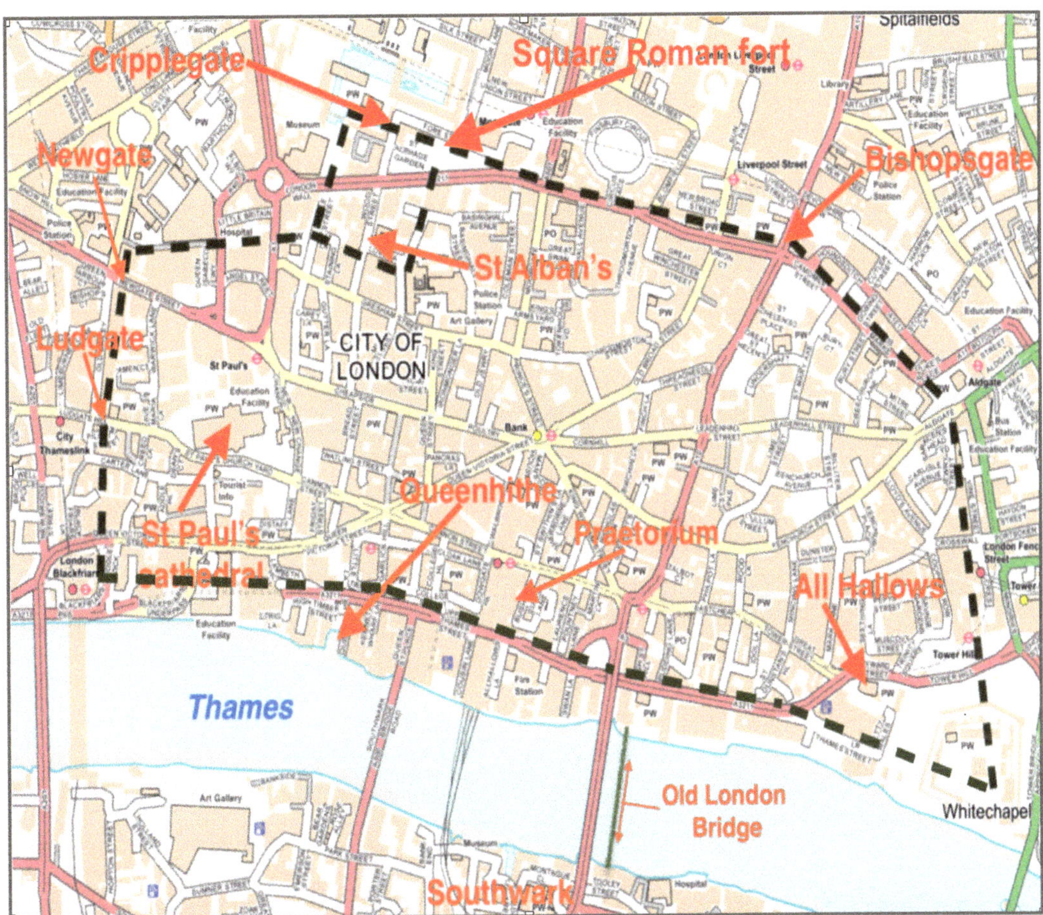

Fig. 20 Places mentioned in the text in relation to London. The indicative route of the Roman walls are shown by the dashed green line. The Roman fort is depicted by this line forming a square at the northern extremity. For simplicity, not all gates are shown.The route of the old London Bridge may not necessarily indicate the route of the Roman or Saxon bridges. Contains OS data © Crown copyright and database right (2018).

we cannot show that this speech took place there must have been some seat of power in London in Alfred's time. It may be that the administrative centre of London at Alfred's time was somewhere near Aldermanbury,[95] and if this was the case then it seems likely that Alfred would have been there at some point. However, this is based on the presence of the Old English *burh* in the name Aldermanbury, and it is not known whether this was acquired after the time of King Alfred. Aldermanbury is immediately to the north-west of the current Guildhall, with Wood Street running north-south through the middle of it. It is possible, based on the 13th century Matthew Paris quoting an 11th century source, that there had been a Saxon royal palace at Aldermanbury near the site of the former church of St Alban on Wood Street.[96] Although we cannot show that any palace here would have been present in Alfred's time, there must have been at least one royal residence and there are few other potential locations within the circuit of London's walls. The church of St Alban was a victim of the 1940 Blitz and all that remained, with the exception of the tower, was demolished in the 1950s. The tower, now a private residence, still stands in splendid isolation in the middle of Wood Street. if it was still standing, the church would extend eastwards into where the police station is located. It is also perhaps significant that this area appears to have been a particularly important part of Roman London, with the site of St Alban's church being within the outline of the Roman fort, and also very close to the amphitheatre. You may not wish to miss the remains of the amphitheatre, which are located beneath the Guildhall Art Gallery. If St Alban's church, or indeed the whole of the former Roman fort, was indeed the site of the palace, King Alfred would have been familiar with the Cripplegate, a gate in the north wall of the Roman fort. There is nothing ancient there now, but if you continue further north up Wood Street, crossing the intersection with the modern traffic artery called London Wall (the actual wall is slightly to the north), you will come to a blue plaque, on a building called Roman House, which declares this to be the site of the Cripplegate, demolished 1760. If you turn right here you will find yourself at St Alphage Garden where there is a surviving section of the ancient wall.

I also thought that it was possible that the royal location could have been at the site of the Roman praetorium (governor's residence), the site of which now lies beneath Cannon Street Station and the area immediately to the east. Although it is unknown how much of this would have remained by Alfred's time (whereas the walls of the fort would probably have still been standing), this may have been a symbolic, and therefore desirable, location to have a base. There is some evidence that the nearby London Stone was considered to be the very centre of London since Roman times, with all distances measured from it. If the site of the praetorium had been appropriate for the Roman governor of London, then perhaps King Alfred felt it was appropriate for him as well, planting himself at not only the former seat of Roman power, but also at Roman London's symbolic geographic centre. The London Stone can be viewed on the other side of Cannon Street from the main entrance to the station, but it is worth noting though that there is no proof that this stone dates to Roman times, let alone the Saxon period. I think the site of the Roman fort is more likely to be the location of Alfred's residence, simply because with the risk of Viking raids he would have been safer in a walled area that also benefitted from quick access to an escape route out of the city through the Cripplegate. Of course, it cannot be ruled out that Alfred's residence was an entirely different building, perhaps wooden, of which no trace remains.

King Alfred's access to and from the west (and therefore perhaps the most important one) would presumably have been through either Newgate or Ludgate. Both of these gates have been long since demolished, but at least the locations are marked by pleasant blue plaques. There is some evidence that there may have been royal palaces to the west of London at Brentford and Chelsea in the 8th century,[96] but I could not find any information to indicate whether they could have been still in service at the time of King Alfred.

We shall see in the next chapter that in 895 King Alfred went to a location on the River Lea approximately 20 miles north of London. I think it is significant that the Roman route of Ermine Street, which starts at the Roman London gate of Bishopsgate, goes straight to potentially relevant locations (Ware and nearby Hertford) for his activities there. As King Alfred technically had London under his control (although formally under the control of his son-in-law Æthelred) I find it plausible that Alfred would have exited London through Bishopsgate to travel north up what is now the A10 via today's Shoreditch, Stoke Newington and Tottenham. There is no remaining evidence of the gate above ground, but it is my understanding that the bishop's mitre set on the wall above a shop on the road called Bishopsgate indicates where the gate would have been. The long-disappeared (at this location) Roman wall would have extended east and west from here and it is thought-provoking to stand here and imagine it disappearing into the modern buildings.

It seems that at least a couple of other places of worship would have been present within the outline of the walls in Alfred's time. A predecessor to St Paul's would have been present at or near the site of today's cathedral, as this had been founded in 604, and All Hallows by the Tower shows evidence of Saxon work.[95]

We know that there must have been a Saxon burgh on the south side of the Thames, because Southwark is mentioned in the Burghal Hidage, a document listing defended settlements and issued in the reign of Edward the Elder after Alfred's death. Indeed, it is possible that a London Bridge, as a replacement or a repair of the earlier Roman structure, may have been built, perhaps during Alfred's lifetime, in order to connect the two burghs on either side of the river and to act as a defence against Vikings trying to proceed upstream.[96] Indeed, the Anglo-Saxon Chronicles record the presence of a bridge in 1016. I am not aware of any evidence pointing to precisely where the burgh of Southwark would have been, but the area around the cathedral must be a possibility. In the 1980s, when I was a student studying dentistry at Guy's Hospital, I spent much time in Southwark and I had no idea that Borough Market, the George Inn and the bleak-looking waterfront warehouses might have all been built over one of King Alfred's burghs.

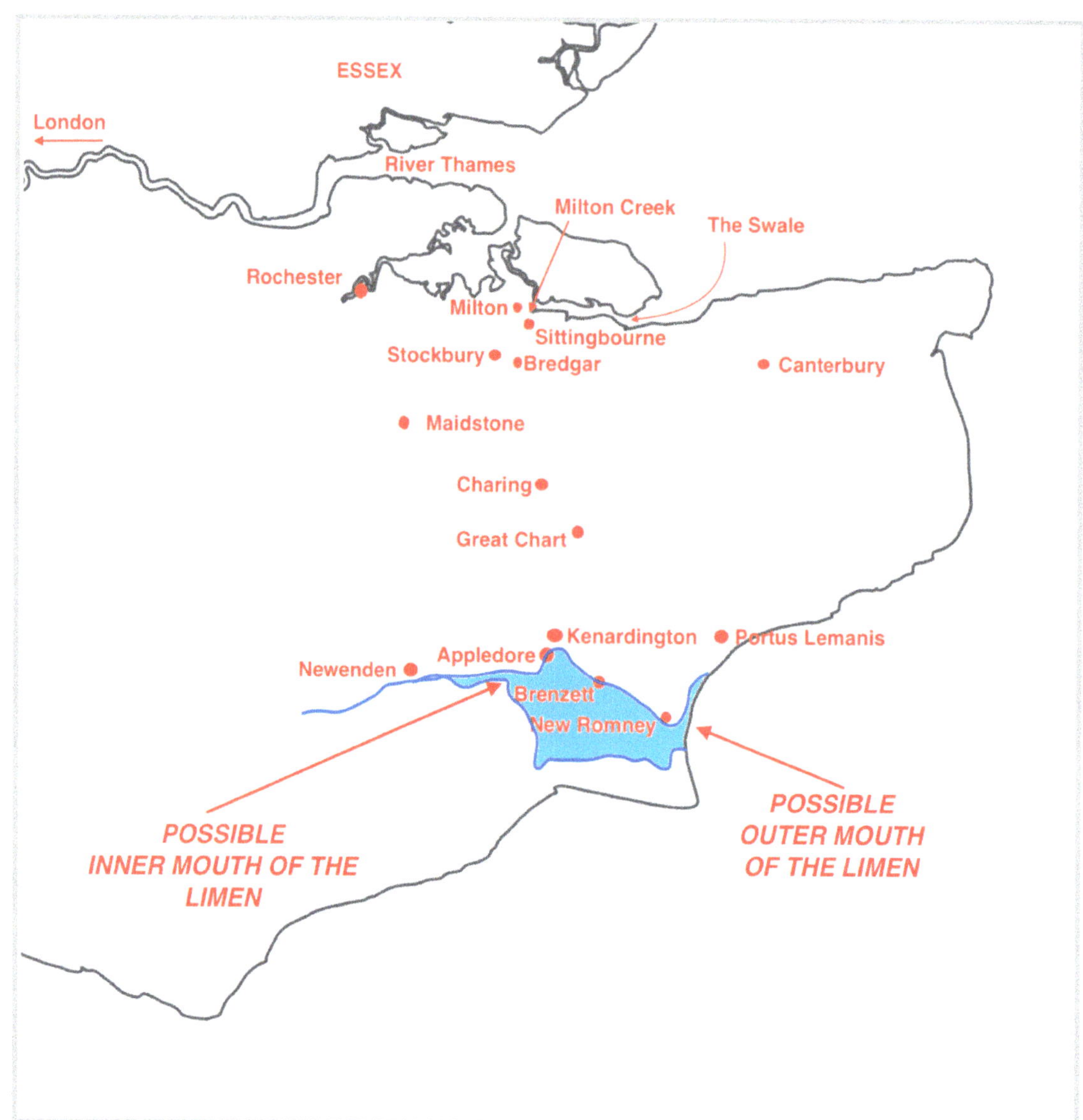

Fig 21 Places in Kent referred to in the text, placed on a map of the modern outline of Kent. Also showing the possible inner and outer mouths of the River Limen in Roman times (which may have changed by Alfred's time), inspired by a map in Robert Furley's 1871 A history of the Weald of Kent with an outline of the early history of the county. Volume 1. Contains OS data © Crown copyright and database right (2018)

The Vikings return to Kent (892 AD)

In 892 a Viking force of 250 ships sailed from Boulogne, France, to the south coast of Kent. In the same year another Viking force of 80 ships came to the north coast of Kent at Milton (now called Milton Regis, part of Sittingbourne). However, this was more than just an emergency for Kent. It was possible that the Viking forces could, as they subsequently did, attack eastwards, and also because they might combine with Viking forces already established in East Anglia and Northumbria. These Viking landings in Kent also must have made Alfred worried about an intention to seize Canterbury. The Anglo-Saxon Chronicles tell us that Alfred camped with his army between the Vikings that landed on the north and south coasts but, intriguingly, there is no record that this led to any subsequent hostile engagements in Kent. Perhaps the absence of any recorded attack on Canterbury at this time was down to Alfred's deployment in Kent, and this might even be why the Viking forces decided to attack eastwards, perhaps as some sort of plan B. It is also possible that Alfred dared not attack to either the north or the south as whichever of these he chose might have given the other Vikings an advantage.

Of course, another major prize for the Vikings would have been London. However, it is notable that the 80 ships that came into Milton could have carried on up the Thames to London, but they chose not to. It is possible that London had become sufficiently well defended to make it not worth attacking, or perhaps the Vikings preferred attacking north and south Kent with a pincer movement to taking London. After all, it appears that Viking forces in East Anglia had not already been able to take London.

Before we look more closely at Kent, it is worth bearing in mind that the Vikings that landed here later proceeded to bases in East Anglia, and sometimes appear to have been assisted by East Anglian forces. There had been significant changes in East Anglia just before the 892 Viking landings in Kent, and I shall try to explain the potential relevance of these below.

The Role of East Anglia

It may seem strange to start discussing East Anglia in this chapter on London and Kent. However, I think it is worth exploring the possibility that events in East Anglia may have caused a de-stabilisation that had made the attack on Kent more likely.

Guthrum, the Viking who had control of East Anglia, including Essex, died in 890, just two years before the 892 Viking landings on the north and south coasts of Kent. This was the same Guthrum who had been baptised by King Alfred, and given a new

Christian name of Æthelstan, after the Battle of Ethandun. When he died, he was succeeded in East Anglia by King Eorhic. Eorhic's rule may have been less effective than Guthrum's, and perhaps the Vikings' arrival in Kent in 892 took advantage of this. It is interesting to take a brief look at the year 904, about five years after Alfred's death, where the Anglo-Saxon Chronicles tell us that Eorhic died in a battle in which he had sided with Alfred's nephew, Æthelwold (the son of Alfred's older brother called Æthelred) against Alfred's son and successor King Edward the Elder. I suggest that because Eorhic later supported a rival to King Alfred's son it is possible that, after he replaced Guthrum in 890, he may have earlier been disloyal to Alfred as well, potentially opening the door to Viking collaboration that Guthrum may have hitherto kept closed. Indeed, I have seen no evidence to indicate that Guthrum had been disloyal to Alfred after his settlement in East Anglia after 878. However, it is recorded in the *Liber monasterii de Hyda* that Eorhic had been killed by fellow East Anglians because he had been uncivil in handling them, which is clearly open to interpretation. Perhaps there was a battle between East Anglians who supported Æthelwold and those who supported Alfred's son King Edward the Elder, and maybe this represented a division between Viking and non-Viking East Anglians. Perhaps there was even a civil war in East Anglia at this time. Incidentally, the 904 battle also claimed the life of Æthelwold, thus removing this challenge against the rule of Alfred's son King Edward the Elder.

Viking Encampments in Kent

I now turn our attention back to Kent and to where the Anglo-Saxon Chronicles tell us that Alfred camped with his troops between the two raiding armies. In trying to locate Alfred it therefore seemed necessary to find out where these two raiding armies were located. This at first seemed quite straight-forward because The Anglo-Saxon Chronicles also tell us that the North Kent Vikings were at Milton and that the South Kent Vikings were at Appledore, which would mean that Alfred would have been between these two places, perhaps on the Greensand Ridge, or even at Charing, where there is an Archbishop's Palace associated with Canterbury that dates back to the 8th century.[97] However, as we shall see, there are complications.

It is perhaps important to point out that although the Anglo-Saxon Chronicles indeed tell us that Alfred camped between the two raiding armies, they do not specify that these two raiding armies were the same Viking armies that had landed on the north and south coasts of Kent. However, because this passage in the text comes shortly after the earlier passage, I believe that this was most likely to have been the case. Nonetheless, with other hostile Viking forces ready to enter the arena (e.g. from Northumbria and East Anglia) it is possible that the two raiding armies were something different. Although I shall return to this matter later, most of my analysis will relate to what I believe to be the most likely scenario, which also seems to be the prevalent interpretation of other writers. An exploration of the potential locations of the Vikings in Kent in 892 therefore follows, and I shall start with the army that came to the south coast of Kent.

Viking locations in the south of Kent

In 892 a Viking force of 250 ships sailed from Boulogne, France, and came to the mouth of the River Limen (now called the Rother) on the south coast of Kent. However, the south coast of Kent would have been different to how it appears today. The changing routes of watercourses and the gradual drainage of Romney Marsh over an extended period makes it difficult to establish the location at which the River Limen would have met the sea in 892. Finding this location is important as we will see later that the Vikings proceeded four miles upstream, and it would be good to know from what point to count the miles from.

It is possible that the Limen exited to the sea at Hythe, New Romney and Rye in sequence over time and it seems to me that it is most likely that in Alfred's time the Limen emerged just to the west of New Romney. Indeed, driving west along the A259 from New Romney to Old Romney takes you right across where it would have once flowed. There is also evidence that there was a Saxon settlement at New Romney,[98] and there may well have been an associated harbour. It must have been quite a shock to the small Saxon settlement to witness the sudden arrival of 250 Viking ships in 892. It seems probable to me that the Vikings would have taken New Romney, and possibly nearby Lydd,[99] keeping some ships there to defend against any attempt by Alfred's forces to trap them in the River Limen after the remainder of the Viking forces proceeded further upstream. Indeed, a few years later, in 895, Alfred would successfully trap the Vikings in the River Lea to the north of London (see Chapter 9).

Confusingly, an inlet that in Alfred's time would have passed to the south of the former Roman site of Portus Lemanis (see later) was also called the Limen, but this name seems to have been left over from a time before the river changed its course to exit at New Romney instead of Hythe. Evidence suggests that the Romans abandoned Portus Lemanis by about 370, possibly because of the silting up of the harbour.[100] It seems that this silting up continued in the Saxon period, which lends weight to the route of the Limen having changed its course to exit at New Romney by Alfred's time.

There is a footpath marked on Ordnance Survey maps called the Saxon Shore Way, but it seems to me that this should not be taken as an accurate depiction of the coastline of this part of Kent in Alfred's time. For example, we know that there were Saxon settlements at New Romney and at Lydd,[99] which are well beyond this footpath.

The *samworht* fort

The Anglo-Saxon Chronicles tell us that the Vikings took their boats four miles up the River Limen from its outer mouth (*fram þæm muþan uteweardum*), up to the great *Andred* wood, and destroyed a fort that was in marshland and is described as *samworht*, which seems to mean that it was half-built. We are also told that there had been a few peasants present, but we are not told what happened to them. Does all this allow us to work out the location of the *samworht* fort, and would solving this help to provide a better picture of what happened next? At this stage I ask the reader to bear with me when I keep referring to this structure as the *samworht* fort. To me it sounds much more elegant than "half-built fort."

The Anglo-Saxon Chronicles suggest that what happened next was that the Vikings arrived at Appledore. This is because the Anglo-Saxon Chronicles mention Appledore later on in the narrative than they mention the *samworht* fort, although they do not explicitly state that the Vikings went to the *samworht* fort and then left and went to Appledore. It cannot therefore be absolutely ruled out that they had already set up camp at Appledore before they made a foray to destroy the *samworht* fort. However, I believe this to be unlikely because it appears that Appledore was more than four miles up the Limen so they would have had to go back downstream to destroy a fort that they had already passed. It therefore seems most likely that the Vikings arrived at Appledore after they left the *samworht* fort.

The settlement of Brenzett corresponds to the four miles from the mouth of the Limen's estuary. Is this the site of the *samworht* fort and where the Vikings initially brought their ships to? I have read that Brenzett (*Brensete* in the Domesday Book) may have been derived from the Old English for a burnt house. Indeed, it seems plausible to me that *Brensete* could derive from "burned settlement," which could be consistent with the destruction of a fort. Maps aimed at demonstrating the coastline and rivers in Saxon times[98] indicate that the River Limen would have gone either through, or close to, Brenzett. Both Asser and the Anglo-Saxon Chronicles indicates that the *samwohrt* fort was in marsh land, which would appear to fit with Brenzett. Both sources also tell us that the Vikings had arrived at the huge *Andred* wood at this point. However, it appears that the edge of the wood in this area has not been determined, with various maps disagreeing. It seems unlikely that Brenzett would have been up against *Andred* wood because Brenzett would have been surrounded by marshland. Incidentally, *Andred* wood became known as the Weald and stretched from Kent to as far as Hampshire. The Anglo-Saxon Chronicles tell us that it was at least 120 miles wide and 30 miles broad.

It has been suggested that the location of the *samwohrt* fort and Appledore are actually the same place. However, Appledore was about eight miles from the mouth of the Limen and not four and it does not seem that Appledore would have been in marsh land. Æthelweard's account[101] is problematic as he does not mention any location four miles up the Limen and has the Vikings going to Appledore (calling it *Poldre*) where they then destroyed a castle. Æthelweard mentions that there were some peasants at the castle, suggesting possible confusion with the Anglo-Saxon Chronicles' mentioning of peasants at the site of the *samwohrt* fort. There is always the possibility that a writer of the Anglo-Saxon Chronicles underestimated the distance to Appledore as four miles, so that the *samwohrt* fort and Appledore are one and the same. Or perhaps there is both a lost Saxon fort and a lost Viking camp at Appledore! However, because Æthelweard was a later writer, and because Asser tells the story in a similar way to the Anglo-Saxon Chronicles, I feel that the evidence points to the *samwohrt* fort not being at Appledore.

The Anglo-Saxon Chronicles describe Appledore as being at the mouth (*muþa*, with *þ* pronounced as "th") of the Limen. However, this does not initially appear to make sense as we know that Appledore must have been inland at this time, as it is now, because there was a Saxon settlement on what really was the coast at New Romney some 8 miles away. It also helps to recall that the *samwohrt* fort was described as being four miles from the *muþan uteweardum*, which translates to being four miles from an outer mouth. It therefore appears that the confusion may be caused by the River Limen having two separate mouths, one where it entered the sea and the other being further upstream where it flowed into an inland body of water. It seems plausible that Appledore was on this latter inland mouth. Indeed, a map attempting to display the geography of this area in Roman times[102] shows the River Limen doing just this, with the inner mouth being near Appledore I have included these features in Fig. 24). It is possible that a remnant of such a lake was still present in Saxon times. It is interesting that when the Anglo-Saxon Chronicles describe the boats being taken four miles upstream to the *samwohrt* fort, the Old English word used for the waterway is *ea*, which seems to have usually meant "river", indicating that there was a stretch of river before the inland lake (rather than the inland lake flowing directly out into the sea).

An alternative explanation is that what the Anglo-Saxon Chronicles call the outer mouth is in fact what I am calling the inner mouth on the map. This is quite a contortion and the only advantage of undertaking it is that travelling four miles upstream to the *samwohrt* fort from here would more likely have taken the Vikings to the edge of Andred Wood than would the same distance from New Romney. These four miles (by following the "Reading Sewer", which appears to approximate to the original course of the Limen) take us to somewhere near the hamlet of Reading Street and perhaps as far as the hamlet of Small Hythe. A map based on the presence of place names including "hurst", which relates to woodland,[103] shows that Reading Street and Small Hythe could have been near the edge of Andred Wood. Chapel Bank (formerly the island of Ebony), a short distance down the Reading Sewer is tempting, but it is less than four miles and would not have been a marsh. It is important to note that these locations are upstream from Appledore whereas Brenzett is on the way to Appledore, and that the Anglo-Saxon Chronicles refer to the *samwohrt* fort before any mention is made of Appledore. This seems to support the case for Brenzett as the location of the *samwohrt* fort even if it may not have been adjacent to Andred wood. On balance, I feel that the *samwohrt* fort was at or near Brenzett, and that they went there before they moved on to Appledore.

It has been suggested that a site near St Rumwold's church at Bonnington is the location of the *samwohrt* fort,[104] but I have not been able to corroborate this. It seems that this location would have been, like Portus Lemanis, cut off from Appledore by silting up before 892.

Appledore

Appledore, about eight miles from New Romney, is an idyllic Kent village (of which there are many) and its name is thought to derive from a Saxon word meaning apple tree. The Anglo-Saxon Chronicles, calling it *Apuldre*, tell us that the Vikings came here, and it is implied that they built a fortification. However, I was unable to find any evidence to indicate where this Viking camp at Appledore would have been. Nonetheless, it has been traditionally thought that the Viking camp was where the church of Saints Peter and Paul was built after Appledore had been burnt down by the French in 1380.[105] The churchyard of Saints Peter and Paul, the large size of which is not immediately obvious, extends north and east of the church. Elevated areas can be seen to the east of the churchyard but I am not aware of any evidence that relates this to the Viking camp.

Kenardington

The Anglo-Saxon Chronicles specifically indicate that the Vikings were at Appledore. However, the lack of any evidence of a Viking camp there has led to suggestions that the remains of ancient earthworks to be found around St Mary's church at Kenardington, just a few miles to the north-west, could be the site referred to as Appledore (*Apuldre*) in the Chronicles.[106]

On visiting this beautiful location, it will be immediately appreciated that the site is on high ground and commands views that could have been strategic. Earthworks are referred to in an archaeological report[106] and also on the information board inside the church. I have seen no evidence that there was a church here in 893, although this would not have stopped the Vikings using a suitable location. Although Kenardington overlooks a silted-up waterway[106] (suggesting that the Vikings could have sailed to here), my overall impression is that there is insufficient evidence to outweigh the fact that it is Appledore that is specifically named in the sources as the location.

The church (Grid Ref TQ97473213) is just to the south of Kenardington, near Battle Hill Farm, and I found it a bit tricky to locate. When heading north up the road towards

Battle Hill Farm I noticed that there was a gate on the right (TQ97383201) and it turned out that this was where the Saxon Shore Way footpath heads east. From here it was just a short walk to the church which is in a lovely secluded location. A notice inside the church indicated that it has been "variously held" that the location was a camp of "Hastings the Dane" (I thought this was unlikely because Hæsten is usually associated with the camp on the North Kent coast), that it is the location of a camp built by the Saxons in King Alfred's time (possible, but with no supporting evidence), and that it was the location that was stormed by the Vikings (i.e. the *samworht* fort). It seems unlikely to have been the *samworht* fort because this elevated location would not have been a marsh, there is no evidence that it was adjacent to *Andred* wood, and it is in the wrong position to be four miles up the Limen. All in all, I found that I could not confidently integrate Kenardington into our story.

The Roman site of Portus Lemanis

An alternative site put forward for the *samworht* fort is the earlier Roman fort and port of Lemanis.[107] The site, also known as Stutfall Castle, is on private land, but there are nearby footpaths. However, Portus Lemanis was on an older course of the River Limen (Rother) and by Alfred's time the site of the Roman fort had become cut off from the new course of the river. It therefore does not seem possible that this could have been the *samworht* fort.

The site can be viewed by parking in the car park on the north side of the Royal Military Canal at West Hythe and then proceeding west along the footpath. Eventually there is a path leading north and quite steeply uphill, which provides views of the walls from a different angle. An additional reason for coming up this hill is to appreciate the magnificent views over Romney Marsh and to the coast. I found this helped my appreciation of the coastline in Saxon times as the land is suddenly flat at the base of the hill and all the way to the sea. In fact, walking back along the footpath to the car, there were places where there were seashells at the surface, almost as though the sea had retreated yesterday!

To conclude, I find that site of the Viking camp would most likely have been at Appledore and that they went there after destroying the *samwohrt* fort, which may have been at the settlement of Brenzett. We now turn our attention to the Vikings who arrived on the North coast of Kent.

The Viking camp on the North Kent coast

The task that I had set myself was made easier here because the relevant section of the north Kent coast has changed less dramatically than the south coast since the time of King Alfred. The Anglo-Saxon Chronicles tell us explicitly that the Vikings built a fortification at Milton (*Middletun*) under the leadership of a man called Hæsten. In order to get their 80 ships to Milton they would have sailed past Whitstable to go up the Swale and they would have then needed to sail up Milton Creek, although it isn't clear how navigable this would have been in Saxon times.

I found it helpful to try to appreciate the relationship between the principal waterways in this area, these being the Medway, the Swale and the Thames. One can appreciate the Medway at various locations including Rochester and Maidstone, but I also found Chatham Marina and the less visited Gillingham Pier to provide useful viewpoints. For those who wish to explore the Medway in more detail, there is a Medway Valley Walk that extends from Rochester to Tonbridge. I particularly like Oare, near Faversham, as a viewpoint for looking over the Swale. I once saw some keep-fitters filling their water bottles from a gushing water tap at Oare. They told me it was safe to drink so I filled up and I can tell you that the water was lovely. I learned later that this is an artesian well and people travel miles to fill up. Another personal favourite look-out point is the coastline at the settlement of Grain, at the end of the Hoo peninsula, because one can see both down and across the Medway and also across the Thames to Essex, where the Vikings went on to developed a base at Benfleet (and then at Shoebury). However, I could never find an explanation as to why it is so easy to find bits of smashed up old marmalade pots on the waterfront at Grain.

Milton Regis

This location is referred to as *Middletun* in both the Anglo-Saxon Chronicles' and Æthelweard 's account of events. Milton Regis lies to the north of Sittingbourne, and is now part of that town. It is worth noting that Sittingbourne is not mentioned in the 1086 Domesday book, whereas Milton is. Milton may therefore be older and locations that today seem to us to be more Sittingbourne than Milton may not have seemed that way in Alfred's time. Milton was apparently a significant Saxon site and it is said that Queen Seaxburgh of Kent became a nun at the abbey she founded there, becoming St Seaxburgh, and that her son became king there in 680. But where exactly was the Viking camp? The main reason for working this out is to determine the northern point of the two locations between which Alfred camped. But there is another reason. At some point before Hæsten left Kent, his son would become Alfred's godson, and this tells us that Alfred must have met these Vikings, and perhaps he met them at Milton. Potential sites for the Viking camp are discussed below.

Castle Rough, Milton Regis

This location, effectively just a mound, is to be found just east of Kemsley and to the west of Milton Creek, close to the evocatively named Saxon Shore Way. The earliest reference that I could find for this mound being the camp of the North Kent Vikings was in Edward Hasted's 1797 writings on the history of Kent.[108] It has been suggested that Castle Rough would have been a man-made island, and evidence from a limited examination undertaken by Sittingbourne and Swale Archaeological Research Group[109] indicated that the lowest parts of the mound contained 13th-14th century pottery, and was therefore built after the time of King Alfred. Although this does not rule out this site, because a more extensive examination may have produced more evidence, it does cast doubt upon this being the site of the Viking camp. The location is also moated, which may indicate a date later than the time of King Alfred. Oliver Rackham found that to his knowledge there were no mentions of moats in Anglo-Saxon charters, in place names, or in the Domesday Book.[110] It is therefore possible that moats were a later development. Oliver Rackham also suggested that moats may have become status symbols, which may have been the case here as a moat of this relatively small size would have been largely ineffective against a determined army. It therefore seems that Castle Rough may have been a medieval moated manor, although it does not seem possible to rule out that it was something else previously.

I did not find it easy to observe Castle Rough. I looked north from Swale Way, just after crossing over Milton Creek and the Sittingbourne and Kemsley Light Railway, and I fancied that I could pick out Castle Rough from this elevated position, using my Ordnance Survey map to guide my eye to the approximate location. Whilst conducting research I also came across a rumour that the camp was under a canteen at the Kemsley paper mill (close to Castle Rough), but I have been unable to find any supporting evidence.

Bayford Castle and Bayford Court

The former location of a place called Bayford Castle, on the other side of Milton Creek to Castle Rough, may have been the site of the Viking fortification. However, Edward Hasted, in his 1797 writings on the history of Kent[108] tells us that it was Alfred who built some fortifications against the Vikings on the other side of Milton Creek from Castle Rough at "Baford-castle." It should be noted that Hasted appears to be an early originator (if not the originator) of the legend that Castle Rough had been the Viking fortification.

Bayford Castle appears on older Ordnance Survey maps with an indication that it was erected in 893. By the time of the 1960 map, references to the location had disappeared. There is nothing for the casual visitor to see as the location appears to be approximately where there are now industrial units to the east of a karting track. Although evidence is lacking in terms of this being either a Viking or Saxon site, it is at least in a suitable location being near to Milton Creek. To confuse matters, maps dating to 1590 show that the location of Bayford Castle used to be called Castle Ruffe. I haven't seen anything to explain why the name of Castle Ruffe disappears from the east side of Milton Creek and then a Castle-ruff (later becoming "Castle Rough") appears on the other side of Milton Creek in the 1797 writings of Edward Hasted.

There has been confusion with Bayford Court, which is south of where Bayford Castle appears to have been. This site is located near the centre of Sittingbourne in an industrial area north of Eurolink Way just off Crown Quay Lane. The remains of the Bayford Court moat were marked on my Ordnance Survey map and it was possible to view it. However, as described under Castle Rough, moats may have been a later development, and nor is the moat here sufficiently wide to stop a determined army. I therefore feel that although Bayford Court may be an interesting old location, the evidence is insufficient for it to be seriously considered as a site for the Viking fortification.

It seems that although we know that the Viking fortification was somewhere in the vicinity of Milton Regis, we cannot locate it precisely. It could, of course, have been located somewhere other than the locations described above.

Sites for King Alfred's Camp in Kent

The Anglo-Saxon Chronicles tell us that in 893 Alfred camped with his army between the two raiding armies and therefore it would have been between Milton on the north coast of Kent and Appledore towards the south coast of Kent. Anyone who travels around Kent will soon appreciate how difficult it would have been to monitor these distant locations from a single site. I therefore feel that any central camp must have had additional outposts in order to monitor what was going on over a wide area. This would fit with the Anglo-Saxon Chronicles telling us that *burga* (fortresses), noting the plural, were being held by Alfred. Maidstone seems to be an important contender for being Alfred's nerve centre for this operation, although I think areas around Egerton, Charing and Great Chart should not be discounted.

Maidstone

A crossing of the Medway at Maidstone was developed in Saxon times[111] and it has been suggested that the settlement may have been the focus of a royal estate and would have also played a significant ecclesiastical role.[111] Maidstone has been favoured as the site for Alfred's camp.[19] The town is at the crossing of a Roman route from Rochester to Hastings with a route connecting Ashford to London, which is now the A20 either side of Maidstone. It seems plausible that Saxon Maidstone would have developed around this crossing, which appears to be where Week Street, King Street, Gabriel's Hill and High Street currently meet. The location is also near to the top of a hill, which may have made it strategically useful. However, by Alfred's time Maidstone may have developed beyond the vicinity of this crossing.

Fig. 22 All Saints' Church, Maidstone

The location of the destroyed church of St Mary the Virgin may be an important clue regarding any camp that Alfred might have had at Maidstone. By the 11th century this church by the Medway had become a minster with 17 dependent churches. It seems plausible that there may have been a settlement around this site in Alfred's time because such significance would have taken time to develop. This church no longer exists, but it has been suggested[111] that the site is at the approximate location of, or even beneath, All Saints' Church, which replaced it in the 1390s. The oldest parts of the nearby Archbishop's Palace date to the 14th century, but the location was likely to have been the site of a manor, that we know existed because it was held in 1086 by the Archbishop of Canterbury.[111] It is therefore possible that there had been a manor here at the time of

King Alfred. On visiting this area my attention was drawn to an information board that told me that a track called Knightrider Street led down to the Medway at a point where it could once be forded (The street is still there although the ford isn't). I feel that the possibility of being able to easily cross the Medway at this point adds weight to this part of Maidstone being the location for King Alfred's camp. A pleasant way of gaining an appreciation of this area is to partake in a small circular riverside walk using the Millennium Bridge and Maidstone Bridge crossings.

Maidstone is also close to what appears to have been the original Pilgrim's Way, which itself was on the route of an ancient trackway. In addition, Maidstone may also have offered a direct route to the vicinity of Milton Regis. In the other direction, there may have been access to the area around Appledore as well.

However, Maidstone is much closer to Milton Regis than it is to Appledore, and it is also quite distant from a line running between these two places. We therefore seem to run into trouble with the Anglo-Saxon Chronicles' description of Alfred's camp being between the two raiding armies.

Bredgar, Kent

The village of Bredgar is to be found just south of the M2 motorway, a short distance south-west of Sittingbourne, and it has been suggested that this was the probable site of Alfred's encampment. Bredgar has a lovely church yard, and is somewhat elevated. However, I could see no special reason to consider that this was Alfred's main camp, although it could have been one of potentially many outposts. Bredgar lies close to a line drawn between Appledore and Milton, but it is very much closer to the latter.

Stockbury, Kent

The earthworks at Stockbury, just a few miles west of Bredgar, are thought to be Norman[112] and therefore more recent than King Alfred's time. However, it is possible that the Norman construction may have been built over earlier earthworks, and this may be supported by the possibility that part of the name may derive from the Old English *burh* (stronghold).[107]

To find these earthworks it is easiest to find the church first, which is located a little way east from the centre of the village, adjacent to Church Farm. Although the rings are on private land they are easily viewed from the road and the church yard. In fact, the outermost visible ring appears to clip the churchyard. It is interesting to see how close the church has been built to the earthworks, and this reminded me of Knowlton in Dorset where the church is surrounded by an earthwork! Whilst I accept that the location commands views that could have made it a useful outpost, there did not seem to be any particular reason to believe that this would have been Alfred's camp. Stockbury, like Bredgar, lies close to a line drawn between Appledore and Milton, but it is very much closer to the latter.

Newenden, Kent

There is a feature to the north-east of the village of Newenden that is called Castle Toll, and you can get quite close to it on a public footpath. Whilst Castle Toll is perhaps 13th century, some of the earthworks marked on the Ordnance Survey map to the south are thought to be the remains of an Anglo-Saxon burgh.[113] However, I found that there is little left to see and you may need to use your imagination as you look across from the footpath. It has, however, been suggested that this was the site of *Eorpeburnan*, a previously lost burgh that is listed in the Burghal Hidage, a document compiled in the reign of Alfred's son, Edward the Elder. An argument against these earthworks being *Eorpeburnan* is that the Burghal Hidage does not seem to have included Kent. It is interesting to note that the River Rother (Limen) flows nearby, and excavations in 1971 showed that in some aspects the burgh was incomplete, which could tempt us into thinking that this was the *samworht fort*. However, this site is well over four miles from potential locations for the mouth of the Limen (it is about ten miles west of Appledore). However, it must be possible that there would have been an unrecorded engagement between the Saxons and Vikings in this area because this burgh was only ten miles from Appledore.

I got to Castle Toll via the village of Newenden, where I parked and walked down to the small sewage works (marked on my Ordnance Survey map), then followed the track around the back and proceeded to where the path meets the River Rother. I then headed north east along the footpath across fields, resisting the temptation to follow another path that hugs the curve of the Rother. There was a wooded area directly before I got to Castle Toll that was not shown on my map, but I decided to press on and I did eventually find my way through to Castle Toll. Although this may be only 13th century, locating this was helpful in locating the earlier Anglo-Saxon defences, because these are a short distance directly due south from here and not otherwise easy to pick out in the landscape. I therefore retraced my steps and I fancy that I could just make out the undulations of the Anglo-Saxon earthworks in a field.

Newenden is not at all on a line connecting Milton Regis and Appledore, so, although I believe it may have played a role, it does not fit the description of Alfred's camp.

Other possible sites of King Alfred's camp

When the Vikings landed on the north and south coasts of Kent, I feel that Alfred must have been concerned that Canterbury may have been a target. When I disregarded previous suggestions (for which there is no real evidence) and considered an approximate line between Appledore and Milton Regis, I found that there were a few places that could have better met the description of being between these locations and which may also have allowed easier access to Canterbury. I considered three locations in particular: The two villages of Great Chart and Charing, and the landscape feature known as the Greensand Ridge.

It is known that in King Alfred's time there was a settlement at Great Chart under the ownership of the Archbishop of Canterbury. Interestingly, there has been a legend that Great Chart had been burned by the Vikings, and this led to the subsequent development of Ashford.[114] I have been unable to corroborate the entry in the church booklet that indicates that these were the Vikings that had been at Appledore and it seems geographically impossible for this to have been the location of the *samworht* fort.

The Greensand Ridge would have offered strategic vantage points. I explored the area around the lovely village of Egerton, but other parts of this ridge may have been equally suitable for Alfred's needs.

Charing is approximately half way between Milton and Appledore and has an Archbishop's Palace associated with Canterbury that dates back to the 8th century.[97] One could be misled into thinking that Alfred's piety may have led him here because of a legend that the block on which John the Baptist had been beheaded had been located at the church.[115] However, the tradition is that this was brought to England by King Richard I, well after the time of King Alfred.[115] Nonetheless, I feel that this location is the strongest contender for the location of Alfred's camp. It is located on an approximate line between Milton and Appledore, without being too close to either, and is located by the ancient track to Canterbury that later became known as the Pilgrims' Way.

An alternative Interpretation of Alfred's Location

Although the Anglo-Saxon Chronicles tell us that Alfred camped between the two raiding armies, we are not told what these armies were, and it is easy to assume that the text refers to the forces at Appledore and Milton. However, by not naming the armies the text permits the possibility that the two raiding armies may have been Northumbrian and East Anglian Vikings, who appear to have been attacking Wessex at the same time as the Appledore and Milton Viking forces. Whereas we know that the Milton and Appledore forces were at Milton and Appledore, we do not know where the

Northumbrian and East Anglian forces were, so if the Chronicles were in fact referring to these armies, we would not know the locations that Alfred had been between. It seems that around the time where the Anglo-Saxon Chronicles describe Alfred as camping between two raiding armies, Wessex may have been under attack from Vikings in North Kent, Vikings in South Kent, and Vikings from Northumbrian and East Anglian land contingents, with East Anglian and Northumbrian sea-borne contingents soon to follow, and with all of this possibly being coordinated.

Later that same year (893) the East Anglians and Northumbrians are described as sailing around the coast to besiege Devon. It is recorded even later in the same year that the East Anglians and Northumbrians had joined forces with the Viking forces that returned from their defeat at Buttington, so we know they were prepared to work together.

It seems more likely that the Anglo-Saxon Chronicles intend to express that Alfred was between Appledore and Milton. However, I don't think that the alternative discussed above can be ruled out. Of course, this could pull locations, like Maidstone, that might be ruled out because they are not between Appledore and Milton, back into the frame.

Farnham in Hampshire

The Vikings in Kent raided to the west, but on their way back east, this time to Essex, they were caught up with and in 893 defeated at Farnham in Hampshire. We do not know where they had been raiding but they could have been in the vicinity of Winchester as it appears that they had travelled most of the distance to that place. It appears that it was the Appledore contingent that carried out this raiding because Æthelweard tells us that it was done by the army that arrived from Gaul (the Anglo-Saxon Chronicles indicate that the Appledore force had sailed from Boulogne; however, there is no record to tell us where Hæsten's forces had sailed from, which therefore could also have been Gaul!) and that they proceeded through an immense *Anderedesuuda* (*Andred* wood). This makes more sense for Appledore than it does for Milton, because moving west from the latter location would not have entailed crossing this wood. The victory at Farnham is generally attributed to Alfred's son, Edward the Elder, and this is supported by Æthleweard's chronicle. However, we cannot rule out Alfred's presence at Farnham because a document called the Annals of St Neots, albeit written later, states that he fought there. After their defeat at Farnham the Vikings were pursued across the Thames and up the River Colne. They were besieged by Wessex forces on an island that Æthelweard calls *Thornige*, and which the Anglo-Saxon Chronicles refer to as an islet in the River Colne. It has been speculated that this islet was at the settlement of Thorney, near Iver (Buckinghamshire), and not far from Heathrow Airport. The Anglo-Saxon Chronicles tell us that while Alfred was on his way to this location, the contingent that had been besieging the Vikings had set off homeward because they had finished their tour of duty and had run out of food. This casts doubt on the description provided in the Annals of St Neots because it is difficult to see how Alfred could have been involved in the conflict and at the same time ride with troops towards it! We are not told whether Alfred reached the islet on the Colne, where the Vikings remained because they could not move their injured king, but we are told that Alfred diverted to Exeter when he became aware of Viking attacks in Devon. The Anglo-Saxon Chronicles indicate that Alfred took all the army with him except for a *swiþe gewaldenum* (very powerful) contingent that went east to London. The power of this contingent might explain why the Viking fort at Benfleet, near the south coast of Essex, was then successfully defeated, with booty, including ships, being taken back to London or Rochester.

It is possible that the Viking attacks in Devon could have been coordinated with the attacks in the east in order to stretch Alfred's forces. Æthelweard's chronicle indicates that the Vikings on the Colne were picked up by their ships that came round from a Limen port (which could therefore have been Appledore) and taken to *Meresige* in Kent. I feel that the location of *Meresige* might be an error as it may well relate to Mersea Island in Essex, and we know that there was a regrouping of Viking forces in Essex. Mersea in Essex is recorded as *Meresig* in the early 10th century.[14] I have seen it suggested that the Farnham referred to above was not the Farnham in Hampshire, but Farnham in Essex. However, this does not fit with the Anglo-Saxon Chronicles' description of the Viking movements where we are told that they crossed the Thames before arriving at the Colne. This would not have been necessary if they had come from Essex.

At some point in 893 Hæsten crossed to Essex, heading for Benfleet and then Shoebury. Although this was followed by raiding and military engagements there is no evidence that Alfred was present. These events are briefly summarised in the Appendix. Nonetheless, the Vikings re-enter our story just a couple of years later when they build a fortress on the River Lea, and it is this area that is the subject of the following chapter.

9

Fortifications and obstruction. The River Lea

I have always been fond of the River Lea, which is perhaps because I was brought up very close to its source in the town of Luton. In order to get to sixth form college, I used to walk along a stretch of its upper reaches twice a day for two years. Of course, I knew that it flowed to London but the fact is that I didn't think very much about it at the time. It therefore came as a pleasant surprise to find that my exploration of the journeys of King Alfred would take me back to this wonderful waterway.

It is worth remembering that the whole length of the River Lea was part of the boundary between what became known as the Danelaw (it did not gain this name until the 11th century) and Anglo-Saxon controlled territory. This boundary became formalised in a treaty between Alfred and the Viking leader Guthrum, probably around 886. The Anglo-Saxon Chronicles tell us that in 895 some Vikings left Mersea Island in Essex and built a fortress by the River Lea at a point about 20 miles north of London. They were then attacked by garrisons loyal to Alfred, which were in turn beaten back by the Vikings, with some loss of life. We are then told that later that year, at harvest-time, King Alfred himself arrived and camped in the vicinity of the Viking fortification in order to prevent the Vikings from stopping the locals from reaping their corn. The Anglo-Saxon Chronicles also tell us that after this, but still in the same year, Alfred rode (up) along the River Lea to see where the river could be obstructed (*forwyrcan*) in order to block the Viking ships in. I have bracketed "up" because, although the Old English text uses this word, it seems unclear whether this would have then meant upstream as it would to us today. Nonetheless, the Anglo-Saxon Chronicles record that the river was indeed obstructed and that Alfred had also started to build a fortification on either side of the river. The Vikings abandoned their ships because they realised that they were being trapped, and fled overland all the way to Bridgnorth on the River Severn in what is now Shropshire. We do not know whether the ships were being physically hemmed in or whether they were being immobilised because of some sort of drainage of the river. Ranulf Higden's beautifully named *Polychronicon*, written in the 14th century, states that Alfred and the Londoners hampered the flow of the river by dividing it into three streams.[11] This method is also mentioned in the earlier 12th century account by Henry of Huntingdon,[83] which Ranulf Higden may have used as his source. Both of these works were written a long time after the events of 895 and may therefore be unreliable.

Nonetheless, this technique could be compatible with the Old English *forwyrcan* because this word does not necessarily mean obstruct. It has a wider meaning of doing harm to something. The Anglo-Saxon Chronicles tell us that before the Vikings fled to Bridgnorth in Shropshire they managed to get their women to safety in East Anglia, which suggests that they may have been intending to settle.

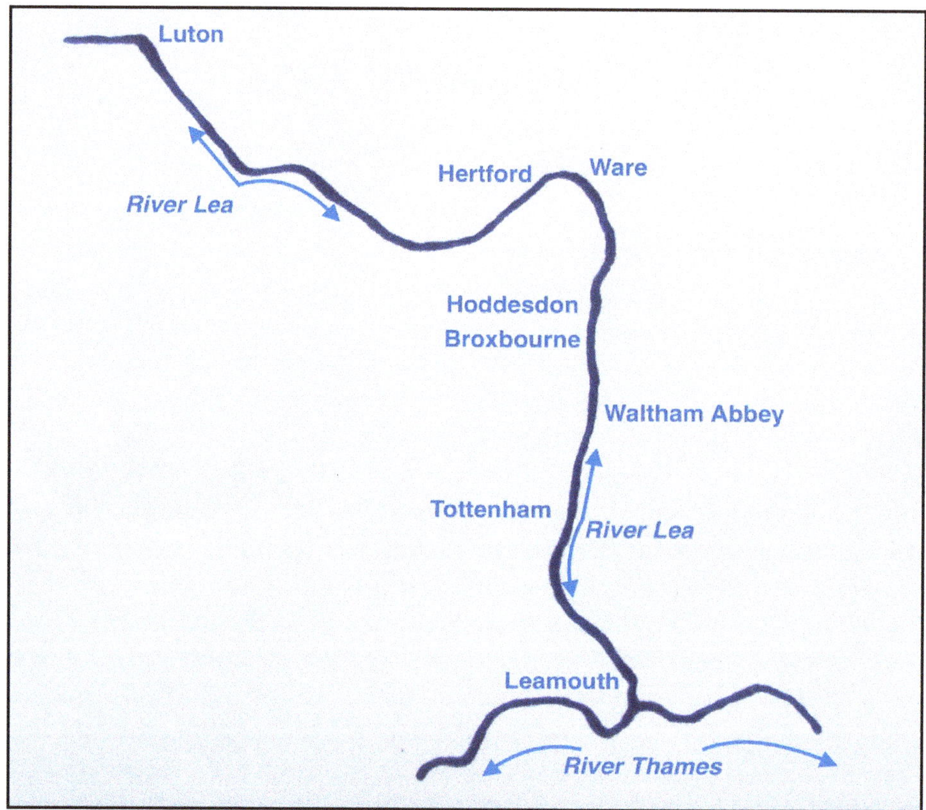

Fig. 23 Schematic illustration of the course of the River Lea, including places mentioned in the text

The River Lee Navigation (the river is variably called "Lea" or "Lee", whereas the man-made navigation is always called "Lee"), which runs the whole stretch of our area of interest from Hertford, in Hertfordshire, to London, was cut in 1770.[116] However, before 1770 there were at least four streams, and there may have been as many as seven,[116] so it seems difficult to establish with certainty the course of the River Lea in Alfred's time. Nonetheless, when I looked at my Ordnance Survey map, I could see a river marked as "Old River Lea or Lee" north of the town of Waltham Abbey, with this appellation (but with the "Old" dropped) also appearing near Broxbourne a few miles further upstream. However, if in Alfred's time the total volume of water was anything like it is today, feeding through different streams and large lakes, the river must have been much wider than the remnants of what today are said to be original course of the Lea.

So, we have four things that it would be nice to locate. The Viking fortification, Alfred's camp, the point where the river had been obstructed, and Alfred's pair of incomplete fortifications on the River Lea. Remembering that we cannot be certain about the distance represented by a mile (see Introduction), or how accurate measurement was at the time, I feel that it would be sensible to consider the distance for the Viking fortress of twenty miles north of London as approximate. Twenty miles takes us to somewhere just south of Hertford, and perhaps the stretch of the river near Hoddesdon and Broxbourne. Only slightly further on are the towns of Hertford and Ware and I think these deserve serious consideration because they are approximately twenty miles from London. We do not know whether Alfred's initial camp was on the river because all we are told is that it was near the Viking fortification, but the location at which Alfred obstructed the river must clearly have been downstream from the Viking fortress. The Anglo-Saxon Chronicles mention the fortress that Alfred had built on both sides of the river immediately after stating that the obstruction was carried out, implying that the fortress was either side of the obstruction, although this remains uncertain.

I shall start by exploring the adjacent towns of Ware and Hertford. I think it is likely that the events took place there, with the Viking stronghold being at Ware or Hertford, and Alfred's initial camp, the obstruction of the river and the pair of fortifications being almost anywhere between (and including) Hertford and Waltham Abbey. I have been told by others that in Saxon times the River Lea was navigable to longboats as far as Hertford. It is important to note that whether the Vikings built their fortress at Ware or Hertford, they would have been on the side of the river that had been under Viking control since about 886. It is, however, a mystery as to why they would flee to Shropshire instead of into their own territory. It is possible that the disruption of the harvest on the Saxon side of the river was part of a military tactic to threaten the food supply for London, and they could quite easily do this from the Viking side of the river. It is also possible that this border area was not particularly well policed by anybody and a Viking fortification may have been seen as a threat to be removed even if it was just into Viking territory. It is maybe possible that Alfred was trying to maintain a Viking-free zone, including the discouragement of new Viking settlements close to London.[117] Perhaps the border was not that well respected and people continued harvesting on either side of the river regardless of whether they had a Viking or a Saxon allegiance.

Ware, Hertfordshire

The town of Ware, famous for its reputedly haunted Great Bed that can accommodate at least eight people (now in the Victoria and Albert museum), is about 24 miles north of London and I found it a thoroughly pleasant place to spend some time. The little museum, staffed by volunteers and partly housed in a World War Two bunker, is a delight and I enjoyed chatting with the staff about King Alfred and the Vikings. I have seen it claimed that the Vikings spent six months at Ware after which they were attacked by Alfred, who lost and retreated to Waltham Abbey,[118] with all this taking place before the period in which the Anglo-Saxon Chronicles tell us that Alfred first turned up to protect the harvesting. The Anglo-Saxon Chronicles indeed record that the Viking base was attacked in this period, although we are neither told that the location was at Ware nor how long the Vikings had been there, and there is no recording of Alfred's presence. If Alfred had not been present then he could not, of course, have retreated to Waltham Abbey. Nonetheless, this must have been a significant engagement as the Anglo-Saxon Chronicles record that four of the king's thegns (noblemen in the king's service) were killed. Overall, it seems to me that Alfred was not at this engagement.

I have seen it written that most archaeologists believe that Alfred obstructed the river at Ware,[119] and that the name Ware derives from the weirs Alfred built (the town is called *Waras* in the Domesday Book, meaning weirs[14]). However, it has been argued that it was the Vikings who built a weir here and they used the dammed water to protect their fort, but Alfred then starved the location of tidal water both by building a wall and by dividing the river into three "near Waltham").[120] It is interesting to note that there are later historical records that demonstrate the plausibility of blocking the river. In 1275, in a dispute between Ware and Hertford, the river between these two towns was indeed blocked by a weir,[121] and there is evidence that by 1300 there were problems with the river being blocked by boats being placed across it.[121]

Although it was not named as such on my Ordnance Survey map, the small waterway north of the broader River Lee Navigation south-east of Ware is part of the old River Lea, and is called this on the 1880 Ordnance Survey map. The maps show weirs on this stretch of the River Lea although, as already indicated, the river must have been much wider in Alfred's time in order to accommodate the water that now flows along different routes. It therefore seems to require a stretch of the imagination to believe that the current locations of wears would correspond to the position of wears in Saxon times.

But why might the Vikings have wanted to go to Ware? It is perhaps significant that Ware was on the London to York Roman road known as Ermine Street, although there is no visible indication of this at surface level today. Evidence suggests that in Alfred's time Ware would have been larger than Hertford and perhaps there was something at Ware that was worth obtaining. Perhaps it was a location where they could control the food supply by river and road at the same time in order to increase what was available to them or to reduce the supply to London.

I therefore decided to explore the location of the Roman road in relation to the Lea at Ware. Although my explorations were inhibited by a heavy downpour, when walking along the River Lea path at approximately the correct location I could see no indication as to where Ermine Street would have run up to the river and crossed it, probably by a bridge.[122] This would have been 200 metres east of the lock marked on the Ordnance Survey map and to the west of the current centre of Ware. Evidence of a Roman site has been found near this road although there is little to suggest that this was significantly inhabited after the Roman period. The focus of settlement appears to have moved east,[122] closer to what is now the centre of Ware, with there being evidence of significant settlement after 850AD around Baldock Street, with this being related to trade, ecclesiastical significance, or something else not yet determined.[122] In 1086, at the time of the Domesday Book, Ware was of significant size and wealth. All of this might have meant that Ware could have been a target for Viking attack in 895. It is possible that a bridge carrying Ermine Street over the River Lea was used up to 1191 because there is a record of the men of Hertford breaking up a bridge at Ware in that year.

There is an Iron Age hillfort at Widbury Hill (Grid Ref TL37211383), east of Ware and north of the Lea and local people told me that this was where the Vikings set up camp. It is difficult to disprove this location, although it seems more likely that their base would have been closer to the water and their ships. I was told that Viking objects may have been found here, although I was unable to corroborate this. There is a footpath that goes past the fort and it is also possible to look up to the location from the River Lea path just south of Ware.

It has also been suggested that the Viking camp was where there are two burial mounds (Grid Ref: TL37221777) north of the River Rib, which flows into the River Lea near Hertford. This is a short distance to the east of the hamlet of Wadesmill (Hertfordshire). However, this suggestion may be based on a mistaken belief that the burial mounds were Viking instead of what they have now been determined to be, which is Roman.[124] Furthermore, there is no supporting evidence that the Vikings went up the River Lea and then went up the River Rib.

Hertford, Hertfordshire

Hertford is about 25 miles north of London and is upstream from Ware on the River Lea. I was brought up just across the border in Bedfordshire and I became familiar in my younger days with much of Hertfordshire, but not Hertford. To us that was distant Hertfordshire, almost as far as Essex. I now realise that I was missing out on a lovely place (and I came to love Essex too).

Fig. 24 The River Lea running through Hertford

There has been speculation regarding how the course of the River Lea through Hertford may relate to the events of 895, with attention being paid to the bifurcation of the river just north-east of Mill Bridge to form Hertford's Folly Island. However, it is difficult to imagine that the route of the river through Hertford would have been the same as in 895 and that this bifurcation is where King Alfred divided the river in order to trap the Viking boats. Nonetheless, the bifurcation can be easily observed near the road called Bull Plain. I have seen reference to the course of the river in Roman times lying to the north -west of its current course, although it may have been in its approximate current location in Alfred's time because a Viking sword was found in modern times when the River Lea was dredged in the centre of Hertford. However, as this was border territory, and because precise dating may be impossible, we should not assume that it is connected to the events of 895. Although many Viking weapons are found submerged,[125] it is also possible that the sword found its way into water as the river changed its course. I also saw a reference to remains of Viking ships being found near Hertford and Stanstead Abbots, although I was unable to corroborate this.

Although I saw a reference to King Alfred in relation to Hertford Castle, it appears that the first fortification on this site was constructed by King Edward the Elder in 912 after Alfred had died. However, the flint walls that you see are more recent (although still very old) and go back to the time of Henry II.

The1881 Ordnance Survey map of Hertford shows an area called "Englefield" lying to the east of Bengeo Street and to the north of Warren Park Road (Grid Ref TL32431336). Readers may recall that there was a battle of Englefield near Reading in Berkshire in 871, with the name Englefield probably meaning the land of the Angles. The same map also shows an area called "Daneshill" (Grid Ref TL32361323) lying to the south of Warren Park Road, with some nearby land to the north-east being called "Danesbury" (Grid Ref TL32691345). There has also been speculation that the former location of the cricket ground, which used to lie to the east of the pronounced curve of Warren Park Road (Grid Ref TL32611346), could have been a Viking camp. Was there a Viking fortification in this area and did Alfred set up his camp at Englefield? Although we must be cautious of the possibility that antiquarian speculation influenced the place names on the 1881 map, I find the juxtaposition of names potentially referring to Vikings and Anglo-Saxons intriguing. In the absence of definitely-established locations for any Saxon or Viking camps I feel this area must be worth considering. The Anglo-Saxon Chronicles also tell us that in 912, after Alfred's death, King Edward the Elder built a stronghold at Hertford. However, the description of the location places this stronghold on the other side of the River Beane to the aforementioned Hertford locations of Englefield, Daneshill and Danesbury. Just a short distance east of these locations lies the 12th century St Leonard's church. I was told that the current building may have been built on an even older structure that might relate in some way to the Vikings or King Alfred, although I was unable to find any supporting evidence.

As is the case with Ware, it is uncertain why the Vikings would have gone to Hertford. However, the Anglo-Saxon Chronicles tell us that in 673 a synod took place at Hertford (*Heorotford*, or *Herutford* in Bede's Latin). Indeed, there is a memorial stone associated with this event in Hertford Castle Gardens. There was also a royal mint here as early as the 920s.[126] Although the mint dates to slightly after the time of Alfred, the record of both a synod and a mint suggests that Hertford was an important place in Anglo-Saxon times, perhaps more important than nearby Ware, and it also indicates that Hertford might have been attractive to the Vikings because of its possessions. However, it is possible that the synod took place at the similarly named Hartford in Cambridgeshire instead. This seems plausible because the Bishop of London, in which diocese Hertford seems to have been located, was not present. However, a person called Bisi appears to have been presiding with a certain Theodore, and Bisi's diocese was Dunwich, in which Hartford in Cambridgeshire may have been.[127]

Locations south of Ware

Sections of the old River Lea can be traced near Waltham Abbey and further upstream at Hoddesdon and Broxbourne. However, as stressed previously, the river must have been much wider than the remnants of what today are said to be its original course. So, the excitement of finding sections of the river that could potentially be sites for Viking or Alfredian activities must be tempered by the possibility of the river being significantly different in Alfred's time.

Hoddesdon, just downstream from Ware, is about 20 miles north of London, and is therefore a good fit with where the Anglo-Saxon Chronicles tell us that the Vikings set up their fortification on the River Lea. However, walking north past Hoddesdon along the River Lee Navigation, the old course of the River Lea seemed to me to have been lost. However, after St Margarets the old course of the River Lea is to the east of the adjacent reservoir, following the line of the parish boundary marked on the Ordnance Survey map, although I couldn't see any public access to this stretch.

A small walkable stretch of the Old River Lea (also known as the Broxbourne Mill Stream) can be found at Broxbourne, just a short distance downstream from Hoddesden and where a 'mill' is indicated on the Ordnance Survey map. If you find Broxbourne South Meadows car park (Grid Ref TL37160672) you will be near the right place. It is not possible to follow the river very far, but a mill was recorded here in the 1086 Domesday Book, suggesting that the course of the river may have ran through here in Alfred's time. However, it is also possible that there was a cut made from the original course to bring water to the wheel. There is a King's Weir to the south of Broxbourne and it has been suggested that this was where King Alfred drove back the Vikings,[128] although I could not find any evidence to support this.

Waltham Abbey is downstream from Broxbourne and the town and abbey, where King Harold II is said to be buried, are well worth a visit. There is evidence that there has been a place of worship here going back perhaps to the seventh century[129] and it is quite possible that Alfred would have visited a location of this significance (although being on the Essex side of the River Lea may have caused complications). It has been suggested that the islands in the River Lea near Waltham Abbey were the result of King Alfred dividing the River Lea in order to strand the Viking boats. Although the waterways in this area are several and complex, I have seen nothing to indicate that this was anything to do with King Alfred's activities. The old course of the River Lea to the north of Waltham Abbey was marked on my Ordnance Survey map and, although no footpath was shown on the map, I found that I could walk some distance along the east bank. Looking at the map, it was tempting to think that one could connect through to Fishers Green car park in order to walk further along the Lea. I had the bit between my teeth. I wanted to walk as far along the River Lea as I could. However, I could not find a way through, so I returned to Waltham Abbey via the Cornmill Stream, which runs parallel to the Lea (not to give up I tried walking this stretch of the River Lea in the other direction but failed to connect through again. Then I did give up). It seems that quite a bit of the land here is out of bounds because it is associated with the nearby and hugely important former gunpowder factory. One can certainly catch glimpses of mysterious brick buildings through gaps in the vegetation. Now known as the Royal Gunpowder Mills, some of the site now opens to the public but I had the misfortune to turn up on a day that it was closed.

Travelling further downstream to what is now London, it has been suggested that Alfred had the Lea drained at Leamouth, which is in Tower Hamlets, and there has been another suggestion that the River Lea was blocked at Tottenham. I have not found anything to support these suggestions, which seem unlikely to be correct because the Anglo-Saxon Chronicles tell us that the Vikings went twenty miles north of London and that Alfred camped close to their fortification.

West of Hertford

The Anglo-Saxon Chronicles tell us that the Saxon army pursued the Vikings as they fled west over land to avoid being trapped in the River Lea. However, it is only in the account of Henry of Huntingdon, written more than two hundred years after the events took place, that we are told that Alfred himself accompanied the army. Nonetheless, it seems plausible that Alfred would have been with the pursuing army for at least some distance, so I spent some time thinking about the route the Vikings might have taken, with Alfred in pursuit.

If the Viking fortification had been, which seems more likely, on the Viking-controlled side of the river it seems plausible that their route to Bridgnorth may have initially involved staying on this side of the River Lea as far as Luton, where they could join the Icknield Way, which would then connect them to the Watling Street Roman road at Dunstable. Watling Street goes all the way to Wroxeter (Shropshire) but in doing so it passes to the north of Bridgnorth. This route would have the advantage that they would have remained in Viking-controlled territory, or at least near the border, for much of the journey (Dunstable to Stony Stratford would have been in Saxon territory). If they had wanted to stay in Viking controlled territory, they could have continued from Luton to Bedford and then followed the River Ouse to Stony Stratford (Buckinghamshire) to connect with Watling Street. However, this seems to be more circuitous and it seems likely that they would have taken the more direct route. Had the Viking fortification been on the other side of the River Lea they could have fled to St Albans and taken Watling Street from there. It seems plausible that Watling Street and the relevant section of the ancient trackway known as the Icknield Way would have been in use at the time, because much of the former is in use as the A5/A5183 and the latter still exists as a main road from Luton to Dunstable. It is, however, perhaps worth bearing in mind that we do not know whether Bridgnorth was a location that the Vikings set out for rather than this being a location that they ended up at.

There is no evidence that King Alfred or any Saxon army went as far as Bridgnorth, where we are told that these Vikings over-wintered before splitting up and going in different directions. However, any respite in Wessex from Viking attacks was very short lived as the Anglo-Saxon Chronicles tell us that in 896 Viking boats were attacking the South Coast. I shall look at this more closely in the following chapter.

10

Three mysterious naval Engagements

In this chapter I bring together in chronological sequence three naval engagements that I could not comfortably accommodate elsewhere. Although there did not appear to be much to discover about the first two, the third has been written about more extensively, largely because the text of the Anglo-Saxon Chronicles provides us with some geographical clues. Although there is no evidence that Alfred was present at this third engagement, I have included it here as it is a great unsolved puzzle that nonetheless ends with King Alfred hanging some of the enemy fleet at Winchester.

1. The location of this sea battle is not known, but it took place in 875 in a period after the Vikings had moved from Repton (Derbyshire) to Cambridge but before they arrived at Wareham in Dorset later in the same year. The Anglo-Saxon Chronicles say that Alfred himself went out to sea to battle against seven ships, capturing one, and putting the other six to flight. It is tempting to suspect that the battle took place somewhere along the south coast when the Vikings were making their way to Wareham. However, we should recall that when the Vikings left Wareham, they did so with a fleet of at least 120 ships. Alfred could of course have been dealing with a detachment from this fleet but perhaps the seven ships had an entirely different origin.

2. The Anglo-Saxon Chronicles tell us that in 881 King Alfred went out to sea and fought against four Viking ships. We are told that Alfred captured two of these ships and all the Vikings aboard were killed. The other two ships surrendered after those on board had been badly wounded. Unfortunately, there seems to be no evidence to indicate where this engagement took place.

3. The Anglo-Saxon Chronicles tell us that in 896 there was an engagement between Alfred's fleet and a Viking fleet of six ships that had arrived at the Isle of Wight and had caused harm all along the coast including as far as Devon. It seems that Alfred could not have been present at this engagement because some of the fleeing Vikings were captured and taken to him at Winchester where he had them hanged. The few geographic clues provided by the Anglo-Saxon Chronicle have encouraged speculation about the location for this engagement.

Dr Ryan Lavelle, using a 1942 analysis of the events by a certain Francis Peabody Magoun,[130] considered both Poole Harbour and Christchurch Harbour, although preferring the former, as potential sites for this engagement.[131] However, much depends on the interpretation of the Old English of the Anglo-Saxon Chronicles. For example, Magoun refers to *ufeweard muða* (*ð* is pronounced "th") as meaning "upper harbour." However, I find it striking that there is an area on the north side of the harbour in Christchurch called Mudeford, with a River Mude running through it and into the harbour. Could this be the *muða* referred to in the Anglo-Saxon Chronicles? Although I have seen it claimed that *muða* could also mean river, we know from elsewhere in the Chronicles and other documents that rivers were sometimes referred to by their name and that *muða* appears to usually mean mouth (the similarity between *muða* and mouth is not a coincidence) with the term for river generally being *ea*. Furthermore, if *muða* had been a generic term for river, we might expect to find other survivors such as is the case with the Brittonic language-derived Avon. However, I have been unable to find any other examples of a River Mude in England.

The Anglo-Saxon Chronicles tell us that Alfred's ships blocked the Viking ships in so they could not get to the *uter mere*. It seems unclear to me whether *uter mere* means "outer lake" or "outer sea". However, the usual term for the sea in the Anglo-Saxon Chronicles is *sæ*, with *Mere* usually meaning a lake. Nonetheless, the Vikings had been blocked into the river and when the tide went out three ships were beached at the upper river mouth and three came forward to attack (making six, matching the number recorded as coming to the Isle of Wight). It appears that at least two Viking ships managed to escape from the trap because the Anglo-Saxon Chronicles tell us as that two of the fleeing Vikings crews came ashore in Sussex because their ships were in a poor state. King Alfred had these men hanged at Winchester. It has been suggested that they came aground while trying to get past Selsey Bill. It seems to me that "row out around Sussex" is an acceptable translation of the Old English *Suð-Seaxna lond utan berowan*, and therefore Selsey Bill would make sense in the absence of anything else substantial in Sussex to have to row "out around." These Vikings would therefore have come aground in Sussex somewhere between East Wittering and Selsey. That they came ashore in Sussex perhaps also makes it less likely that the battle had taken place in distant Devon, after which they would have had to round Portland Bill (or drag their boats across the causeway), near Weymouth in Dorset, first.

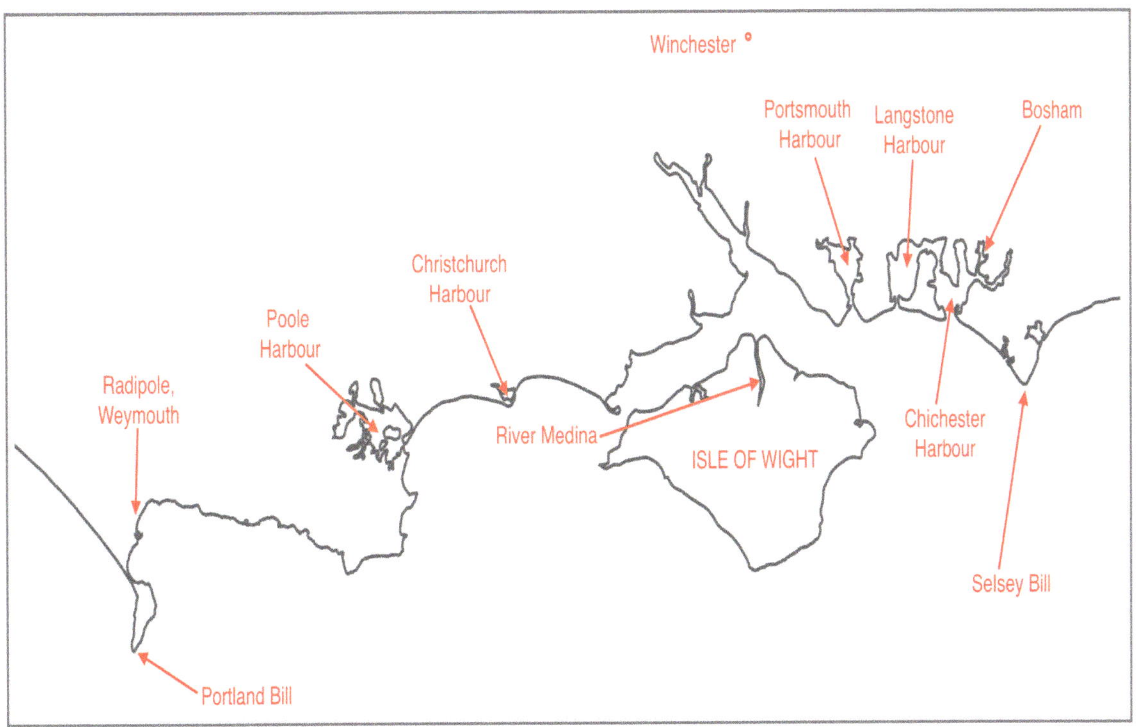

Fig.25 Possible sites for the 896 sea battle. Contains OS data © Crown copyright and database right (2018)

Perhaps the clue to potential locations for this battle lies in the fact that there were only six ships. We know that Wareham (with access to Poole harbour) and Christchurch are listed in the Burghal Hidage (a list of places defended by King Alfred after 878), and would therefore probably have been defended by 896. It does not seem to make sense to me that the Vikings would have ventured close to defended locations with just six ships. Perhaps the Dorset coastal town of Weymouth should be regarded as a possible site. Radipole Lake, fed by the River Wey, is connected to the sea via the town harbour, and one of Athelstan's charters refers to all the water within the coast of Weymouth, indicating that there was an inland body of water here in Anglo-Saxon times. Indeed, it is thought that the Romans may have had some sort of port at the head of this body of water, and a Roman road ran north from near here to Dorchester. At least parts of this route appear to have remained in use today, which suggests that it might have been in use in 896, thus providing access to any Vikings that intended to raid Dorchester. This area is no stranger to Viking threat. In 840 the Vikings landed at nearby Portland, with fatal consequences for the locals, and in 2009, during construction of the Weymouth Relief Road, fifty-four skeletons of executed Vikings were found, although these dated to a later period than that of King Alfred. It is even claimed that the first Viking raid on England was at Portland in 789 and, although the Anglo-Saxon Chronicles record an engagement at an unnamed location, we learn from Æthelweard's Chronicle that it took place on the coast near Dorchester and the 12th century Annals of St Neots tells us that the location was Portland. Weymouth was not in the Burghal Hidage, perhaps indicating that it was a less defended weak point.

However, it seems to me that it is more likely that the events took place at one of the main rivers, including the River Medina, that flow into the Solent on the north coast of the Isle of Wight. The Anglo-Saxon Chronicles do not state that the engagement took place during a Viking raid on the coast of the mainland, although it is easy to assume this because the Chronicles tell us that the Vikings had been undertaking such raiding. It is an interesting coincidence that the Old English term for the River Medina was *Meðume,* not terribly different from *muða.* An old map of the Isle of Wight suggests that the main waterways may have had constricted entrances to the sea, thus meeting the description of the location in the Anglo-Saxon Chronicles. It seems to me that Alfred's improved naval force had managed to root out a small Viking base that had set itself up on the Isle of Wight.

A further possibility is that this was a failed and unrecorded Viking attack on the Saxon settlement of Bosham (West Sussex). Bosham lies on the Bosham Channel of Chichester Harbour. There is some evidence that there would have been some sort of religious establishment at Bosham in the time of King Alfred and this, to the Vikings, might have meant that there was something worth raiding. Bosham would go on to have strong associations with King Harold Godwinson, and the church is even depicted on the Bayeux Tapestry. It seems unlikely that it would have suddenly have become such a significant place and it seems more likely that it had a prior but under-recorded importance.

Although I favour the River Medina on the Isle of Wight, it seems impossible to determine where this sea battle took place. Almost any inlet could be considered. I could not find a special reason to include Langstone and Portsmouth harbours, but these locations cannot be ruled out either. However, it seems likely that Portsmouth Harbour may have been protected by Portchester, a defended settlement listed in the Burghal Hidage. Henry of Huntingdon's 12th century account states that the events took place in Devon, and this cannot be ruled out either.

11

Other Places of Interest

This chapter explores some additional locations that I could not comfortably accommodate in the preceding chapters. I will then explore Winchester separately in the final chapter, which seems appropriate as this will include the events that took place there after King Alfred's death.

Shaftesbury, Dorset

Shaftesbury is a historic hilltop settlement in the north of Dorset, close to the Wiltshire border. Asser tells us that Alfred ordered the building of a nunnery near Shaftesbury's east gate (which is no longer present) and that Alfred's daughter Æthelgifu was appointed abbess. The location initially seems wrong because the remains of the the Norman abbey, which is thought to have been built over the site of the nunnery,[132] are south-west of the current centre of Shaftesbury, leading us to expect that the nunnery would be near a west gate and not an east gate. However, the modern centre does not align well with Alfred's burgh. This was to the west of the current centre and when we accommodate this shift the nunnery would have indeed been at the eastern aspect of the settlement![133] Unfortunately, Asser does not tell us when the nunnery was built. However, Ranulf Higden's *Polychronicon*, potentially unreliable because it was written at least four hundred years later, indicates that the nunnery was built after Alfred had restored London, and we know from the Anglo-Saxon Chronicles that Alfred took control of London in 886. This suggests that the nunnery may have been built in 886 at the earliest and 893 at the latest (because it had to be present at the time Asser was writing, believed to be 893).

However, Higden also tells us that around the time that Alfred restored the settlement of Shaftesbury in 880, Pope Marinus sent Alfred a piece of the "true cross."[11] Manuscript E of the Anglo-Saxon Chronicles indicates that this was sent in 882. I found out that Marinus was pope between December 882 and May 884, indicating that the item could only have been sent in December 882. This led me to change my mind from believing that the abbey was built between 886 and 893 to a belief that it was in use by 882 or 883 because it seems plausible that the fragment of the true cross had been destined for either the new and important nunnery at Shaftesbury or the new abbey at Athelney, which was built at about the same time. In a generous attempt to make everything fit, one could argue that the nunnery might have come into use before its completion, with this being in the period after King Alfred had restored London, although this itself must have taken some time to complete. The current location of this piece of the "true cross" is not known, although there is a reputed fragment of the true cross, which could be different to the one sent to Alfred, in St Michael and St Gudula Cathedral in Brussels, Belgium. It seems that Alfred restored Shaftesbury before he founded the nunnery. This is because Asser tells us that Alfred had the nunnery built at the east gate, which may not have existed before Alfred's restoration of Shaftesbury.

Shaftesbury was clearly a very important place. In 980 the nunnery became the resting place of King Edward the Martyr after he had been murdered at Corfe Castle in 978 (he was initially interred at Wareham). His shrine became a focus for pilgrimage, and perhaps this was what King Canute was undertaking when he died at Shaftesbury in 1035. In 944 the site also became the burial place of Ælfgifu, who was the first wife of King Edmund who also became venerated as a saint. Elisabeth, the wife of Robert the Bruce, King of Scotland, was also briefly held here.

Although the later Norman abbey is now a ruin, it is a delightful and evocative place to visit. It is thought that the Normans generally constructed churches on, or adjacent to, existing venerated sites,[132] which lends weight to the location of the abbey being at the same location as the nunnery. There is a fascinating museum at the site, and in the grounds there is a statue of Alfred with a glint in his eye. It is a peaceful sanctuary with blooming roses spilling their scent on to the paths and an old-fashioned herb garden resting in the full sun. On a sunny day one can get lost in time. It seems that the nunnery at Shaftesbury and the abbey at Athelney were inaugurated before the man perhaps most associated with Alfred's religious life appears on the scene. This man was called Asser and the story of their first encounter takes us to Dean in Sussex.

Dean, Sussex

Asser tells us that he first met King Alfred at a place in Sussex called Dean, and it has been suggested that this was probably in 885.[5] It was at Dean that Alfred asked Asser to work for him, although Asser was not prepared to make a commitment at that time. Dean is also mentioned in Alfred's will and it has been suggested, although not universally,[55] that the location was probably East or West Dean in West Sussex[5] and not East or West Dean near Eastbourne in East Sussex. The case for the West Sussex option was strengthened when I became aware that an estate there had been known in the early eleventh century as *Æðelingadene*.[5] *Ætheling* means prince and the name of *Æðelingadene* (*"ð"* is pronounced *"th"*) is therefore evidence of a royal connection for that area.

Singleton, which lies between East and West Dean, should perhaps not be overlooked as it has a church that goes back to Saxon times, and at the time of the Domesday Book the manor of Singleton contained both East and West Dean.[134] Because Singleton lies between East Dean and West Dean, one wonders whether this whole area at some time might have been called Dean.

The church of St Andrew at West Dean is Saxon, but I found no evidence that the church of All Saints at East Dean is as old. This made me think that it was more likely, putting to one side my nagging doubt about Singleton, that Asser had been referring to West Dean rather than East Dean. On visiting the church at West Dean, I was struck by how close it was to the large adjacent estate that is now West Dean College. I wondered whether there might have been a much earlier Saxon estate here associated with this church. West Dean was recorded in Domesday as a hunting park,[135] and it is therefore possible that it had still been a hunting park in the time of King Alfred, and we know from Asser that Alfred engaged in hunting. Is this *Æðelingadene*? The evidence of a former hunting park, together with the presence of Saxon elements at the church suggest to me that West Dean is the most likely location of the place called Dean referred to by Asser and contained in King Alfred's will.

Leonaford

Asser initially returned to Wales after Alfred had requested his services. He tells us that when he came back to Wessex, he was with Alfred at a place called *Leonaford*, and it has been suggested that this would probably have been in 886.[5] This location has remained unidentified, but Landford in Wiltshire and Linford in Berkshire have been suggested. However, when I started to investigate, I could find no evidence of a place called Linford in Berkshire. However, there is a Lyford that is now in Oxfordshire, and which used to be in Berkshire, and which is named as *Linford* in a charter dating to 944. Clearly, however, *Linford* is not the same as *Leonaford*, so this after all may not be the place referred to by Asser. Although Asser records that *Leonaford* was a royal manor (*villa regia*), there is no name similar to *Leonaford* in Alfred's will, although it could of course have been under the control of another "royal" at Alfred's death. At face value the name seems to mean a ford across a River Leona, but I could not find any rivers of that name. I did some investigations and it appears that there were Celtic deities called Alauna and Alaunus, both recognised on the near continent and whose names had become associated with rivers. This led me to consider the River Allen, which flows through Wimborne in Dorset, although it has been argued that the name is of more recent origin and may derive from a person called Aldwine.[136] Furthermore, there was a royal site at Wimborne, referred to in the Old English as *Winburn*, so it seems less likely that there would have been an additional site there that went under a different name.

I think a case, although perhaps not a strong one, can be made for Lingfield in Surrey. The will of an ealdorman, also called Alfred, and dating to a period between 871 and 899, indicates that Lingfield must have been a place of some importance because the will, which included land at Lingfield, was witnessed by the Archbishop of Canterbury. However, Lingfield is referred to as *Leangafeld*, which although not terribly dissimilar to *Leonaford*, suggests that the place-name is derived from a field and not a ford.

It is also plausible that the *leon* component could suggest that the location might relate to a St Leonard. There is a St Leonard's church with Saxon components near the Thames in Wallingford, but this may just be coincidence. I was eventually unable to determine that any particular location was likely to be *Leonaford*, although I have a romantic preference for a lost ford across the River Allen somewhere upstream from Wimborne in Dorset.

Dorchester (Dorset)

Dorchester is the county town of Dorset and I know this place well as I have lived nearby for many years. It is an important market town on the River Frome surrounded by colourful agricultural land and grazing cattle where the farming economy played, and still plays, an important part in the Dorset economy. This part of Dorset is inextricably linked with the life and works of Thomas Hardy and much of the archaeology in the surrounding countryside is of world importance. Evidence from charters (legal documents showing transfers of land or rights) indicates that King Alfred came to Dorchester and presumably he would have had some sort of base there. But where exactly was this?

Clues about Dorchester's Saxon past are scant, and this includes any evidence that might help us establish the location of a Saxon royal residence at the time of King Alfred. My personal speculation, which I have heard others suggest as well, is that the royal site would have included the location on the northern edge of the town where the current prison buildings are sited (Grid Ref: SY69199090), where we know that the Norman castle was also located. It seems to make sense that if a site was deemed defendable by the Saxons (which a royal site would need to be) then it would hold a similar appeal for the Normans. It therefore seems plausible that the Normans would have built their castle on the site of the previous Saxon fortification / royal residence. There is a very pleasant footpath that follows the River Frome and which passes below the site of the former castle. From there one can understand how elevated (and therefore defendable) the site would have been. In 2017 archaeological investigation was being carried out in the area of the prison, but I was told that, although further investigations were to be carried out, no evidence had been found for a Saxon royal residence.

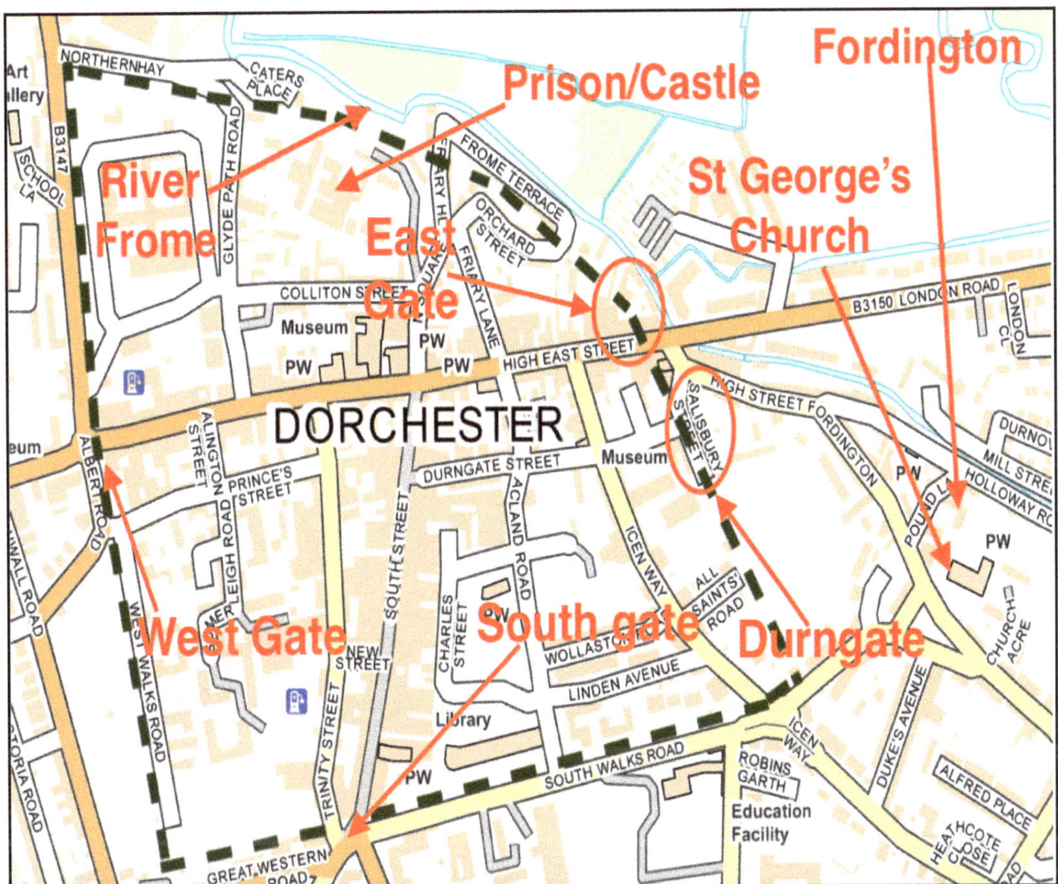

Fig. 26 Locations in Dorchester referred to in the text. The Roman walls are indicated in dashed green. The north-eastern section remains speculative. Contains OS data © Crown copyright and database right (2018)

It has been suggested that King Alfred spent every Christmas at a royal manor at Fordington, which is now part of Dorchester but was once a separate settlement to the east.[138] I have also read that Fordington became a royal manor after the Romans left and that the first church there had been built about 857, and that this was a royal church dedicated to St George.[138] Although the earliest parts of the current St George's church date to the 11th century, it is located at the site of a Roman cemetery[139] so the location was clearly a significant one stretching back to ancient times, which makes the presence of a church being there in 857 seem more plausible.

So, we have two potential royal locations that are close to each other, one in the centre of Dorchester at the site of the former prison, and the other at Fordington. Although the evidence from charters (see below) suggests that Dorchester really was a royal location, I am not aware of any charters having been issued from Fordington. It is perhaps possible that a royal residence at Fordington would have been close enough to Dorchester to go under that name, or that the residence was at Fordington while the charters were signed at nearby Dorchester. Fordington is so close to Dorchester that I found that I could walk, at a brisk pace, from St George's church in Fordington to the closest point of Dorchester's former Roman walls in a matter of three minutes. It seems to me that the Roman walls (perhaps replaced or repaired in places) would have been present in Alfred's time and would have probably continued to define and defend the town. This is supported by the fact that even today much of the line of the walls can still be followed. The exception to this is the northern section stretching between Northernhay and Salisbury Street where it is possible that there was no wall at all, with the River Frome providing defence instead. My personal opinion is that there would have been a wall here as well, which has long since been destroyed and built over. A recognition that the town was walled leads to a discussion about the location of gates through which King Alfred might have passed, which isn't just relevant to Alfred's signing of charters or the legend that he spent Christmas at Fordington. It seems likely that in 876, when Alfred was pursuing the Vikings from Wareham to Exeter, he would have passed through Dorchester, travelling west down the Roman road and through the east and west gates (see Chapter 3), possibly on a line running through the current buildings just a little bit to the south of the current main road, something to think about when enjoying a meal in one of the several restaurants there. The 1888 Ordnance Survey map declares the West Gate to have been at the top of the current High West Street. This seems plausible, although it may have been just a little to the south of here because the discovery of a tessellated pavement under the current road suggests that it does not lie exactly on the line of the Roman road. It seems to me that the East Gate would have cut across the eastern end of the current High East Street at a location where there is no remaining wall visible. As elsewhere (the walls of Winchester and Exeter) you have to imagine the wall passing through the more recent buildings on either side of the road. There was probably a North Gate somewhere near the prison, and Alfred may have used this as well if this area was indeed the location of the royal estate. The South Gate was near the south end of South Street (Grid Ref: SY69189033), marked approximately by, unintentionally I think, a couple of horse chestnut trees. There was an additional entrance called the "Durngate", which is worth mentioning as its purpose was to connect Dorchester with Fordington. We have already seen that Alfred has been associated with Fordington, so it is possible that he passed through that gate. There is still a Durngate Street in Dorchester, although if you go down it you will find a row of buildings and no gate. I suggest, however, that this road must at least lead in the correct general direction for this gate.

Alfred appears on a charter granting privileges to Sherborne, issued on the 26th December 864 at Dorchester (*Dornwara ceaster*, ruling out Dorchester on Thames, which had a different name). This charter was in the reign of his elder brother King Æthelberht, but Alfred is confusingly listed as being a son of the king. After making enquiries I was told that this probably meant son of his deceased father King Æthelwulf. Although he was not king at the time, the date fits with the legend that Alfred spent Christmas at nearby Fordington. Of some concern is that a later charter of Edward the Confessor in parts has identical wording in parts, although it is possible that the 864 charter could have been rewritten to conform with later standards, and therefore the information provided may not be wrong. A further charter, perhaps slightly more disputed, listed an Alfred, again as a son of the king, present in Dorchester (*Dornwara Caestrae*) in 868, when his brother Æthelred was king.

Plush and Sutton Poyntz (both in Dorset)

There is a charter signed by Alfred that dates from 891 and which records an exchange of land between himself and a man called Berthwulf. We are told that Berthwulf obtained land at a place called Plush and that King Alfred obtained land at a place called Sutton, which can be assumed to be today's Sutton Poyntz because the charter describes the location as being by the sea in Dorset. In all the transcriptions of this charter that I could find the first word that is written is *Plyssche*, followed by a full stop. This suggests to me that this charter could have been issued at Plush, which might not be surprising as the charter indicates that King Alfred owned some land at Plush. Although many charters of this period have had their authenticity questioned, I nonetheless feel that King Alfred may have been at Plush, a lovely Dorset village that I have visited many times, mainly in order to visit the excellent pub.

Old Wardour, Wiltshire

We can pin Alfred down at this location near Tisbury in Wiltshire because of a letter about a property dispute that also tells us at one point, perhaps surprisingly, that Alfred was in his bed chamber at Old Wardour washing his hands. Old Wardour still exists as the ruined 14th century Old Wardour Castle, with apparently nothing above ground remaining from Alfred's time.

This is without doubt a lovely place to visit, and popular with families on sunny days especially as adults and children alike can explore the extensive ruins. Although the remains are 14th century, I did wonder whether the origins of the well that can be seen inside the ruined house might be older, perhaps dating back to the previous structure in which Alfred had his bed and washed his hands. Old Wardour is adjacent to what is now the Wessex Ridgeway footpath, which could have been a downland route in the time of King Alfred and indeed might explain the location of the castle. Be careful not to confuse Old Wardour Castle (Grid Ref: ST93862633) with the nearby 18th century Wardour Castle.

Swinbeorg, Wiltshire

Alfred tells us in his will that an assembly had taken place at a location called *Swinbeorg* at which inheritance matters were discussed. Unfortunately, we cannot be certain of the location of *Swinbeorg*. The context indicates that the meeting would have taken place after the Viking emergency of 870-871 had commenced (see Chapter 2) but before Alfred's brother, King Æthelred, died after Easter (or over Easter) in 871. It has been speculated that this would have been at the presumed Anglo-Saxon meeting place called Swanborough Tump (Grid Ref SU13136008), which is to be found near the Manningford villages in Wiltshire. Although this seems tempting, the vowel change is problematic as even in 987 the place-name began with "Swan" and not "Swin." However, I am not aware of any other proposed location and it seems to me that this site could indeed be *Swinbeorg*. A plaque at the location indeed declares this to be the case.

Oxford

A fourteenth to fifteenth century document called The *Liber Monasterii de Hyda* (originating from the former Hyde Abbey in Winchester) has a section that refers to Alfred founding Oxford University in 886, with Grimbald and St Neot also having seats there).[94] Furthermore, Ranulf Higden's 14th century *Polychronicon* states that Alfred established schools in Oxford on the advice of St Neot.[11] However, Higden also indicates that when he was writing St Neot's remains were still at St Neot in Cornwall, although we know that his remains had been transferred to St Neots Priory in Cambridgeshire prior to 1020 (some 300 years or so earlier). It therefore seems that Higden is not a reliable source on matters relating to St Neot. Furthermore, although we know from the writings of Asser that Alfred knew Grimbald, there is no evidence that he knew St Neot. The current consensus seems to be that King Alfred did not found Oxford University, which is consistent with the absence of any mention of the foundation of a school at Oxford in the Anglo-Saxon Chronicles and the writings of Asser, Æthelweard, Gaimar and King Alfred himself.

Seaford

There is a work called the *Proverbs of Alfred* that is a collection of various sayings that legend would have us believe King Alfred told to an audience at a place called Seaford (the Middle English in which the documents are written call the place *Siforde, Sifforde* or *Seuorde*). It is thought that this may be Seaford, a coastal settlement in East Sussex. However, there is no evidence that these proverbs were either composed or uttered by King Alfred. Indeed, it seems that the earliest that any of the four versions of this work could date back to is the twelfth century.

Cheddar and Axbridge, Somerset

Although I have seen no evidence that Alfred had been at Cheddar or Axbridge, these were significant places in Anglo-Saxon times and a few words seem appropriate. Cheddar was an important royal site, and nearby Axbridge is listed in the Burghal Hidage, possibly having gained importance through defending and acting as a trading centre for Cheddar and Wedmore, with the River Axe flowing through the open space between these two towns upstream from Axbridge. Confusingly, the current town of Axbridge is not on the river Axe, which runs a short distance to the south. This may be because the river has changed course or even because the settlement itself has moved. Indeed, no archaeological evidence of Axbridge's burghal defences have been found[140] and it has been suggested that the burgh may have been outside the current town.[140] The Axe starts around Wookey Hole, on the edge of the Mendips, and emerges near Uphill, close to Weston-Super-Mare on the Somerset coast. Undoubtedly, the Vikings would have been aware of this river, the course of which would take them close to the important Saxon locations of Axbridge, Cheddar and Wedmore. However, I came across no evidence of Viking attacks here in King Alfred's time. Perhaps Axbridge performed its defensive job well, or at least acted as a deterrent.

It is interesting to note that, after his baptism, Guthrum was taken by Alfred to Wedmore instead of nearby Cheddar, which might be thought of as being the more important Saxon location. However, it is possible that Cheddar became more important relative to Wedmore after the time of King Alfred. Cheddar is mentioned in Alfred's will, but in a way that suggests that it may not have been under royal control in Alfred's time. Alfred's will simply asks that Cheddar accepts his son Edward in the way that had been previously agreed (although the will does not specify what this was). Alfred may therefore have had limited control over Cheddar. Furthermore, Wedmore may also have been safer than Cheddar, which may have been vulnerable to attack from the Mendips to the north and via the River Axe.

A Saxon royal location has been discovered in the grounds of the Kings of Wessex Academy at Cheddar, but it is uncertain whether this could date back to King Alfred's time. The general location is between Station Road and the banks of the Cheddar Yeo.[141] Stones have been laid out in the grounds of the Academy to indicate the site of the Anglo-Saxon palace. Those visiting Cheddar may wish to visit the famous Gorge and caves, or even the disused lead mines near Charterhouse, where the Roman road that originates at Old Sarum terminates. This is the same Roman road that passes through Kingston Deverill and the crossing near Pertwood (see Chapter 6).

Somerton, Somerset

Although there is no evidence to connect Alfred with Somerton, it was an important place in Anglo-Saxon times and I consider it likely that he would have been here at some point. It has been considered that the Saxon burgh was north of St Michael and All Angels church or at the Millands, an open space to the east of the town that is crossed by footpaths.[142] We know that a royal assembly was held at Somerton in 860, when Alfred was about 11, owing to a charter issued when his brother Æthelbert was king. However, Alfred is not listed as being present, which could have perhaps been because of his young age.

It is interesting to note that there is a part of Somerton (to the west) called St Cleers where tradition has it that the kings of Wessex had a residence. Although this area has now been developed, it seems that ruins were visible in 1579.[143] Readers may recall from Chapter 1 that there is a possible link between King Alfred and a Cornish king called Doniert/Dungarth and that a King Doniert's Stone lies by the roadside near St Cleer in Cornwall. However, I have no evidence to indicate that this is anything other than coincidence. Furthermore, one must be cautious about the significance of ancient saints popping up in various locations. For example, there is a chapel dedicated to St Nectan in St Andrew's church at Cheddar. St Nectan was a celtic 5th century saint who is largely associated with Hartland in North Devon. However, documentation inside the church indicates that this saint crops up in Cheddar as a result of the efforts of the Fitzwalter family as late as the 15th century and therefore has nothing to do with our post-Roman or early Saxon history.

Kingston upon Thames, Surrey

Kingston upon Thames, just 10 miles from the centre of London, is known to be a location where Saxon kings were consecrated, including Æthelstan, Alfred's grandson, and other later Saxon kings. Although we do not know where earlier Saxon rulers, including Alfred, formally became kings, Kingston upon Thames must remain a possibility. There is indeed evidence that Kingston upon Thames was significant prior to King Alfred's time because in 838 King Egbert issued a charter from there (with its authenticity contested by some), although charters were issued from many other places as well. The so-called "Coronation Stone" can be easily visited in central Kingston, outside of and next to the Guildhall. This stone block was recovered from St Mary's church, which collapsed in 1730 after its foundations had been compromised by grave-digging.[144] It has been believed that the later Saxon kings were crowned in this church, although there is no evidence that there was a church there before 1050, thus making it less likely that Athelstan (ruling from 924), let alone Alfred, became King at this location. It has, however, been suggested that St Mary's had been built next to the ruins of an old Saxon church that is now the site of All Saints' church,[144] the construction of which commenced in 1120. A piece of a tenth or eleventh century cross has been found at the location of All Saints',[145] which indicates there may indeed have been a church there then. All Saints', which is a short distance north of the Coronation Stone, is well worth a visit. I have also heard that the Coronation Stone may at some time be moved from its current location to the churchyard of All Saints church. Finally, it is worth considering that the ceremonies may have taken place outside at a symbolic location not connected with any particular church.

Eashing, Godalming and Guildford (Surrey)

These three locations are close to each other and are all on the River Wey, which flows into the Thames. Although there is no record of Alfred having been at any of these places, it nonetheless seems likely that he would have been in this area at some point. King Alfred's will includes estates at Guildford, Godalming and Eashing, and the Burghal Hidage (a list of Alfred's defended settlements after 878, but drawn up under his son, King Edward the Elder) includes Eashing. This is a different River Wey to that which flows to Weymouth on the Dorset coast, and mentioned in chapter 10. Alfred's connection to this part of Surrey is remembered in one of several beautiful stained-glass windows in the Victorian church of St John the Baptist in Busbridge, just a couple of miles south of Godalming. He is depicted above an image in the same window of a Saxon church at a place called Tuesley.[146] Tuesley, just to the south-west of Busbridge, is the site of this now lost 7th century Saxon church (Grid Ref: SU96964230), and it may be that there was a site of worship here going back to pagan times. It seems that Tuesley derives from the name of the pagan god *Tiw*, from which we also get "Tuesday". It has been suggested that the settlement at Tuesley was a predecessor to the settlement at Godalming although, as Tuesley is still present by the time of the Domesday book in 1068, the settlement would still have been present in Alfred's time. The location of this church is now a shrine to the Virgin Mary and is on land now owned by Ladywell Convent. At the time of writing there is access to this location every day except 21st December. It is a peaceful and beautiful site and I highly recommend a visit. We know that Alfred was pious and if he was in this area, I think he would have come to this significant church. The shrine is on the other side of the road to the convent, and the access is through a gate down a very short track.

In Godalming there is evidence that a church on the current site of the church of St Peter and St Paul would have been present in the 9th century,[147] while King Alfred was alive, and it seems plausible that the church would have been associated with the royal estate there. The royal estate may therefore have been in this part of Godalming, potentially around Church Street and to the south of the church. I was told that an archaeological investigation had been carried out before some new buildings were built to the south-west of the church and that hundreds of Anglo-Saxon skeletons had been discovered. However, when I visited Godalming's delightful museum I found out that more mid to late-Saxon pottery had been found at the site of what is now a supermarket on Bridge Street than anywhere else in Surrey and it was now thought that the "Royal Manor" could have been there instead of near the church. For clarity I will repeat here what I said in the introduction, which is that it seems impossible to tell whether particular estates that Alfred left in his will comprised the whole of that named place or just a part of it. In other words, he might have left the whole of Godalming because he owned all of it. In this situation, looking for a separate "Royal Manor" would be a mistake.

We cannot be certain of the location of the royal estate at Guildford but it seems most likely that it would have been located where evidence suggests there was a Saxon presence. Indeed, following the argument applied to Godalming, Alfred may have owned all of what comprised Guildford at that time. It appears that the Saxon settlement at this time would have been in the area around St Mary's church[148] and there is evidence that this building may have been preceded by a timber structure.[148] I found it pleasant to wander around this part of Guildford, which is essentially around Quarry Street and where the remains of Guildford's Norman castle are also to be found.

The location of the fortified site at Eashing has been identified (Grid Ref: SU94774369),[149] and is immediately to the east of the famous thirteenth century Eashing Bridges, which were marked on my Ordnance Survey map. Indeed, it may be significant that the fortified site would have been able to defend a crossing over the River Wey at the location of the current bridges. There is no public access across the site of the former fortification, although a combination of roads and footpaths delineate the perimeter. It was easy to find the two sides that benefit from a footpath. I parked at the small car park on the other side of the historic bridges, walked across and then up the path on the west side of the burgh. From here I could really appreciate how the burgh was in an elevated position above the River Wey. But I could only see the site of the burgh when I got to the path that runs across the north of the site. You will find it necessary to use your imagination because the location is now just an open space, and it is thought that this is because Guildford replaced it as the regional centre.[149] I decided not to follow the road for the two remaining sides of the square as it looked like a potentially dangerous endeavour.

Three charters

Charters are generally documents in which a power (such as a king) grants rights and privileges. We are lucky in that some of these have survived and come down to us, and we are even more fortunate because some of them carry Alfred's name and the place where the charter was issued. However, it should be noted that almost all charters from this period are disputed on some point or other, including claims of outright forgery or of changes and insertions made in later time periods. The information provided by these should therefore perhaps be taken as a lead to follow up rather than as proof that something happened at a particular place and time.

In 882 King Alfred issued a charter from what others have claimed to be Epsom (the charter refers to it as *Hebbeshamm*) in Surrey. It appears that this charter was produced while Alfred was on a campaign because it includes the Latin term *in expeditione*. Asser tells us that Alfred had a victory in a sea battle against the Vikings that year and, although Asser provides us with no location, it is possible that this was part of this otherwise unknown campaign. Nonetheless, despite the fact that it seems to have been drawn up whilst on a campaign, the impressive array of counter signatories indicates that this was a significant gathering. I looked closely at the area of Epsom to see if I could identify a potential location for this event. The only thing I could come up with was a road and a farm marked on the Ordnance Survey map to the south of Epsom that carried the name Ebbisham. However, because these names were not present on older maps, I could not tell whether these names were acquired in a period after someone had determined Epsom to be *Hebbeshamm*.

There is a further charter carrying King Alfred's name that was issued in 898 from a place called *Wulfamere*, which has been claimed to be Woolmer in Hampshire. There is indeed an area called Woolmer Forest that still exists today just west of Liphook. However, there is a later document that describes witnesses being brought before King Æthelred II (the "unready", and not to be confused with Alfred's younger brother) at a place also called *Wulfamere*. This case was referred to the shire moot (ancient meeting place), which was at what is known today as Scutchamer Knob, then in Berkshire (now Oxfordshire), but importantly nowhere near Liphook in Hampshire. Could there really have been two independent places both called *Wulfamere* and both fit for a Saxon king to be in attendance there? I could not find a fit with the place name *Wulfamere* in the vicinity of Scutchamer Knob except, albeit about 20 miles away, a short track called Woolmer Drove, north of Ogbourne St George, which did not appear to be sufficiently significant, although it connects with a Roman road that is still in use today. I eventually decided that the location of *Wulfamere* should be categorised as unsolved.

The final charter is one of uncertain date, but signed by Alfred when he was king and issued at Malmesbury in Wiltshire. The authenticity of this charter is, however, perhaps more contested than the two preceding ones. Malmesbury is mentioned in the Burghal Hidage, drawn up in the time of Alfred's son King Edward the Elder, so it might be expected that King Alfred would have been there at some point. It was, or at least became, sufficiently important for Alfred's grandson King Æthelstan to be interred there.

There remains one further important location that is relevant to the story of King Alfred both in life and death. That place is the city of Winchester in the county of Hampshire and it is to there that we now turn our attention and our travels.

12

Winchester and Alfred's Remains

Alas, we now reach the closing stages of our journey into the life and travels of King Alfred the Great, which means that we now have to discuss his passing away. Although we know that King Alfred passed away in 899, we do not know where he died or how. Wherever he died, he was buried at Winchester and there is indeed much more material relating to King Alfred's relationship with Winchester after his death than during his lifetime. Much of what follows will therefore be about the period after his death, although I have also included in this single chapter the events that relate to Winchester while he was alive.

Let us start with a couple of events that took place during the future king's younger life. The Anglo-Saxon Chronicles tell us that Winchester had been destroyed by a ship-army in 860, although the attacking forces lost. Asser tells us that these attackers were Vikings, which perhaps comes as no surprise. However, we do not know the whereabouts of Alfred, who would have been about eleven, at this time. The young Alfred may have also been present at Winchester in 861 when he and his family may have attended the funeral of Swithun, bishop of Winchester, who, according to version F of the Anglo-Saxon Chronicles, died in 861, although modern sources claim this to have been in 863.

Although I have seen other writers claim that Winchester was Alfred's "capital," there is little evidence to indicate that Alfred's court had been centered on a particular location in Wessex.[2] However, we know that Alfred was at Winchester in 896 because he ordered the hanging of captured Vikings after they had run ashore on the Sussex coast. It has also been suggested that Alfred became king in Winchester, although I have seen no supporting evidence.

It seems that there must have been a royal estate at Winchester in Alfred's time. Winchester does not appear in Alfred's will, although it is possible that a royal estate there might not have been owned by him personally or was under the control of the church. Winchester is, however, listed in the Burghal Hidage, which is the record of defended settlements drawn up in the reign of his son, King Edward the Elder. Indeed, it shared first place (with Wallingford in Oxfordshire) as the largest settlement in that document. It is indeed possible that the Old Minster (discussed later in this chapter) and

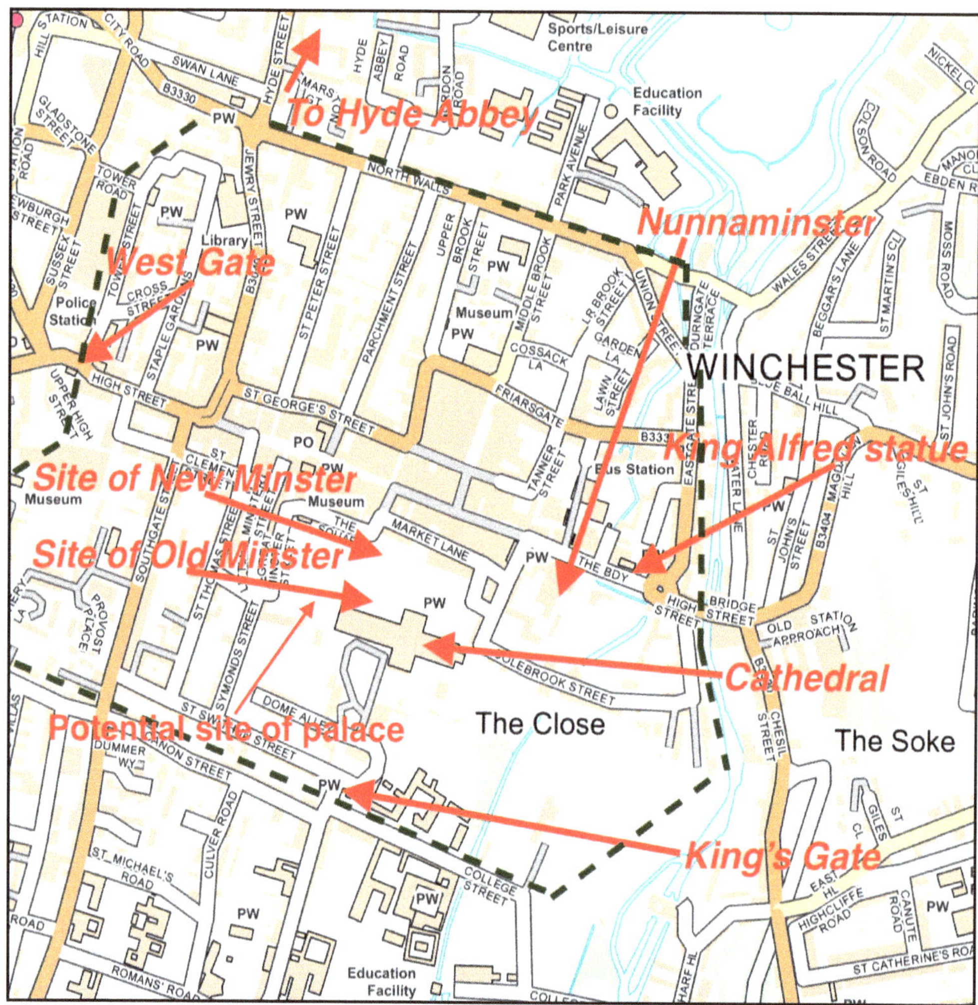

Fig. 27 Locations in Winchester mentioned in the text. The approximate route of the Roman walls is depicted in dashed green. Contains OS data © Crown copyright and database right (2018)

the royal residence were part of the same complex, and it is worth noting that Martin Biddle[150] places the royal palace in the area directly to the west of the Old Minster (and therefore also directly west of the current cathedral). I have sat on the lawn here (many do) to enjoy my lunch, without having the faintest idea about what might have once been there. As the tourists make a bee-line for the cathedral they may be unwittingly traversing something of competing significance.

Winchester had Roman walls and, although there is some evidence that the area within the walls became depopulated in the early Anglo-Saxon period, it seems that this area may have become repopulated by the time of King Alfred. I have seen it stated that the King's Gate (or Kingsgate), to the south of the cathedral, had been the entrance through the walls that provided access to the royal palace. This seems reasonable as this would have been the closest gate to both the Old Minster and the site immediately to the west proposed by Martin Biddle as that of the royal palace. The present gate is a later construction but it seems that it could well be on the site of the original gate, and it is therefore not beyond the bounds of possibility that King Alfred himself may have used it. I strongly recommend the nearby Wykeham Arms as a location in which to consolidate your thoughts, and if that is not to your taste then perhaps visit the small church of St Swithun-upon-Kingsgate that is built into the walls above the gate.

It is generally accepted that what is now called High Street would have been the main street through Winchester in Alfred's time, and following this to the west brings one to the Westgate, which is an impressive structure that includes some Anglo-Saxon fabric. Unfortunately, it isn't possible to walk a circuit of walls like it is in some other places, although this did not stop me trying to walk where the walls once were in an attempt to better understand the layout of the town in Alfred's time. The most pleasant stretch is to the south-west of the city, where there are actually walls to be seen. These are post-Roman, but generally lie on the route of the Roman walls. Indeed, at one point the wall has been excavated out to show the Roman wall inside the later wall. Much of the rest of the route of the wall is covered by buildings. There is even a huge multi-story car park on the line of the former walls.

I have already mentioned that King Alfred was buried at Winchester, but at the time of writing the location of his remains are unknown. His remains were moved at least twice and the different religious buildings built at different times can cause confusion in trying to work out where these remains went. I therefore hope that what follows will assist the reader in understanding what happened. Important to our story are three buildings built close to each other in the centre of Winchester. These buildings, in their order of construction, were the Old Minster, the New Minster, and Winchester Cathedral. Today, the only building that remains is Winchester Cathedral. The Old Minster was immediately north of this current cathedral, and it is the outline of this building that you can see marked out today on the cathedral lawn. The New Minster was built in the reign of Alfred's son, King Edward the Elder, to the north of the Old Minster, and this is where he had his father's remains interred. However, the New Minster was not consecrated until 901 (we are told this in version F of the Anglo-Saxon Chronicles), and Alfred, who had died in 899, was therefore initially interred in the Old Minster while the New Minster was being built. It had been King Alfred's intention to have the New Minster built in his reign but by the time he died he had only managed to obtain the land,[94] and this is why the job of building the New Minster fell to his son. Alfred's remains were joined in the New Minster by those of his wife Ealhswith when she died in 902. The Old

Minster continued to exist alongside the New Minster until the cathedral was consecrated in 1093. The Old Minster was then demolished.

In 1109 Henry I ordered that the New Minster be moved to land that he had provided at Hyde, which was then just outside Winchester. It is possible that the New Minster had suffered from a fire prior to 1109, which might have made the move opportune, or perhaps Henry I did not want the Saxon New Minster cramping the style of the gleaming Norman Winchester Cathedral. The re-located New Minster would then become known as Hyde Abbey. Certainly, the New Minster building in the centre of Winchester must have been demolished at some point as nothing remains above ground. Documents indicate that Alfred was transferred to Hyde Abbey in 1110 and that he was interred in front of the altar. Today, Hyde is just north of the city centre and can be easily visited by walking north up Hyde Street, and then turning right into King Alfred Place. This leads to the location of the altar of Hyde Abbey where three stone slabs show where Alfred, his wife and his son were once buried. It is thought provoking to consider that walking between the houses in King Alfred Place, one is walking almost on the line of the aisle of an important but largely invisible abbey. The nave of the abbey runs under the eastern part of King Alfred's Place, and the houses and gardens to the south of this lie over the location of the cloisters. It is worth having a general wander around the area to get a feel for this once very important location. The perimeter of Hyde Abbey covered a large area, with the current King Alfred Place running east-west across it.[151]

It seems that a good starting point for locating the remains of King Alfred would be Hyde Abbey, because the records seem to indicate that they safely arrived there from their previous locations at the Old Minster and the New Minster. But in 1539 Hyde Abbey was destroyed in Henry VIII's dissolution of the monasteries. Furthermore, the Annals of Winchester tell us that Hyde Abbey was burnt in 1141,[152] which fits with another record that tells us that the abbey laid "in ruins" after having been set alight in a battle between King Stephen and Matilda in 1141. Indeed, the Annals of Winchester record at 1182 that a renovation of Hyde Abbey had begun,[152] and it was clearly up and running again up to 1539. It seems possible to me that Alfred's and other important remains could have been relocated in 1141, or prior to the 1539 dissolution. According to Alfred Bowker, writing in 1902[153] Grimbald, a favourite of King Alfred, had been interred at Hyde Abbey in a silver shrine. Bowker also writes,[153] in reference to the events of 1141, that "the bishop seized much of the valuable metal left by the fire." We are not told what happened to these valuables, although Bowker refers to a large "loss to the abbey." Bowker tells us that, according to somebody called Rudbourne, although some rebuilding had taken place in 1182, there had been ruins for a further 130 years. If Bowker is correct in saying that Grimbald was in a silver shrine, then this tomb must have been a target for acquisition, whether legal or illegal, particularly in the context of other valuables having been removed. At the Dissolution, Thomas Wriothesley, a loyal servant of King Henry VIII, recorded the presence of plenty of silver and "rotten bones that be called relics." It seems impossible to know whether these were items acquired in the time after the Hyde Abbey ceased to be a ruin, or whether earlier possessions had managed somehow to survive *in situ* at the ruin, or whether possessions were returned to Hyde from locations of safe-keeping after it was brought back into use. Alternatively, part of Hyde Abbey may have remained functional while the rest was a ruin.

It should be noted that the *Liber Vitae* of Winchester[18] refers to there being ashes of Alfred, casting doubt on whether there are any of his bones left to be found. However, the *Liber Monasterii de Hyda* describes his son Edward moving Alfred from the Old Minster to the New Minster because his spirit had been reentering his body and causing him to walk about.[94] The source reports that these sightings were down to the inhabitants of the Old Minster having moments of delirium. Importantly, this source refers to bones. Furthermore, it seems that the Anglo-Saxons ceased using cremation well before the time of King Alfred.

That Alfred's remains, along with those of his wife and his son Edward, were transferred to Hyde Abbey shortly after 1110 is an assumption, perhaps a relatively safe one because Hyde Abbey was the successor to the New Minster and we know that Alfred had been interred in that building. There is evidence from the Annals of Winchester that religious relics were transferred,[152] and it is of course possible that royal remains would have counted as such. However, Luard points out, in his preface to the above source, that the annals of Winchester contain many errors. There is an interesting entry in John Leland's 16th century "Itinerary." After telling us that Alfred and his son Edward (he makes no mention of Alfred's wife) had been transferred from the New Minster to Hyde and that they had been placed in a tomb before the high altar, he goes on to write that there were "late founde" two small lead "tables" inscribed with their names.[154] I am taking "late found" to mean recently found at the time Leland was writing, which was roughly 1535-1543, and that "table" means tablet. He writes that the bones of St Grimbald and St Judoc had also been at Hyde. The abbey was dissolved in 1538 (and destroyed probably from 1539). Leland refers to the abbey as having "stoode," so Leland must have visited after the dissolution, at which point the tomb may have been opened. These "tables" do not appear to have survived so their former existence is dependent on Leland's unknown source, i.e. the person who found them. According to Hughes, writing around 1871,[155] Dr Richard Fox, bishop of Winchester placed the royal remains into named lead chests and then had these placed on top of a wall he was building to enclose the cathedral's presbytery. According to this account, they stayed there until parliamentary forces took Winchester in 1642, when the chests were broken and the contents spread "all over the cathedral." The account then says that the bones were collected up and placed in a repository in Oxford in a building next to the public library. It has been suggested that Hughes was confused by the rehousing of Anglo-Saxon remains, other than those of Alfred and his son, in Winchester Cathedral by Dr Fox in 1524. Nonetheless, it may have seemed sensible at the 1538 dissolution to, either overtly or covertly, unite the Hyde Abbey Anglo-Saxon remains with the other royal Anglo-Saxon remains that had been rehoused at Winchester just 14 years earlier. Indeed, this may have happened before the

1538 dissolution. There must be a real possibility that Alfred's remains were moved to Winchester in this period and that Alfred's remains are amongst the mixed up remains in the caskets now housed in Winchester Cathedral.

It is also possible that Alfred's bones remained interred at the location of Hyde Abbey after its demolition after the dissolution. With much of the material perhaps used for local building, it is said that the area returned to agricultural use. Alfred Bowker[153] says that a William Cole visited the site in 1723, with Cole writing: "The site of the abbey is a close with pits and holes of foundations." If King Alfred's remains were still present, how secure would they have been at this location, and had the presence of Alfred's remains been forgotten about as the surrounding abbey was demolished? Forgotten about until a man called Henry Howard drew attention to the possibility that the graves that had been destroyed by the construction on the former site of the abbey of a prison, which we know commenced around 1788, might have included those of King Alfred.[153] Apparently, prisoners were used to prepare the ground for building the new prison and a man called Page, writing in 1798, but referring to the events of 1788, stated that some bones that they found had been "thrown about." However, a John Mellor claimed that Page had told a Captain Howard that he had placed the bones near a spring on the site. In 1866, and using Captain Howard's map, Mellor started digging and indeed found skulls and other bones. Mellor sold these bones to a William Williams, vicar of St Bartholomew's, and he buried them, giving rise to the suspicion that an unmarked grave at St Bartholomew's church, which used to be in the grounds of the abbey, might contain the remains of King Alfred. We now know that this is not the case because when these bones were radio-carbon dated they were found not to be from the time of King Alfred. St Bartholomew's church, which appears to have avoided the damage otherwise inflicted on Hyde Abbey at the Dissolution, can be visited on King Alfred Place.

It is interesting to note that the abbot of Hyde in the period leading up to the dissolution was a John Salcot (also known as John Capon), a supporter of King Henry the Eighth's divorce. He appears to have taken advantage of the available voluntary surrender arrangements, after which he became bishop of Salisbury.[156] It is worth noting that voluntary surrender arrangements were generally not voluntary at all because the alternatives to not accepting them could be dire. We do not therefore seem to be looking at a context where King Alfred's remains would have been covertly relocated in defiance of the dissolution, although we cannot be certain that this did not occur or even that it might have been done with permission. Those who signed the deed of surrender received a pension,[156] and they may not have wished to put this at risk. However, it appears that at Shaftesbury Abbey, the venerated remains of Edward the Martyr may have been moved and hidden at the dissolution.

At the time of writing it seems that nobody knows the whereabouts of Alfred's remains. Prior to the radio-carbon dating of the remains from St Bartholomew's church, testing had been carried out in the 1990s on bones from an excavation at the main site of the abbey, and a sample from a male pelvis was dated to 895-1017. Although dating to the correct period, it is not possible to say whether this pelvis once belonged to King Alfred.

It does not seem possible to know why Alfred was interred at Winchester whereas at least two of his elder brothers, who had also been kings, were interred at Sherborne. It is possible that Winchester rose to greater prominence in Alfred's rebuilding programme after 878. I have seen no evidence to indicate that King Alfred's remains were transferred to Sherborne.

For the sake of completion, I point out that I have seen it written that Alfred died at a place called Farndon, and this has been used to support a supposition that Alfred died at Faringdon (Oxfordshire) or Fordington (Dorchester, Dorset). However, the entry for 924 in the D version of the Anglo-Saxon Chronicles states that King Edward the Elder, Alfred's son, died at Farndon in Mercia (which is probably Farndon in Cheshire), so I think that Farndon may at some point have inadvertently became attached to Alfred's story, because I think it unlikely that Alfred and Edward would have both died at places called Farndon.

It is interesting to note that another abbey, the Nunnaminster, was built at Winchester soon after King Alfred's death. Indeed, this was built by King Alfred's widow Ealhswith, and it also became known as St Mary's Abbey. This abbey occupied an area to the east of the current cathedral, but it was demolished after 1539 when it was included (like Hyde Abbey) in King Henry VIII's programme of dissolving monasteries. Part of the site is now a pleasant park, and in 1873 part of it became the site of the Guildhall. If you go down the path leading south off the Broadway, near the west side of the park, you will come to an excavated area (Grid Ref SU48422931) of the Nunnaminster adorned with information boards and where some stone coffins can be seen. Near the east end of the park there are the remains of what appears to be a solitary pillar sticking out of the ground, although I have been unable to establish whether this was from the destroyed abbey.

Near the Nunnaminster, on the Broadway, you will find perhaps the most famous of the statues of King Alfred. It dates to 1899 and commemorates the passing of one thousand years since the death of King Alfred. The statue was designed by Sir William Hamo Thorneycroft, who is also famous for the statue of Oliver Cromwell outside the Palace of Westminster. I can think of no better place to finish this book than at the foot of this statue looking up to the great man as he himself gazes across the town that he restored and in which he was buried, and with the location of his widow's Nunnaminster to his side.

Afterword

Because Alfred's life was so important it seems wrong to end bluntly on the matter of his missing remains. The impact of King Alfred's achievements overshadow his death to such an extent that we can still marvel at them today. In that sense he is immortal, and I think that it is this immortality that makes walking in his footsteps so poignant, causing it to be all too easy for our imagination to slide effortlessly across the intervening centuries.

In a book of this nature, focused on locations, there are some aspects of Alfred's life that I have either omitted or glossed over. Perhaps the most significant is his contribution to literature and education, and I shall say a few words on this matter now. King Alfred instituted a translation programme, from Latin into the English of his time, of the books that he thought were particularly important to understand. These included works by Pope Gregory I (the *Dialogues,* and *Pastoral Care*), *The Consolation of Philosophy* by Boethius, St Augustine's *Soliloquies,* and the first fifty of the psalms. It is thought that King Alfred translated four of these himself (all except Pope Gregory's *Dialogues*), perhaps with assistance. However, some of these works go beyond pure translations and they include additional writing by King Alfred himself. For me, the one that provides the most lucid view into Alfred's mind is his Preface to his translation of Pope Gregory's *Pastoral Care* where he addresses the reader directly in the first person as he laments the state of education and the folly of having books in a language that few could understand. HIs central question in this Preface seems to me to be: How can one follow the path of wisdom if one is not provided with the means of doing so?

It is my hope that this book will encourage people to go out and directly engage with history by visiting locations associated with this great king. In the introduction I suggested that it was possible to mentally compress time so that events that happened a long time ago can seem more recent, and that quiet contemplation at significant locations can assist this process. Many of you reading this may have been involved with the World War One commemorations that took place in 2018 and will understand what I am trying to say. Although the First World War was more recent than the time of the Anglo-Saxons, I argue that what causes pleasure and what causes pain has remained the same; the men, women and children of Wessex were not much different from us, and we must not allow the passage of time to imply decreasing relevance. What happened then was incredibly important and is a part of our heritage that I often find to be neglected. There are, of course, exceptions such as the city of Winchester, which proudly extolls its association with King Alfred. However, the enthusiastic visitor of locations described in this book will soon find out that this is more often not the case, and it would give me great pleasure if this book could be instrumental in changing this. If you believe that this book could help make this possible, then I humbly ask that you encourage others to read it. Above all, I thank you for your attention and I congratulate you on getting to the end.

Appendix.

Knowing the Viking Enemies

In writing this book I found that it was sometimes tricky to keep tabs on who was who, particularly as individuals are sometimes known by different names. I hope to make things easier for the reader by pointing out the main characters and their different names. It seems that all these Vikings were from what we now know as Denmark. Being a summary of complex activities, this section is quite dense. It may be easier to read the rest of this book before tackling this appendix.

The sons of the legendary Ragnar Lothbrok

These three Vikings, Ivar, Halfdan and Ubba, can be connected with the "Great Army" (*micel here*) that arrived in East Anglia in 865, and it may be this same army that had raided across eastern Kent earlier that same year.

There is a legend that their father, Ragnar, had been killed by Ælla, a Northumbrian king, by being thrown into a snake pit. There may therefore have been an underlying current of revenge in the later events perpetrated by his sons, although we must keep in mind that we cannot confirm that Ragnar existed, let alone any legend in which he features. Nonetheless, in the year after arriving at East Anglia (866), this force, also called the "Heathen Army" (*hæþen here* in the Old English of the Anglo-Saxon Chronicles, and referred to as just *pagani* (pagans) in the Latin of both Asser and Æthelweard), attacked York, which was then in Northumbria. The three sons together constituted the leadership of this army (although it may have started off with just Ivar and Ubba). This army then attacked Nottingham in 867, and when repulsed, returned to York. It is at Nottingham where we find the first crossing of the paths of these Vikings and Alfred, who was not yet king (this is covered in Chapter 1). These Vikings then went back to East Anglia, where they killed the local King Edmund the Martyr in 870, after which Ivar appears to have left the trio, either because he had died or because he had re-located to the North of England. Bagsecg (see below) may have become part of this army at this point and, according to the Anglo-Saxon Chronicles, he was involved at the time of the Battle of Ashdown in 871. Ubba appears to disappear from the record between 869 and 878 (see section below on Ubba). The army, seemingly now under the leadership of Halfdan and Bagsecg, later set up camp at Reading and soon after engaged with the Saxons at the Battle of Ashdown. Bagsecg was killed at Ashdown, so at the subsequent

871 battles of Basing and Meretun, out of the three brothers plus Bagsecg, it may have been only Halfdan left in charge. However, it is recorded in the Anglo-Saxon Chronicles that after the Battle of Meretun a large Viking summer fleet (*micel sumorlida* in the Old English of the Anglo-Saxon Chronicles; Asser just refers to it as another pagan army) arrived, and version F of the Anglo-Saxon Chronicles indicates that it came to Reading. As Reading was the base of the "Great Army" / "Heathen Army", it seems reasonable to conclude that they joined forces, and this indeed is what Asser indicates happened. The 871 Battle at Wilton (Chapter 2), which Alfred lost, would therefore have been against the combined forces. Between 871 and 875 the combined forces went to over-winter in London and were then in Mercia and the North of England. More details of these events, and others, will be found in the relevant chapters.

1. *Ivar/Ivarr/Ivar the Boneless/Imar/Igwar/Hingwar*

Æthelweard tells us that the Great Army (the same one that the Anglo-Saxon Chronicles tell us went to East Anglia in 865) was a fleet headed up by Ivar, and that it came from the north. Asser states that it had come from the Danube, but it has been suggested that he had somehow confused Danes with Danube.[5] The twelfth century writings of Henry of Huntingdon indicate that Ivar arrived with Ubba.[83] There is tradition that Ivar was the leader of the attack in which King Edmund of East Anglia (later St Edmund) was killed in 870. However, Æthelweard does not explicitly state that Ivar was present at the location where King Edmund was defeated and killed. Henry of Huntingdon's account indicates that Ivar came down to Thetford (in Norfolk, East Anglia), but there is no mention of Ubba or, for that matter, Halfdan. However, if Ivar was the leader it may not be expected that the others would have been recorded. However, a Canterbury writer at around 1100, in version F of the Anglo-Saxon Chronicles, refers to Ubbe as well as Ivar in relation to this attack on the King of East Anglia.[157] Æthelweard records that Ivar died in the same year as Edmund. However, it is possible that he went via Northumbria to Dublin where he could have died in 873, because the Annals of Ulster indicate a certain "Imar" dying that year. If that is the case it would be possible that Ivar is the same person as the Imar involved in the siege of Dumbarton Rock, in Scotland, in 871.

Investigation of a high-status burial at Repton sparked speculation that the remains of Ivar might have been found, although it may be very difficult to prove that the remains are specifically those of Ivar. Nonetheless, we know from the Anglo-Saxon Chronicles that the Vikings over-wintered at Repton 873-874.

2. *Halfdan/Halfdene/Albann*

Halfdan was one of the two Viking leaders that Alfred and his brother Æthelred engaged with at the battle of Ashdown 870, the other being Bagsecg. Henry of Huntingdon indicates that Halfdan and Bagsecg were the leaders of the Viking forces that had arrived at Reading in 870. However, after the battle of Ashdown in 871, Halfdan may have been the sole remaining leader of this "Great Army" / "Heathen Army" when they engaged with King Alfred at the subsequent 871 battles of Basing and *Meretun*.

After the series of battles in 871 the combined Viking force went from Reading to London, then from London to Torksey (Lincolnshire), and then from Torksey to Repton (Derbyshire). Henry of Huntingdon tells us that it was Halfdan who had led the army north to Torksey, and this seems to make sense. We are not told who the leader was once they had got to Repton but it seems likely that it would still have been Halfdan. Repton was more than just a base. The Anglo-Saxon Chronicles tell us that the Vikings conquered the area and drove out King Burhred of Mercia, who was also the husband of King Alfred's sister Æthelswith (they fled to Rome). After this journey to Repton it appears that Halfdan may have stayed in the North. This is because the Anglo-Saxon Chronicles record that the Viking leaders that came down from Repton to Cambridge in 874 (and then went on to Wareham - see Chapter 3) were three entirely different Vikings called Guthrum, Oscytel and Anund, and we are told that Halfdan went with a division of the army to the River Tyne and conquered that area.

Halfdan died at the Battle of Strangford Lough (Northern Ireland) in 877 in a fight between different groups of Vikings.

3. *Ubba/Ubbe/Hubba.*

Henry of Huntingdon tells us that Ubba was one of the leaders (the other being Ivar) when the great army went to East Anglia in 865. Ubba is also a candidate for being the murderer of King Edmund of East Anglia in 870, and it is also possible that he was jointly responsible along with Ivar. However, Henry of Huntingdon mentions Ivar but does not mention Ubba when the Vikings moved from York to Thetford before King Edmund was murdered. We must, however, remember that Henry of Huntingdon was writing in the 12th century and it may be inappropriate to depend on this source as good evidence that Ubba was not involved in King Edmund's death. Ubba may have been a silent participant in the 871 exploits of the Great Army, such as the Battle of Ashdown, or he may have departed for other exploits.

It is recorded in the Anglo-Saxon Chronicles that a brother of Ivar and Halfdan, and therefore probably Ubba, attacked Devon in 878 at a location that Asser states to be *Cynuit*, in the same winter that Guthrum (and possibly still Oscytel and Anund - see below) attacked Chippenham, which resulted in Alfred going into hiding and eventually building a fortification at Athelney on the Somerset Levels. The two attacks could have been coordinated. The writings of Geffrei Gaimar also indicate that it was Ubba that attacked Devon.

The Anglo-Saxon Chronicles record that the Viking leader, and therefore probably Ubba, died at *Cynuit*. However, the whereabouts of *Cynuit* remains uncertain (see Chapter 4). It is interesting that Geffrei Gaimar refers to a huge mound being built over his grave in Devon. Outside of the south-west, I have seen a reference to Ubbe having been killed at place called Ubbelawe in Yorkshire.[157]

Bagsecg/Beogsec

Henry of Huntingdon indicates that Halfdan and Bagsecg were the leaders of the Viking forces that arrived at Reading in 870.

Bagsecg was one of the two leaders that Alfred and his brother Æthelred engaged with at the battle of Ashdown, the other being Halfdan. Some time after the killing of King Edmund of East Anglia in 870 and the Battle of Ashdown in 871 it appears that the leadership of the "Great Army" changed from the three sons of the legendary Ragnar Lothbrok to that of Halfdan and Bagsecg. The Anglo-Saxon Chronicles tell us that Bagsecg died at the battle of Ashdown. According to folklore he was interred at Wayland's Smithy in Oxfordshire. However, there is no corroborating evidence that he was buried here and the site itself, being Neolithic, is much too old for it to have been constructed for Bagsecg. There used to be a Bag's Tree south of Harwell (still marked on Ordnance Survey maps), but the mere presence of a name claimed to be similar to Bagsecg is weak evidence that it has anything to do with him.

Guthrum, Oscytel and Anund

Although the Anglo-Saxon Chronicles give no names, Keynes and Lapidge [5] suggest that these three came over to Reading in 871, after the battle at *Meretun*, in what seems to translate as a "Great Summer Army" (*micel sumorlida* in the Old English), although it seems that they did not return when the summer was over. This army joined forces with the Great Army that was already based at Reading, although it seems that after the Battle of Ashdown the only remaining leader of the Great Army was Halfdan. It seems reasonable to assume that Guthrum, Oscytel and Anund were the leaders of the "Great Summer Army" because after the combined forces (of the Great Army and the Great Summer Army) went to Mercia and the North between 872 and 874, these three came down to Cambridge from Repton, and the only recorded addition of a significant new

Viking force had been the "Great Summer Army." Furthermore, none of these three are mentioned in relation to the "Great Army" before the arrival of the "Great Summer Army."

The Anglo-Saxon Chronicles tell us that these three were with a large raiding army in 874, and in 875 this army is recorded at Wareham and then at Exeter, although 120 of their ships were lost at Swanage after leaving Wareham (see Chapter 3). After Exeter this army left Wessex and went to Mercia. However, in 878 they attacked Chippenham (see Chapter 4).

It is recorded in Æthelweard's entry for 880 that the same Viking troop that had fought at Ethandun in 878, and then settled for peace with Alfred, eventually moving to East Anglia, went to Ghent (Belgium). Æthelweard also indicates that these were the Vikings that had been at Fulham. This is different to the entries in the Anglo-Saxon Chronicles where it is stated that the Viking force that was at Ethandun settled in 878 in Cirencester for a year (before moving to East Anglia in 879) and an entirely separate contingent of Vikings settled at Fulham, which the Anglo-Saxon Chronicles tell us went to Ghent in 879. The Anglo-Saxon Chronicles are more contemporary with Alfred's time than is Æthelweard's account, so it seems more likely that the Fulham Vikings went to Ghent without going to East Anglia first, and that the Viking force that went to East Anglia did not then go to Ghent.

Guthrum

Guthrum was defeated by King Alfred at the battle of Ethandun at 878. There is no record of Oscytel or Anund still being with Guthrum at this time or after. After his defeat, Guthrum was baptised by King Alfred at Aller (see Chapter 7) after which, having adopted a new name of Æthelstan and becoming King Alfred's godson, he settled with his men in East Anglia. The Anglo-Saxon Chronicles record that Guthrum died in 890, and The Annals of St Neots record that he was interred at *Headleaga*, thought to be modern-day Hadleigh in Suffolk.

Hæsten

The Anglo-Saxon Chronicles record that in 892 Hæsten, presumably after having crossed the channel (he arrived with 80 ships), made a fortification at Milton near Sittingbourne in Kent. There was another Viking army that had crossed from Boulogne and which arrived in the same year and was based at Appledore, but the name of the leader of this contingent does not appear to be known (this is covered in greater detail in Chapter 8). Earlier, in about 860, a man called Hæsten (although we cannot be certain that it was the same man) had teamed up with Bjorn Ironside and departed from the

Loire to raid in the Mediterranean, but mistakenly sacked a place in Italy called Luna because he thought it was Rome. Later, in 866, this Hæsten was backing Salomon, King of Brittany, against the Franks. However, for this Hæsten to be the same person that landed in Kent in 892 would require him to be aged over 70 by that time, which seems quite old for a leader of a hostile force. Whoever this Hæsten was who landed in Kent, we know that he was still the leader when his contingent moved to Benfleet (in Essex) in 893 and built a fortification, from which he raided into Mercia. Hæsten is not mentioned by name after these raids into Mercia (although there is a mention in Æthelweard's Chronicle in relation to Buttington - see later), but it is assumed he remained in charge as it is likely that his death would have been recorded and no replacement leader is mentioned. Hæsten's forces were joined by the Appledore forces, perhaps all arriving from their previously besieged position on the River Colne, or partly from there and partly from a remaining contingent still at Appledore (see Chapter 8). Later in the same year they built a fortification at Shoebury (Essex). It is recorded in the Anglo-Saxon Chronicles that this combined force went up the Thames and were there joined by Viking forces from East Anglia and Northumbria. Clearly, a strong Viking force had developed on the Thames. The Anglo-Saxon Chronicles indicate that they got up the Thames, managed to cross to the Severn, but were caught up by the Saxon forces and defeated at Buttington (just across into Wales and near the River Severn). There is less certainty about Hæsten's presence after Buttington as he is no longer mentioned (although his presence in relation to Buttington is recorded in Æthelweard's chronicle). While the siege at Buttington (893) was taking place, Alfred was at an unknown location in Devon dealing with an enemy fleet. We know that he went to Exeter earlier that same year, so perhaps he was still there. The Viking forces returned to Essex, again received reinforcements from East Anglia and Northumbria, and then broke out again, this time going all the way to Chester, with the year still being 893. Alfred's position at this time is not known, but he may perhaps have still been busy in Devon. Being effectively starved out by the Saxon forces, they moved into Wales in 894, but in the same year went back to Essex, this time to Mersea. The final fate of Hæsten does not appear to be known.

The Fulham Brigade

See also under Guthrum, Oscytel and Anund. The leaders of this force do not seem to be recorded. The Anglo-Saxon Chronicles indicate that this army, after it had arrived at Ghent from Fulham in 879, it was eventually at Amiens in 883, and it was after this, in 884, that it divided in two, with one contingent responsible for the attack on Rochester in 884. The other contingent had remained on the continent.

Other nameless leaders

We must not assume that we have a complete picture because we know the names of significant Viking belligerents. Some, and perhaps many, are not named and many engagements may not be recorded in the sources available to us today.

As indicated above, we do not know the name of the leader of the force at Appledore. Nonetheless, the Anglo-Saxon Chronicles indicate that it was this contingent who in 895 went up the Thames, then up the River Lea to a point about 20 miles north of London and built a fortress. However, the Anglo-Saxon Chronicles also indicate that it was the contingent that had been at Mersea that did this. Perhaps the original Appledore force, still with its unnamed leader, separated out from its merger with Haesten's forces to go to the River Lea. With the direct involvement of Alfred, they were cut off and they departed and crossed to Bridgnorth where they made another fortification. They over-wintered at Bridgnorth and then dispersed in 896, some to East Anglia, some to Northumbria, and some across the Channel to the River Seine.

Nor do we know the leaders of the forces that rode down from East Anglia and Northumbria to support Hæsten in the Thames in 893. The same goes for the leaders of the East Anglian and Northumbrian forces that in 893 caused Alfred to go to Devon to deal with their attacks on both the North and South coasts (Exeter) there. It seems possible that, because in the same year (893) the attackers in Devon and the reinforcements of Hæsten on the Thames are both stated in the Anglo-Saxon Chronicles to be from Northumbria and East Anglia, this was a co-ordinated approach in order to stretch Alfred's forces by attacking on multiple fronts. The Anglo-Saxon Chronicles record that the force that besieged Exeter raided near Chichester (W. Sussex) on the way home, but they were seen off by the local garrison.

A Timeline

849	Alfred is born
853	Alfred's first trip to Rome
855	Alfred's second trip to Rome
858	Death of Alfred's father, Æthelwulf
868	Alfred marries Ealhswith
	Alfred assists in removing the Vikings from Nottingham
870	The Vikings set up camp at Reading
	The Battle of Englefield (Alfred not present)
871	The Battle of Reading
	The Battle of Ashdown
	The Battle of Basing
	The Battle of *Meretun*
	King Æthelred dies and Alfred becomes king
	The Battle of Wilton
875	The Vikings arrive at Wareham
876	Alfred makes the Vikings swear to leave Wareham and Wessex
	The Vikings flee to Exeter
	Alfred confronts the Vikings at Exeter and they leave Wessex
878	The Vikings arrive at Chippenham
	Alfred retreats to Athelney
	The Battle of Ethandun
884	The Vikings besiege Rochester

885	King Alfred relieves the Viking siege of Rochester
886	King Alfred takes control of London
892	The Vikings arrive in North and South Kent
	King Alfred camps between the North and South Kent Vikings
	The Battle of Farnham (Alfred not present)
895	The Vikings build a fortress on the River Lea
	King Alfred obstructs the river and the Vikings flee
899	The death of King Alfred
	Alfred's remains are interred at the Old Minster in Winchester
901	Alfred's remains are transferred to the New Minster
1110	Alfred's remains are transferred to Hyde Abbey
1141	Hyde Abbey badly damaged by fire and/or military activity
1539	Hyde Abbey dissolved and destroyed
1788	A prison is built on the site of Hyde Abbey

References

1. Taylor C. Roads and Tracks of Britain. Orion; 1994.

2. Macdonald J. Travel and Communications Network in Late Saxon Wessex: A Review of the Evidence. DPhil. Centre for Medieval Studies, University of York. 2001.

3. Swanton M. The Anglo-Saxon Chronicles. Translated and Edited by Michael Swanton. Phoenix; 2000.

4. Giles J. Old English Chronicles. London: George Bell and Sons; 1906.

5. Keynes S, Lapidge M. Alfred the Great. Asser's Life of King Alfred and Other Contemporary Sources. Penguin; 1983.

6. Stenton F. Anglo-Saxon England. 3rd Ed. Oxford University Press; 1971.

7. Holbrook N, Thomas A. The Roman and Early Anglo-Saxon Settlement at Wantage, Oxfordshire. Excavations at Mill Street, 1993-4. Cotswold Archaeological Trust.

8. Garnish L. Alfred's Palace. Vale and Downland Museum - Local History Series.

9. Prentice M. Martin Tupper [title]. Vale and Downland Museum - Local History Series.

10. Nelson, J (translation and annotation). The Annals of St. Bertin. Ninth-Century Histories, Volume I. Manchester University Press; 1991.

11. Lumby J. Polychronicon Ranulphi Higden Monachi Centrensis; Together with the English Translations of John Trevisa and of an Unknown Writer of the Fifteenth Century. Vol VI; 1876.

12. Sargent A. A misplaced miracle: the origins of St Modwynn of Burton and St Eadgyth of Polesworth. Keele University.

13. Harris R. Steyning. Historic Character Assessment Report. August 2004. Sussex Extensive Urban Survey (EUS).

14. Hanks P. The Oxford Names Companion. Oxford: Oxford University Press; 2002.

15. Allen J. History of the Borough of Liskeard and its Vicinity; 1856.

16. Smyth A. The Medieval Life of King Alfred the Great. A Translation and Commentary on the Text Attributed to Asser. Palgrave; 2002.

17. Historic England. The Doniert Stone, accompanying cross shaft and underground chamber 650m SW of Common Moor. List entry number: 1010873

18. De Gray Birch, W (ed). Liber Vitae: Register and Martyrology of New Minster and Hyde Abbey *Winchester.* London and Winchester: Simpkin and Co.; 1892.

19. Abels R. Alfred the Great. War, Kingship and Culture in Anglo-Saxon England. Longman; 1998.

20. Wessex Archaeology. Sutton Courtenay, Oxfordshire. Archaeological investigation and assessment of results, 2010.

21. Brennan N, Hamerow H. An Anglo-Saxon Great Hall Complex at Sutton Courtenay/Drayton, Oxfordshire: A Royal Centre of Early Wessex? Archaeological Journal. 2015;172:325-350.

22. Burrows B, Cuttler R. Excavation at St. Mary's Gate/Warser Gate, Nottingham, Post-Excavation Assessment 2005-2006. Birmingham Archaeology; 2006

23. Walker I. Mercia and the Making of England. Stroud: Sutton Publishing; 2000.

24. Man J. The History and Antiquities, Ancient and Modern, of the Borough of Reading on the County of Berks. Snare and Man. Reading; 1816.

25. Doran J. The History and Antiquities of the Town and Borough of Reading in Berkshire, with some Notices of the most Considerable Places in the Same County. Edmund Yorke. Reading; 1838.

26. Historic England. Uffington Castle: a univallate hillfort immediately north of the Ridgeway on Whitehorse Hill. List entry number: 1008412.

27. Grinsell L. The Blowing Stone 1993. Leaflet available at the location in 2017.

28. Historic England. Alfred's Castle univallate hillfort. List entry number: 1015551.

29. Nash Ford D. Royal Berkshire History. Ashbury. Arthur, Alfred and plague asylum. Nash Ford Publishing. Available at: http://www.berkshirehistory.com/villages/ashbury.html. Accessed June, 2019.

30. Page W., Ditchfield P. (Eds). The Victoria history of the county of Berkshire, Volume 4. London; 1924.

31. Barradell-Smith J. A local battle: The Battle of Ashdown. The Astons. Tirrold and Upthorpe community website. Available at: https://www.theastons.net/history/the-battle-of-ashdown Accessed July, 2019.

32. Edwards B. Old Basing. Medieval Settlement Survey. Produced for Basingstoke and Deane Borough Council.

33. Hinton D. The placing of Basing in mid-saxon history. Proceedings of the Hampshire Field Club and Archaeological Society. 1986;42:162.

34. Brown R. Doing battle with the Danes. Basingstoke Gazette. 10th December 2007.

35. Williams-Freeman J. A topography of Alfred's wars in Wessex. Proceedings of the Hampshire Field Club & Archaeological Society. 1953;18:103-118.

36. Hawkes C. Old roads in central Hants. Proceeding of the Hampshire Field Club and Archaeological Society. Vol 9. Part 3; 1925.

37. Gover J, Mawer A, Stenton F. The place names of Wiltshire. English Place-Name Society. Volume XVI. Cambridge: The University Press; 1939.

38. Crowley, D. (Ed.) The Victoria History of Wiltshire. Volume XVI. Oxford University Press; 1999

39. Wright G. Roads and Trackways of Wessex. Moorland Publishing Co Ltd. Ashbourne; 1988.

40. Pauli R. The Life of Alfred the Great. Translated from the German. George Bell and Sons. London; 1889.

41. Wiltshire Community History. Available at: https://history.wiltshire.gov.uk/community/getcom.php?id=246 Accessed July 2019

42. Crittall, E. (Ed). The Victoria history of Wiltshire. Volume VI. Oxford University Press. 1962.

43. Mcmahon P. The Archaeology of Wiltshire's Towns. An Extensive Urban Survey. Wilton. Wiltshire County Archaeology Service, Wiltshire County Council. Trowbridge; 2004.

44. Gaimar G. Estoire des Engleis. Edited and Translated by Short, I. Oxford University Press; 2009.

45. Bellamy P, Davey J. Dorset historic towns survey. Wareham. Part 3: Town context. Dorset County Council; 2011

46. Bellamy P, Davey J. Dorset historic towns survey: Wareham. Wareham historic urban character area 4. The town walls. Dorset County Council; 2011.

47. Bellamy P, Davey J. Dorset historic towns project. Wareham. Historic urban characterisation. Dorset County Council; 2011.

48. Bellamy P, Davey J. Dorset Historic Towns Survey: Wareham. Wareham historic urban character area 8 Bestwall Road. Dorset County Council. 2011.

49. Blaylock S. Exeter city wall survey. Exeter Archaeology. Exeter City Council; 1995.

50. Historic England. Roman, anglo-saxon and medieval defences called collectively Exeter city walls. List entry number: 1003858.

51. Smyth A. King Alfred the Great. Oxford University Press. Oxford; 1995.

52. Edwards J. The Transport System of Medieval England and Wales - A Geographical Synthesis. A Thesis Presented for the Degree of Doctor of Philosophy. University of Salford. Department of Geography; 1987.

53. Wiltshire Community History. Church of St. Andrew, Chippenham. Available at: https://history.wiltshire.gov.uk/community/getchurch.php?id=266. Accessed July, 2019.

54. Chippenham Conservation Area Statement. Public Consultation; 2004.

55. Stevenson W. Asser's Life of King Alfred together with the Annals of Saint Neots erroneously ascribed to Asser. Oxford University Press; 1998 (first published 1959).

56. Historic England. Earthwork defences of Countisbury Castle promontory fort. List entry number: 1020807.

57. Daily Mail reporter. I've discovered the site of the first Battle of Britain, says writer. Mail Online; 19/9/2008.

58. Spelman J. The Life of Alfred the Great. Thomas Hearne. Oxford; 1709.

59. Vidal R. An inquiry respecting the site of Kenwith or Kenwic Castle, in Devonshire. 1804. Archaeologia. 1806;15:198-208.

60. Smith L. Bloody Corner. Available at: http://appledore.org/appledore_bloody_corner.htm. Accessed July, 2019.

61. At last, a fitting memorial to Viking warrior Hubba. North Devon Gazette. 6/10/2010.

62. Historic England. Anglo-Saxon occupation site and site of Athelney Abbey on Athelney Hill. List entry number: 1019099.

63. Gathercole C. English Heritage Extensive Urban Survey. an Archaeological Assessment of North Petherton. Somerset County Council. Taunton; 2003.

64. Keynes S. The discovery and first publication of the Alfred Jewel. Somerset Archaeology and Natural History. 1992;136.

65. Page, W (Ed.) The Victoria History of the County of Somerset. Volume II. London. 1911

66. Egbert Stone Trust. Egbert Stone history. 2018. Available at: https://egbertstonetrust.com/egbert-stone-history-1. Accessed July, 2019.

67. Historic England. Part of a roman road 565m north of Abbey Farm. List entry number: 1005421.

68. Wiltshire Council. Upper Deverills. Housing Needs Survey. Survey Report April 2013. Trowbridge; 2013.

69. Rouse, E. Historic Environment Action Plans. Theme 5: Hunting Landscapes. Version 1 (page 4). Cranborne Chase and West Wiltshire Downs AONB. Cranborne; 2010.

70. Peddie J. Alfred the Good Soldier. His Life and Campaigns. Millstream Books. Bath; 1989.

71. Macfayden G. Alfred the West Saxon King of the English. J.M. Dent & Co. London; 1901.

72. Costen M. Anglo-Saxon Somerset. Oxbow Books. Oxford; 2011.

73. Skinner K. Michael Wood on Alfred the Great and the Battle of Edington. Wiltshire Local History Forum. Online resource unavailable as at July 2019.

74. Historic England. Henge monument 350m north-east of Long Ivor Farm. List entry number: 1010471.

75. Jackson J. The Wiltshire archaeological and natural history magazine. 1871;13.

76. JMM [no further author information provided]. Battle of Ethandun. In: Brayley E. Ed. The Graphical and Historical Illustrator: An Original Miscellany of Literary, Antiquarian, and Topographical Information. J. Chidley. London; 1834.

77. Archaeology of Wiltshire's Towns. an Extensive Urban Survey. Wiltshire County Archaeology Service. Wiltshire County Council. Warminster.

78. Pugh R., Crittall, E (Eds.) The Victoria history of the County of Wiltshire. Volume VIII Oxford University Press; 1965.

79. Foard G. Conflict in the Pre-Industrial Landscape of England: A Resource Assessment. University of Leeds; 2008.

80. Pugh R., Crittall, E (Eds.) The Victoria history of the County of Wiltshire. Volume VIII. Oxford University Press; 1965.

81. Maddock S, Mahon P. A Romano – British prone burial from Bratton, Wiltshire. Wiltshire archaeology and natural history magazine. Vol 99 pp 190-203; 2006.

82. Laslett G. Edington. the Bishop's Legacy. The Hobnob Press. East Knoyle; 2010.

83. Forester, T (transl. and ed). The Chronicle of Henry of Huntingdon. Henry G. Bohn. London; 1853.

84. Dunning, R. (Ed.) A history of the County of Somerset: Volume VIII. The Poldens and the Levels. Boydell & Brewer. 2004.

85. Whitaker J. The Life of St Neot, the oldest of all the Brothers to King Alfred. London; 1809.

86. St Clair Baddeley W. Place-Names of Gloucestershire. John Bellows. Gloucester; 1913.

87. Marston Acres W. A brief history of Wedmore. Available at: http://www.theisleofwedmore.net/wp-content/uploads/2018/03/2017-05-10-brief_history_wedmore.pdf. Accessed July, 2019.

88. Somerset Archaeology, 2003. Webster, C. (Ed.) Somerset County Council, Historic Environment Service.

89. Whitelock D. English Historical Documents C. 500-1042. Eyre and Spottiswood. London; 1955.

90. Payne G. Roman Rochester. Archaeologia Cantiana. 1895;21.

91. Kent Historic Towns Survey. Rochester. Archaeological Assessment Document. Kent County Council. Maidstone.

92. Milne G. King Alfred's plan for London? London Archaeologist. Volume 06:08. pp. 206-207 London Archaeologist Association; 1990.

93. City of London. Local development framework. Fleet Street Conservation Area. Character summary & management strategy SPD. City of London Corporation.; 2016.

94. Edwards E. Liber Monasterii de Hyda. Longmans, Green, Reader and Dyer. London; 1866.

95. City of London. Local development scheme. Historic environment strategy. City of London churchyards. Statements of significance; 2017.

96. The Archaeology of Greater London. an Assessment of Archaeological Evidence for Human Presence in the Area Now Covered by Greater London. Museum of London Archaeological Service; 2000.

97. Historic England. The archbishop's palace. List entry number: 1011028.

98. Kent historic towns survey. New Romney. Archaeological Assessment Document. Kent County Council; 2004.

99. Kent Historic Towns Survey. Lydd. Archaeological Assessment Document. Maidstone: Kent County Council; 2004.

100. Kent historic towns survey. Hythe. Archaeological Assessment Document. Kent County Council; 2004.

101. Æthelweard. Giles, J. (Ed.) Ethelwerd's Chronicle. in: Old English Chronicles. George Bell and Sons. London; 1906.

102. The forest of Anderida during the Roman occupation of Britain. Available at: https://commons.wikimedia.org/wiki/File:The_Forest_of_Anderida_during_the_Roman_Occupation_of_Britain.jpg. Accessed July, 2019.

103. Simon M. Silva-Anderida/Andredsweald boundary map implied by village names containing hurst. Available at: http://saxonhistory.co.uk/Location_Anderida.php. Accessed July, 2019.

104. Great Chart. The Great Chart millennium sign and the early history of the village. Available at: http://gtchart.tripod.com/greatchart/. Accessed July, 2019.

105. Hasted E. The history and topographical survey of the County of Kent. Volume 7. EP Publishing Limited in collaboration with Kent County Library; 1972 (first published 1797).

106. Kent Historic Towns Survey. Appledore. Archaeological Assessment Document. Maidstone: Kent County Council; 2004.

107. Baker J, Brookes S. Beyond the Burghal Hidage: Anglo-Saxon Civil Defence in the Viking Age. Brill; 2013.

108. Hasted E. The history and topographical survey of the County of Kent. Volume 1. EP Publishing Limited in collaboration with Kent County Library. 1972 (first published 1797).

109. The Castle Rough Training Project - 1972, part 1. Kent Archaeological Review. 1973;31.

110. Rackham O. The History of the Countryside. J.M. Dent. London; 1987.

111. Kent Historic Towns Survey. Maidstone. Archaeological Assessment Document. Maidstone: Kent County Council; 2004.

112. Historic England. Ringwork and baileys at Church Farm. List entry number: 1009949.

113. Historic England. Castle Toll Saxon burgh and medieval fort. List entry number: 1013041.

114. Hasted E. The history and topographical survey of the County of Kent. Volume 7. EP Publishing Limited in collaboration with Kent County Library. 1972 (first published 1797).

115. Sayer J. Charing church. Archaeologia Cantiana. 1886;16.

116. Powell, W. (Ed.) The Victoria history of the County of Essex. Volume V. Oxford University Press. London; 1966.

117. Jones, A. Herts. Past and present. No 9; 1969.

118. Wrong turning, fixing the border. London's Metropolitan Essex. Essex Hundred Publications. Available at: http://www.essex100.com/wrong.html. Accessed July, 2019.

119. Ware Town Council. Town history. Available at: https://waretowncouncil.gov.uk/about/town-history/Accessed July, 2019.

120. Chauncy H. The Historical Antiquities of Hertfordshire. JM Mullinger and BJ Holdsworth. London; 1826.

121. Page, W (Ed.) The Victoria History of the County of Hertford. Volume three. Constable and Company; 1912.

122. Bryant S, Seddon V, Marlow C. Ware. Extensive urban survey project assessment report. Hertfordshire County Council. 1998.

124. Historic England. Youngsbury Roman barrows. List entry number: 1018271.

125. National Museum Copenhagen. Viking swords. Available at: https://en.natmus.dk/historical-knowledge/denmark/prehistoric-period-until-1050-ad/the-viking-age/weapons/swords/. Accessed July, 2019.

126. Bryant S, Seddon V. Hertford. Extensive urban survey project assessment report. Hertfordshire County Council; 1999.

127. Page, W (Ed.) The Victoria History of the County of Hertford. Volume three. Constable and Company, 1912.

128. Chris Blandford Associates. Harlow Area Landscape & Environment Study. Volumes 1-3; 2005.

129. Historic towns in Essex. Waltham Abbey. Historic towns assessment report. Essex County Council. 1999.

130. Magoun F. King Alfred's naval and beach battle with the Danes in 896. The Modern Language Review. 1942;37:409-414.

131. Lavelle R. Alfred's Wars. Sources and interpretations of Anglo-Saxon warfare in the Viking age. Boydell Press. Woodbridge; 2010.

132. Davey, J. Bellamy, P. (Ed.) Dorset historic towns project: Shaftesbury. Part 5: Historical analysis. Dorset County Council; 2011.

133. Davey, J. Bellamy, P. (Ed.) Dorset historic towns project: Shaftesbury. Shaftesbury historic urban character area 1. Bimport. Dorset County Council; 2011.

134. Salzman, L. (Ed.) The Victoria history of the County of Sussex. Volume 4, the Rape of Chichester. Dawsons; 1973.

135. Historic England. West Dean. List entry number: 1000190.

136. Fagersten A. The Place Names of Dorset. EP Publishing Limited; 1978.

138. Ungley J. History of Fordington and St. George's church. Discover Dorset. 2010. Available at: http://www.dorchesterdorset.com/blog/general/history-of-fordington-and-st-georges-church/ Accessed July, 2019.

139. An Inventory of the Historical Monuments in Dorset, Volume 2, South East, Part 3. Royal Commission on Historic Monuments; 1970.

140. Richardson M. English Heritage Extensive Urban Survey. an Archaeological Assessment of Axbridge. Somerset County Council; 2001.

141. Historic England. Roman settlement site, Anglo-Saxon and Norman royal palace, and St Columbanus' Chapel. List entry number: 1017290.

142. Somerton Web Museum. Saxon royal town. Resource unavailable as at July 2019. http://www.somertonmuseum.org.uk/index.php?table=subcat&idnum=13. Accessed 2017.

143. Dunning. R (Ed.) A history of the county of Somerset: Volume III. Oxford University Press; 1974.

144. All Saints Kingston. St Mary's Chapel. Available at: https://www.allsaintskingston.co.uk/heritage/st-marys-chapel. Accessed July, 2019.

145. The corpus of Anglo-Saxon stone sculpture. Vol IV: South-East England. Available at: http://www.ascorpus.ac.uk/catvol4.php?pageNum_urls=63. Accessed July, 2019.

146. Bailey J. History of St. John the Baptist Church, Busbridge. Busbridge and Hambledon Church. 2016. Available at: https://www.bhcgodalming.org/history-of-st-john-the-baptist-church-busbridge. Accessed July, 2019.

147. Poulton R. Extensive Urban Survey of Surrey. Godalming. Woking: Surrey County Archaeological Unit; 2004.

148. Robertson J. Extensive Urban Survey of Surrey. Guildford. Woking: Surrey County Archaeological Unit; 2003.

149. Historic England. Anglo-Saxon fortified centre at Eashing. List entry number: 1017720.

150. Biddle M. The Search for Winchester's Anglo-Saxon Minsters. Winchester Excavations Committee; 2018.

151. Hyde 900. Map of the archaeology in the Hyde Abbey precinct. Available at: http://www.hyde900.org.uk/about/communityarcheology/map-of-the-archaeology-in-the-hyde-abbey-precinct/. Accessed July, 2019.

152. Luard H. Annales Monasterii De Wintonia. in Annales Monastici Vol II. Longman, Green, Longman, Roberts, and Green. London; 1865.

153. Bowker A. The King Alfred Millenary. A Record of the Proceedings of the National Commemoration. Macmillan and Co. Ltd. London; 1902.

154. Smith L. The Itinerary of John Leland in or about the Years 1535-1543. Parts I to III. George Bell and Sons; 1907.

155. Hughes T. Alfred the Great. 2nd Ed. Macmillan and Co.; 1871.

156. Doubleday A, Page W (Eds.) A History of Hampshire and the Isle of Wight. Volume two. Victoria County History; 1903.

157. Whitelock D. Fact and fiction in the legend of St. Edmund. Proceedings of the Sussex Institute of Archaeology. Vol 31. Part 3; 1969

Index

N

O

P

Q

R

S

T

U

V

W

Z

www.ingramcontent.com/pod-product-compliance
Ingram Content Group UK Ltd.
Pitfield, Milton Keynes, MK11 3LW, UK
UKHW061954290726
14090UKWH00021B/1230